19th Edition

# Alaska's
# INSIDE PASSAGE
## TRAVELER

## See More, Spend Less!

## Ellen Searby

Windham Bay Press
Occidental, California

Also from Windham Bay Press:

*Vancouver Island Traveler* by Ellen Searby
*The Costa Rica Traveler* by Ellen Searby
*The Panama Traveler* by David Dudenhoefer

Alaska's Inside Passage traveler : see more, spend less! / by Ellen
    Searby. Occidental, California: Windham Bay Press
    v. : ill., maps ; 22 cm.
    Annual

    ISSN: 1046-5871 0736-9298
    Inside Passage traveler
    Description based on: 14th ed. (1992-1993).
    Continues: Inside Passage traveler 0736-9298 (DLC)sn 83001988
(OCoLC)8469819

        1. Alaska--Description and travel--1959---Guide-books.  2. Inside
    Passage--Description and travel--1959---Guide-books.   I. Searby,
    Ellen.  II. Title:   III. Title: Inside passage traveler.

**Front Cover:** *M/V Malaspina* approaches Haines.
**Back Cover:** Visitors enjoy the Mendenhall Glacier near Juneau.

Photos by Ellen Searby unless otherwise noted.
Maps by Ellen Searby and Henry Jori.

While the author and publisher have worked diligently to make the information and advice in this book accurate when the book went to press, they accept no responsibility or liability for any delay, inconvenience, loss, or injury from any cause sustained by anyone using it.

Windham Bay Press
Box 1198, Occidental, California 95465 U.S.A. (707) 823-7150, Pacific Time.

Web site for Travelers' Tips with latest information on areas we publish, new in summer 1999, http://www.metro.net/windham

                                                                    Key title: Alaska,
Printed in the USA.                                        Inside Passage, ferries.

# Foreword For 1999

After three summers as a U. S. Forest Service shipboard naturalist, answering (or trying to answer) all the questions that over 30,000 people aboard the Alaska ferries could ask, I thought it would be worthwhile to put the information into book form. Many questions concerned not forest and wildlife, but towns, routes, and ferries. I hope that knowing what is in Southeastern Alaska, how the ferry system works, and how you can make best use of it will help you have a really great trip.

The Alaska Marine Highway started in 1963, with the twin missions of providing transportation for Alaskans, their vehicles, and possessions while being an essential and enjoyable part of tourism in Alaska. Since Alaskans as well as tourists travel most in summer, it has not been easy.

In this nineteenth edition of the book, I have used the information and suggestions some of you have provided, what I learned as a member of the ferry crew from 1978 to 1990, and current information collected in research. Henry Jori, my husband, has redrawn and improved most street maps of the towns. Please note that prices are the 1999 summer rates, as known at presstime.

Tourism has grown rapidly in the Inside Passage recently. While downtowns are often crowded with tourists in summer, there are miles of unpopulated forest and ocean. Now, in most towns there are kayak and bicycle rentals as well as more hotel rooms, b&b's, rental cars, and charter boats. With concern for the weight of this book you will carry, as well as the fact that they change so often, I do not list many individual charter boats and b&b's, though I list their associations and reservation services.

*Special Events:* Alaska celebrates its first 40 years of statehood in 1999—watch for events and displays statewide. Alaska and the Yukon have been celebrating the centennial of the discovery of gold and the Klondike Gold Rush that followed. The year 2000 will be the centennial of the completion of the White Pass & Yukon Railroad from Skagway to Whitehorse.

Please send suggestions and information you think others would find useful to Windham Bay Press, Box 1198, Occidental, California 95465. I apologize for not having time to answer questions or to plan readers' trips, but a 24-hour day isn't long enough. For the same reason, my e-mail address, ellnsearby@aol.com, is a good place to leave your comments or a request for our latest catalog, but please don't expect replies.

Many thanks again to all the nice people in towns, visitors' bureaus, the ferry system, and passengers on the ships who helped gather and update the current information we all need.

Have a wonderful time! I hope the sun shines for you.

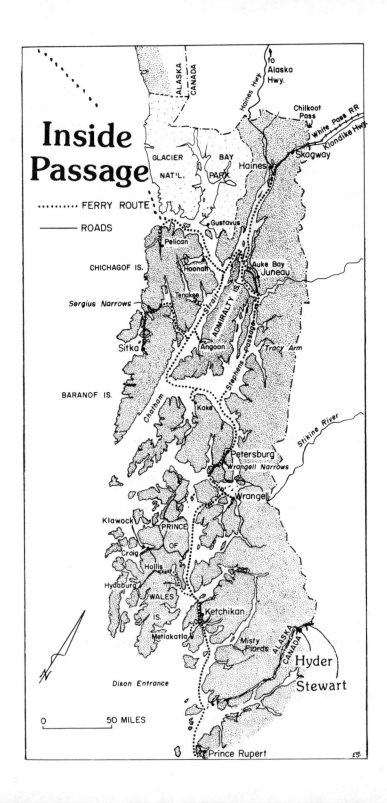

# Inside
# Passage

......... FERRY ROUTE

——— ROADS

ALASKA / CANADA

to Alaska Hwy.

Haines Hwy.

Chilkoot Pass

White Pass RR

Klondike Hwy.

Skagway

GLACIER NAT'L.

BAY PARK

Haines

Gustavus

Pelican

CHICHAGOF IS.

Hoonah

Auke Bay

Juneau

Tenakee

Sergius Narrows

Strait

ADMIRALTY IS.

Sitka

Angoon

Tracy Arm

Stephens Passage

BARANOF IS.

Chatham

Kake

Stikine River

Petersburg

Wrangell Narrows

Wrangell

Klawock

PRINCE OF

Craig

Hollis

Hydaburg

WALES IS.

Ketchikan

Metlakatla

Misty Fiords

ALASKA / CANADA

Hyder

Stewart

Dixon Entrance

0        50 MILES

N

Prince Rupert

ES

# TABLE OF CONTENTS

# MAPS AND TABLES

# TABLE 1

## AVERAGE PRECIPITATION BY MONTH
### (in inches)

|           | KETCHIKAN | JUNEAU |
|-----------|-----------|--------|
| January   | 12.79     | 4.94   |
| February  | 13.35     | 7.10   |
| March     | 13.46     | 6.17   |
| April     | 13.15     | 6.43   |
| May       | 9.70      | 6.23   |
| June      | 7.74      | 3.58   |
| July      | 7.50      | 5.34   |
| August    | 12.17     | 7.58   |
| September | 12.84     | 9.59   |
| October   | 24.96     | 13.01  |
| November  | 17.90     | 10.02  |
| December  | 18.83     | 10.11  |
| **Annual** | 164.39" (over 13 ft!) | 90.10" |

## AVERAGE TEMPERATURE BY MONTH
### (Degrees Fahrenheit)

|           | KETCHIKAN | JUNEAU |
|-----------|-----------|--------|
| January   | 34.0      | 25.8   |
| February  | 36.5      | 30.9   |
| March     | 37.7      | 33.9   |
| April     | 43.4      | 41.0   |
| May       | 50.3      | 48.9   |
| June      | 54.7      | 55.4   |
| July      | 58.7      | 58.9   |
| August    | 58.7      | 57.0   |
| September | 54.4      | 51.8   |
| October   | 47.3      | 47.3   |
| November  | 40.7      | 37.3   |
| December  | 37.2      | 32.1   |

Good luck picking the weather for your trip!

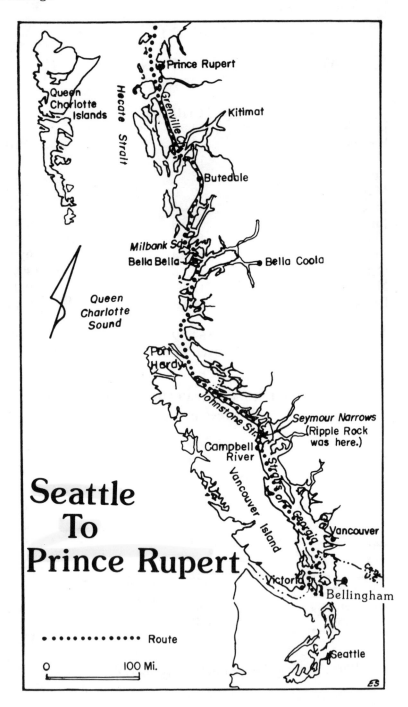

Queen Charlotte Islands

Hecate Strait

Prince Rupert

Grenville

Kitimat

Butedale

Milbank Sd.
Bella Bella

Bella Coola

Queen Charlotte Sound

Port Hardy

Johnstone Str.

Seymour Narrows
(Ripple Rock was here.)

Campbell River

Strait of Georgia

Vancouver Island

**Seattle To Prince Rupert**

Vancouver

Victoria

Bellingham

Seattle

•••••••••• Route

0       100 Mi.

The Mendenhall Glacier and mountains are the backdrop for Juneau Airport and the float pond for sea planes.

## SOUTHEAST ALASKA

Welcome to Southeast Alaska, the northern Inside Passage, the Alaska Marine Highway, and the Tongass National Forest. Here are hundreds of miles of sheltered waterways, islands, mountains, glaciers, fiords, and thick spruce/hemlock forests, with all the wildlife that can live on land and sea. Scattered throughout an area larger than Massachusetts, are just seven towns and a dozen villages— fewer than 60,000 people. That leaves a lot of uncrowded country and clean air!

The scenery and climate are comparable to the coast of Norway, but much closer to home. The Inside Passage is one of few places on earth where you can be among mountains and glaciers with no physical exertion, keeping your cardiovascular system at sea level, and without even getting seasick. For the athletic, there are waterways to kayak, mountains to climb, and the Chilkoot Trail to hike.

There are two kinds of weather here: the one that makes the area what it is, and the one you hoped it would be. Rain and clouds are common, but the climate gets drier as you travel north. The sunny days are worth it all! June and July are the driest months, while October is the wettest. Do bring rain gear so you can get out and explore, no matter what the weather. For city streets and organized tours, a raincoat, a hat, and waterproof shoes or rainboots are enough. For trail or cross-country hiking suggestions, see our Chilkoot Pass and Off the Beaten Track sections.

Most towns in Southeast Alaska are on islands, with water that is often 1000 feet deep between them. There are no roads connecting the main towns, as the expense per capita is simply too great. Water can be an obstacle, or it can be a well-marked freeway, built by nature and maintained at small cost by tides and the Coast Guard.

Alaska has used her natural waterways to provide a transportation system among the people of "Southeast," as it's often called (and you thought this was northwest!), and to link Alaska with the "Lower 48" states. Using ships instead of buses and trucks, Alaska has developed the most enjoyable public transit system in the world—the Alaska Marine Highway.

Expressive figures carved in cedar totem pole at Sitka National Historical Park.

The *Aurora* docked at Sitka in winter.

## THE ALASKA MARINE HIGHWAY
### What It Is

The Alaska Marine Highway is Alaska's answer to surface transportation for people and vehicles on the Southeast Alaska coast. People traveling in Southeast Alaska drive, but between its towns they ride the ferries. Your fellow passengers may include the circus, the carnival, Scout troops, and Little League teams.

Sailing the world's longest ferry route, 1060 statute miles in Southeast Alaska, Canada, and Puget Sound, the Alaska Marine Highway System began service in 1963 with three new ships named for Alaskan glaciers: *Malaspina, Taku,* and *Matanuska.* The *Columbia,* largest and fastest of the fleet, was added in 1974. The *Kennicott,* new in 1998, serves Southeast Alaska and makes runs across the Gulf of Alaska to Valdez and Seward. Ferries now sail weekly, from Bellingham, Washington, and several times weekly from Prince Rupert, B.C., north to Skagway, stopping at Ketchikan, Wrangell, Petersburg, Sitka, Juneau, and Haines. Thirty-six years later, the ferries still offer a great experience!

The *LeConte* and *Aurora,* smaller ferries, provide local service to Hoonah, Pelican, Tenakee Springs, Angoon, Kake, Hollis, Metlakatla, and Hyder, as well as to several mainline ports.

Serving most towns and villages in Southeast Alaska, these ferries run through narrow passages close to shore. In Wrangell Narrows and Peril Strait, passengers are near enough to see bald eagles on their nests and sometimes bear and deer on shore. The ferries run all year, though they make fewer trips in winter as ships take turns in the shipyard for annual maintenance.

Two additional ships, the *Tustumena* and *Bartlett*, also are operated by the Alaska Marine Highway. They serve South Central and Southwest Alaska, including Kodiak Island and the Aleutian Chain. Their routes connect with those of the Southeast ships only with monthly summer sailings of the *Kennicott* and occasional winter runs of the *Tustumena* between Seward and Juneau. These ships and their routes are discussed briefly in

The *Matanuska* sails out of Auke Bay on a sunny day, leaving Juneau.

the Southwestern section of this book.

## The Ships

The gleaming blue and white ships of the Alaska fleet may change your image of a "ferry". Despite running continuously, they are nearly spotless, thanks to the stewards and deck crew.

On the five mainline ships you will find cabins with two or four berths (some with three and five berths on the *Matanuska*), a cafeteria, cocktail lounge, gift shop, and a forward observation lounge. All have closed-circuit TV on which documentary films are played. There is a recliner lounge

Passengers can enjoy the view from the *Kennicott's* dining room.

airline-type chairs for sleeping if you don't have a cabin. Free showers and baggage lockers are provided. You can bring your own or rent towels, pillows, and blankets (with a deposit). The *Taku* has the fewest staterooms but has several lounges with tables for writing or playing cards and it provides plenty of seating even in summer.

The car deck holds more than 100 standard-size cars, or their equivalent in vans and campers. You may go to your vehicle while the ferry is in port, or with a crew escort during car deck calls, but Coast Guard regulations do **not** allow you to stay on the car deck while the ship is underway. If you really need something from your vehicle which can't wait until the next port or car deck call, you can ask at the purser's counter for an escort to the car deck. Pets must remain on the car deck in vehicles or in secure containers provided by their owners.

Each Southeastern ferry has a glassed solarium astern of the bridge on the top deck. It is roofed, somewhat heated, and open to the rear for a clear view of scenery and wildlife. The clean Alaskan air is a real treat. You can lounge in the solarium, and even sleep there in dry comfort if you bring a good sleeping bag, a plastic sheet or tarp, and perhaps a foam pad. Some chaise lounges are provided. On warm days passengers sun-

On to Alaska! The *Columbia* sails out of Bellingham, WA on Friday evening.

bathe and sometimes even fly kites.

The new *Kennicott* has some additional features. She can serve as an emergency operations center for oil spill cleanups or earthquakes. She is also built for open ocean sailing with stabilizers. There's a vehicle elevator topped by a helipad on her stern, giving her a boxy look and limiting the size of the solarium and its view (tents are not allowed). She has several types of staterooms and roomettes. The roomettes, with two bunks, are similar to some on Amtrak, come with or without linen, and are inside or outside (with window). They offer a very economical bed with privacy, but you shouldn't expect the space and facilities of a stateroom. Note the deck diagrams we have later in this section.

All seven Southeastern ferries have passenger elevators, located forward on the car deck. A powered baggage cart hauls baggage between the car deck and the terminal building. Passengers are responsible for all other handling of their baggage. It is convenient to have what you will need en route packed separately to bring to upper decks (including medicines, cameras, film, binoculars, etc.) so you can leave the rest in your vehicle. Baggage should not be left on the cart unless you are getting off at the next port. There is space on the car deck to stow it (ask the crew).

Many passenger bring snack food with them, and there are several places on the ships where brown-bagging is allowed, including the solarium. Fire regulations do not allow cooking aboard ship except in the galley. The steward's department will heat baby bottles and fill thermoses, if you bring them, so you can have hot coffee in your cabin. They will also

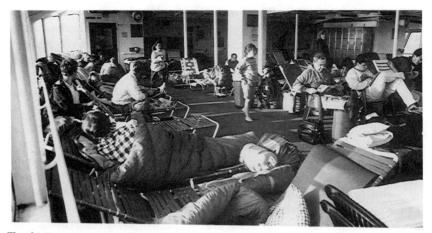

The ship's campground, the *Columbia's* solarium, with heaters overhead, baggage lockers, chaises and space claimed early by passengers headed for Alaska

heat special diet foods you bring, but are not equipped to provide them. Prescription medicines, which need refrigeration, can be stored in the galley, but food and fish cannot.

Cooks prepare at least three entrees for each lunch and dinner as well as fresh salads, sandwiches and soup. Seafood is featured at each meal, often locally caught salmon or halibut. The *Columbia* offers seated dining service in the dining room and also has a snack bar serving hamburgers, salads, etc. The other ships have cafeterias.

Alaskan law limits smoking in public facilities, allowing smoking on outside decks of the ships and in a few designated areas, including staterooms, inside.

If you need any help or information, you can ask those incredibly patient pursers (on the cabin deck forward), the watchmen and other crew members, and, in summer, the U.S. Forest Service interpreter. The ferries do not have a doctor or nurse on staff, but the pursers are qualified in first aid.

The *LeConte* and *Aurora* have no cabins, as these ships usually serve shorter distances between ports. However in summer it's possible to ride the *LeConte* from Juneau to Petersburg via Sitka and other stops and the *Aurora* from Hyder to Hollis on Tuesdays. If you'll be on the ferry overnight, you may want a blanket or sleeping bag. Both ships sell a package with a lightweight blanket and small pillow for $10. The ships have free showers (bring your own towel and soap), solariums, small cafeterias, and cocktail lounges. They are really just miniatures of the big ships.

## How The Ferry System Works

The Alaska Marine Highway is a public transit system (think of a marine bus), not a cruise ship fleet. Its routine is designed to provide the best possible service to an otherwise inaccessible area, which just happens to have fantastic scenery and wildlife. The terminals usually are not downtown, and may even be several miles away. The location of each terminal, and what is within walking distance from it, will be discussed separately for each port.

A ferry may dock at a civilized hour, allowing you to see the town and its surroundings, or it may dock and depart in the middle of the night. This you can discover from the ferry schedule. Stopovers are the solution to untimely landings in towns you want to explore, and will be discussed in the next section. Ferry schedules for summer are available the preceding autumn, and for winter, by the end of August. Early reservations (December) are advised for summer vehicle and cabin space.

The Marine Highway is not quite as predictable as the Los Angeles Freeway. Fog may slow ferries, and reliable as they are, ships do occasionally need repair. When there is a capacity load on the car deck, loading takes longer, and sometimes a ship misses the tide. This doesn't happen often, but you will be more relaxed if you don't plan tight air or rail connections, especially at Prince Rupert and Ketchikan, where the airports are on other islands that must be reached by boat. As there are several areas of tide constraint on the Bellingham run, it's best to allow at least 8 hours for south bound air and rail connections in Bellingham. If you allow 6 to 12 hours at the Skagway end, you will have time to see the town and not miss a bus connection to Whitehorse if the ship is late.

Tides may have more than 20 feet of range between high and low here. Your ship requires at least 5 feet of water under her keel in Wrangell Nar-

The *Kennicott* heads north from the Ketchikan terminal.

Campers load onto the *Malaspina* at Haines.

rows, and slack water at the tide change when she goes through Sergius Narrows near Sitka. The captain will adjust the schedule as needed for these conditions, borrowing time from port stops to get back on the printed schedule. Occasionally these adjustments allow enough time at an otherwise short stop, like Wrangell or Petersburg, for a walk to town or a visit to a museum. Making up time from port stops may leave no time for exploring some towns, especially in summer when loading the car deck takes longer. If you really want to see a town, plan a stopover.

Because most ferry docks are out of town and the ships often arrive outside open hours, shopping en route can be difficult. In Ketchikan there is a shopping center 1/4 mile north of the dock, with a 24-hour grocery store—the easiest spot on the whole route for you to resupply with ice if you need it in your RV. The Sitka stop is long enough, but shopping may mean not going on the sightseeing tour. The gift shops on the larger ships have some supplies and toiletries, as do coin-operated vending machines on board. It's wise to bring what you will need en route, including supplies for children's activities if you bring children.

## RESERVATIONS AND PEAK SEASONS

In summer the cabins and car decks are full, requiring either reservations or considerable flexibility in your schedule. Reservations are advisable **any** time for cars and cabins. For summer travel you should make these reservations by December 1 to be sure of getting your choice of date. Flash! The ferry systemhopes to start acting on reservations for summer

)vember 1, 1999 and on reservations for winter and spring 2000 ₵ 15, 1999.

on standby" with a vehicle can mean getting up at 3 a.m. to see if yѵ going to get dropped off at a port to wait for the next day's ship. Standby vehicles usually have to unload at each port and remain in the terminal area for reloading during the port stop. Walk-on passengers without vehicles or staterooms usually don't need reservations between Southeast Alaskan ports though you should have them on the Bellingham run. Even in peak season there often is car space north of Ketchikan as far as Juneau, though not always between Juneau and Haines.

The staterooms are often fully reserved, though there may be some no-shows. If you don't have a room but want one, sign the purser's wait list as soon as you board the ship. In Bellingham the list is available in the terminal. After the ship sails, any available rooms are sold in order from the list.

Sometimes the ferry system offers temporary promotional or excursion fares for some destinations. You should ask if there are any in effect that you could use. We don't list these as they're not known at presstime.

The ferry system accepts applications for reservations any time they are sent in, acting on them in the order received starting the first working day of November. For example, in September 1999, you could apply for ferry reservations for July 2000, and your application would be held until November 1999, but would be acted on before those received in October 1999. Note: at the same time a full staff of phone operators starts taking reservations, putting them on the same computer. Very shortly some sailings from Bellingham have all staterooms booked.

If you have only one or two available dates, you may want to write in early or fax (907) 277-4829, but also call on the first working morning in November if you can get a line. You'll find an automatic redialing phone useful. A toll-free reservation phone system has been installed in Juneau with additional agents for reservations and information, (800) 642-0066 inside and outside Alaska and TDD (800) 764-3779. To call from Canada, use (800) 665-6414. The system operates 10–12 hours a day in heavy demand times, so you may get through outside normal working hours. Alaska time is one hour earlier than Pacific time, standard or daylight.

You can also call any ferry reservation office you can get through to, such as Bellingham, (360) 676-8445 or (800) 585-8445 within WA; Homer, (800) 382-9229; and Kodiak, (800) 526-6731. These offices keep long hours even in winter and are on the ferry computer system.

The Alaska Marine Highway website is helpful and is getting even better. www.dot.state.ak.us/external/amhs/home.html  On it you can use

## REQUEST FOR RESERVATIONS

DO NOT SEND PAYMENT UNTIL RESERVATIONS ARE CONFIRMED

| Full Name | | | CUSTOMER NO. (if any) |
|---|---|---|---|

Travel Agency or Business Name (if applicable)

Mailing Address

City, State/Country, Zip Code

| Daytime Phone ( ) | Home Phone ( ) | FAX ( ) |
|---|---|---|

E-Mail Address

**VEHICLE INFORMATION**

☐ Passenger car/truck
☐ Truck/camper
☐ Camper Van
☐ Motorhome
☐ Vehicle with trailer
☐ Vehicle is Over 6 ft 6 in Tall
☐ Other (describe)

Veh. Height | Veh. Width | Veh. Length*

*This figure should reflect the total vehicle length, including hitch and trailer, if any.

The Alaska Marine Highway System Internet Website address is:

http://www.dot.state.ak.us/external/amhs/home.html

**The following information is required by federal regulations. Omissions may result in booking delays.**

| FULL NAMES OF PERSONS TRAVELING: | AGE (If under 12) A=12 or older S= Senior (65 or older) | Male / Female |
|---|---|---|
| | | |
| | | |
| | | |
| | | |

| ____ Number of Pets | If a cabin is NOT available, are you willing to travel without one? ☐ Yes ☐ No | Approximate date you will ____ be departing your area. |
|---|---|---|

| TRAVEL DATE & SHIP (if important) | FROM | TO | CABIN (yes or no) | ALTERNATE TRAVEL DATES |
|---|---|---|---|---|
| | | | | |
| | | | | |
| | | | | |
| | | | | |

| FOR RESERVATIONS, CALL: | |
|---|---|
| 1-800-642-0066 or 1-907-465-3941 | 1. Port of embarkation/debarkation |
| TDD : 1-800-764-3779 (Text telephone for the speech or hearing impaired) | 2. Full names of all travelers, and ages of those under 12 years |
| FAX: (907) 277-4829 | 3. Width, height and overall length of vehicles (including extensions such as trailer hitches, bike racks, and storage containers) |
| When you call to make a reservation, you will need to know: | 4. Mailing address |

5. Telephone numbers

6. Alternate travel dates (vehicle or cabin space may not be available on your first choice of travel dates)

7. Approximate date you will be leaving your home.

642-0066

Photocopy this form, fill out, and fax to apply for a reservation. Used with permission of the Alaska Marine Highway System.

the Ferry Schedules Search Engine to search the dates and port-to-port segments you'd like to sail. It will list your choices in ships, dates, and times that may fit your schedule.

Your reservation request should include your ports of embarkation and debarkation, names of all members of your party, ages of children under 12 years at time of trip, and stopovers if known ahead. You also must supply the width, height, and length *including* bumper and hitch of your vehicle, your mailing address and telephone number, alternate dates if cabin or vehicle space isn't available, and the date you will leave home. You must pay the fare at least 45 days before sailing or the reservation will be cancelled.

Demand for ferry transportation to and from Bellingham greatly exceeds the capacity of the ferry system, especially during peak season. Without building additional ships that aren't needed much of the year, the system can't provide all the staterooms and vehicle space people want. There is some luck as well as early action required in getting those reservations. An alternative, and the pleasure of riding less crowded ships, is finding another way to or from Prince Rupert, British Columbia, using highway, rail, air, or British Columbia ferries, or driving to Hyder, Alaska for the Tuesday sailings of the *Aurora*. These are discussed under "Prince Rupert" and "Driving the Alaska Marine Highway Your Way," the next section. All passengers, including walk-ons, should have reservations to or from Bellingham.

Traffic flow during summer varies as follows:
**Northbound:** Traffic increases through June, peaks in mid-July, then tapers off gradually. **Southbound:** Traffic increases the second week of July and remains heavy until Labor Day, when it drops off rapidly.

Many people avoid crowded ferries and improve their chances of getting cabin and vehicle reservations, even in summer, by going north in May or early June, south in late June or early July. Others go north in August and return after Labor Day. **$Tip**: some airlines and trains, including Canada's Via Rail, offer big discounts for travel in May and June, especially for seniors—useful for ferry connections.

May usually offers **much** better weather than late September or October and longer daylight hours. Some tourist activities such as Glacier Bay tour boat and lodge dates and community summer plays are geared to a mid-May to mid-September season. Ferry service increases in frequency during May as ships end winter layup. Life aboard ship is more relaxed with seats available and no lines in cafeterias during spring.

Even in summer, the smaller ferries, *LeConte* and *Aurora*, are generally less crowded than the mainliners.

The weekends of the Little Norway Festival in Petersburg, May 13–16, 1999, and of the Southeast Alaska Fair in Haines, August 11–15, 1999, fill the ships between Petersburg, Juneau, and Haines even for walk-on passengers (reservations advised). If you plan around the foreseeable peak periods, you will find the ships less crowded and more relaxing. A fringe benefit: more of the passengers will be Alaskans, with lots to tell about their home.

Between October 1 and April 30, most fares are the same as in summer *except* for promotional fares which sometimes include the driver free with the vehicle (most likely at non-holiday times during winter). In winter drivers of ticketed vehicles sometimes get a 75% discount from their fares, and anyone can bring a bicycle free on the ferry.

During peak season, you and your fellow passengers will appreciate courtesy in using seats, especially near windows. There are no reserved seats on the ships, so they cannot be held while you eat or sleep somewhere else. You may want to bring a foam or air cushion for sitting on deck on nice days. If you smoke, please observe the smoking areas and think twice before lighting a pipe or cigar in enclosed parts of the ship.

Some passengers use freestanding tents on the solarium deck, except on the *Kennicott* where tents aren't allowed. It's no problem when the solarium isn't crowded, but in summer can take more than one or two people's share of the space and block others' view of the scenery everyone came to see. The Coast Guard prohibits cooking anywhere on the ship except by the crew in the galley.

Sometimes an all-out effort by the crew in Bellingham or Prince Rupert is needed to fit in all cars. That may mean that it isn't possible to park all vehicles according to their destinations. You may then have to drive off in Ketchikan (and stay with your car during the port stop) so vehicles can be reloaded in the order they will unload farther on.

## TABLE 2
## MILEAGE AND SAILING TIME ON THE ALASKA
## MARINE HIGHWAY FROM BELLINGHAM

| Ports | Travel Times (at 17 knots) | Nautical Miles |
| --- | --- | --- |
| Bellingham to Ketchikan | 36 Hours | 594 |
| Prince Rupert to Ketchikan | 6 Hours | 92 |
| Ketchikan to Wrangell | 5 hours 35 Min. | 88 |
| Wrangell to Petersburg | 3 Hours | 40 |
| Petersburg to Auke Bay | 7 Hours 30 Min. | 128 |
| Auke Bay to Haines | 4 Hours 15 Min. | 68 |
| Haines to Skagway | 1 Hour | 14 |

| | | |
|---|---|---|
| Auke Bay to Sitka | 8 Hours 45 Min. | 131 |
| Sitka to Petersburg | 9 Hours 45 Min. | 151 |
| Bellingham to Skagway "direct" | | 934 |
| Bellingham to Skagway via Sitka | | 1086 |
| Prince Rupert to Skagway "direct" | | 430 |
| Prince Rupert to Skagway via Sitka | | 584 |

Highway—Land Miles

| | |
|---|---|
| Haines to Valdez | 702 |
| Haines to Fairbanks | 653 |
| Haines to Anchorage | 775 |
| Skagway to Whitehorse | 108 |
| Skagway to Fairbanks | 710 |
| Skagway to Anchorage | 832 |

A nautical mile is 1.15 statute miles. A knot is 1 nautical mile per hour. The *Columbia*'s trip takes less time than is shown. However all ferries reduce speed in narrows and congested areas and may adjust speed to reach narrows at a chosen time of the tide. Ships on the Bellingham run do not stop at Prince Rupert north or southbound.

## TABLE 3
## RATES ON THE ALASKA MARINE HIGHWAY

May 1 to September 30, 1999, from the ferry system's full rate schedule.

Staterooms are available on the five major vessels, but not on *Aurora* and *LeConte*. All staterooms have shower, toilet and basin, except the no facilities rooms and roomettes listed separately on the *Kennicott*. Two berth cabins are hardest to reserve in peak season. Berths are upper with ladder, and lower. "Outside" rooms have window.

| | Bellingham to Skagway | Prince Rupert to Skagway |
|---|---|---|
| Passengers, 12 years & older | $ 252 | $ 130 |
| Vehicle 15' to 19' long | 707 | 356 |
| Vehicle 25' long | 1361 | 686 |
| Motorcycle (2-wheel, no trailer) | 213 | 109 |
| Bicycle, Kayak less than 100 lbs. | 42 | 25 |
| Children under 2, free. | | |
| Children 2 through 11 | 127 | 65 |
| Pet (free between Alaskan ports) | 25 | 10 |
| 2 berth cabins, all ships, outside | 271 | 121 |
| 2 berth cabins, all ships, inside | 234 | 105 |
| 4 berth cabins, all ships, outside | 373 | 163 |
| 4 berth cabins, all ships inside | 321 | 141 |
| 3 berth cabin, *Matanuska, Columbia* & | | |
| *Malaspina* (outside) | 304 | 129 |

4 berth with sitting room, outside
*Columbia, Malaspina*               405                 177

*Matanuska*, running between Prince Rupert and Skagway, also has 5 berth combinations, of 2 and 3 berth cabins.

*Kennicott* has cabins as listed above plus the following without facilities:

| | | |
|---|---|---|
| 2 berth cabin outside | 213 | 93 |
| 2 berth cabin inside | 192 | 84 |
| 2 berth roomette outside/no linen | 128 | 56 |
| 2 berth roomette inside/no linen | 106 | 46 |

(Linen may be rented separately or you can bring a sleeping bag.)

*Kennicott* fares for the "intertie" run from Bellingham, Ketchikan and Juneau to Seward and Valdez listed in schedule. Bellingham–Seward: Adult $386, Child 2–11 $194. Juneau–Seward: Adult $148, Child 2–11 $74. Meals and cabins not included.

For rates between other ports see complete schedule. For longer vehicle rates, call (800) 642-0066. Meals are additional. No out-of-state personal checks are accepted. However Visa, MasterCard, American Express and Diners Club are accepted by phone (800) 642-0066 and (907) 465-3941 and at terminals. Payment must be made at least 45 days before sailing to hold reservations. Lower rates apply to vehicles to 10 feet long and subcompacts 10 to 15 feet long. Cancellation fees apply to any change made within 14 days of sailing that results in a reduction of fare.

Reservations are strongly advised for cabins and vehicles. Fares are paid separately for each segment if you plan stopovers. Walk-on passengers boarding in Bellingham or sailing to Bellingham need reservations. Passengers *without* vehicles must check in at Bellingham 2 hours before departure, at all other ports, 1 hour.

At all terminals, passengers with reserved vehicles must check in at terminal *before* lining up in parking lot. Check-in times are 3 hours before departure at Bellingham and Prince Rupert, 2 hours at Ketchikan, Juneau, Haines, Skagway, Kodiak, Seward and Homer, 1.5 hours at Petersburg, and 1 hour at all other ports. Checking in a vehicle late can result in losing your reservation and going on standby. Anyone cancelling anywhere on the route is encouraged to call the terminal or ferry office so others can plan to use the space.

## 1999 SEASON

Most staterooms to and from Bellingham are booked early in the preceding December from June 1 through August, though there is usually some car deck space left. Most staterooms throughout the system are booked and car deck space is filling fast, but there is space for walk-on passengers even out of Bellingham. While there are some no-shows and it's worth signing the purser's wait list for staterooms as early as possible, you can't count on it. In Bellingham the purser's list is in the terminal. For all other ports it is at the purser's office aboard ship.

From Prince Rupert car and stateroom space is limited until late May when the last ships come back from winter maintenance. For the remainder of the summer, this port offers the most car deck and stateroom space as there are 4 mainline vessel sailings per week, daily except Wednesday. Alternatives are traveling south bound during early summer, traveling earlier or later, or flying to one of the Southeast Alaska ports and riding ferries around their route from there. From Prince Rupert the *Matanuska* has the most staterooms, the *Kennicott* and the *Taku* fewer.

Sailing times from Prince Rupert vary with tides to avoid having two ships using docks at the same time, particularly at Sitka. Most Skagway stops are 1 to 3 hours long, allowing time for a walk around town or up to Dewey Lake—making a good one-day excursion from Juneau or Haines.

### Sailings To And From Bellingham

*Columbia*: Friday evenings. Has 91 staterooms and room for 140 cars, though some space is taken by freight vans. Sailings are at 6 p.m. Reserved vehicles must check in before 3 p.m. or risk cancellation. Foot passengers usually start loading about 4 p.m. Southbound Bellingham arrivals are 6–10 a.m. Friday mornings. She leaves Skagway on Manday evenings.

Note: the *Columbia* stops at Sitka southbound, usually in the middle of the day. Arrivals in Juneau are Monday morning northbound.

In winter and early spring either the *Kennicott* or the *Matanuska* leaves Bellingham on Friday evenings.

### Sailings To And From Prince Rupert

*Matanuska*: Wednesday and Saturday. Has 112 staterooms, mostly 2 and 3 berth, and room for 105 cars. Both sailings go only as far as Juneau until mid-September. Goes to Sitka northbound onthe Saturday sailing, arriving about midnight, and southbound Friday morning early.

*Taku*: Monday and Thursday. Both sailings go only to Juneau and turn back to Prince Rupert. Stops at Sitka northbound Friday late afternoon and southbound Saturday evening. In winter she sails between Prince Rupert and Skagway, sometimes going to Hollis. The *Taku* is shorter than the other mainliners, but is a very comfortable ship with 44 staterooms and room for 90 cars. With all its lounge space compared to the number of staterooms and vehicles carried, the *Taku* always has seating even in peak season. Some lounges have tables for writing or playing cards.

Note: Most passengers using these ships north and southbound in summer 1999 will have to stop over in Juneau to connect with the *Malaspina's* daily run or another ship. The Auke Bay terminal is 14 miles north of downtown and is often closed at night when there are no ships. I strongly suggest you plan for this layover and make reservations for rooms in Juneau if you need them.

*Kennicott*: One monthly sailing crosses the Gulf of Alaska to Valdez and Seward with stops at Ketchikan and Juneau. Sailings not going to Valdez stop at Sitka northbound Wednesday in very early morning. In winter she will serve Southwestern routes while the *Tustumena* is in shipyard. Has 109 staterooms and roomettes and room for 120 cars.

## Sailings To And From Stewart/Hyder

*Aurora*: The *Aurora* sails from Hyder (Stewart, B.C.) every Tuesday afternoon June 1–September 14, 1999, arriving in Ketchikan about midnight. You can continue north on the *Kennicott* Wednesday evening. No staterooms, but has showers. Most service is between Ketchikan and Metlakatla and Hollis.

## Northern Panhandle

*LeConte:* Has no staterooms but has showers. Takes cars and vans. Leaves Petersburg Tuesday and Thursday and sails to Juneau via Kake, Sitka, Angoon, Tenakee, and Hoonah. Has three runs to Sitka per week with stops at most of the villages listed above. Usually arrives at Sitka in daylight.

She goes to Pelican at least once a month all year, but twice a month in summer on Sundays, May through September. For additional information, see the section on Pelican. With a 1-2 hour layover at Pelican and passage through areas where you may see humpback whales or sea otters, this is a scenic, enjoyable excursion from Juneau.

*Malaspina*: Has 84 staterooms and room for 105 cars. Most outside rooms are 4 berth and most inside rooms are 2 berth. In summer 1999 through September 12, runs daily round trips from Juneau to Haines and Skagway. She arrives southbound in Juneau at 10 p.m. Most passengers continuing south will have to stop over in Juneau. Travelers flying into Juneau will find this daily ship service in daylight a fine way to make short trips to Haines and Sakagway.

## Alaska—Sitka Run in 1999

The days each ship goes to Sitka are noted in the earlier section on sailings from Bellingham and Prince Rupert. The smaller *LeConte* sails to Sitka three times a week and turns around after a stop Saturday on a round trip from Juneau, a good weekend excursion. Check the schedule as the length of time in Sitka varies from 1 hour to 6 or more. Bus tours are available for arrivals after 5 a.m. until late September! Sitka really does welcome you!

## Winter

Winter rates are effective October 1 through April 30. During that period drivers of vehicles traveling on the ferry will receive 75% discounts from their adult passenger fare. Any ticketed passenger can bring a bicycle free during winter.

*Always* ask (even in summer) if there are any special promotional fares such as discounts for drivers of cars towing trailers, excursion fares to Pelican, or special round trip fares anywhere on the routes.

## British Columbia Ferries
## Port Hardy to Prince Rupert

The British Columbia ferry, *Queen of The North*, (750 passengers, 157 cars) sails between Port Hardy on northern Vancouver Island and Prince Rupert. In summer 1999 she is running all-daylight 15-hour cruises between Port Hardy and Prince Rupert, with all departures at 7:30 a.m. and all arrivals about 10:30 p.m. There is a short weekly stop at Bella Bella. Note that a shipload of passengers can fill accommodations in Port Hardy the night before and the night after the ferry's arrival. We have listed motels in Port Hardy and advise making reservations. Port McNeil, a few miles farther south, also has several motels.

| Schedule: | Lv Port Hardy | Lv Prince Rupert |
|---|---|---|
| June | odd dates | even dates |
| July | odd dates | even dates |
| August | even dates | odd dates |
| September | odd dates | even dates |

October: Southbound2, 4, 6, 8, 10, 12, 14, 16. Northbound—1, 3, 5, 7, 9, 11, 13, 15, 17.

The *Queen of the North* has food and drink service, elevators, day rooms for one-way travelers and staterooms on the boat deck which may be reserved for round trips, including 4 equipped for wheelchairs. It has observation decks and lounges and a children's play area.

### 1999 Summer Fares, Port Hardy to Prince Rupert
### (lower in May, October, and winter), Canadian $

| | |
|---|---|
| Passenger, 12 years & older | $104 |
| Vehicle to 6'8" high, 20' long | 214 |
| Vehicle over 6'8" high | 356 |
| Motorcycle | 107 |
| Motorcycle with sidecar or trailer | 157.50 |
| Bicycle | 6.50 |
| Kayak/canoe | 17.50 |

Surcharge for vehicles over 20' long, $17.80 per ft. over 20', depending on whether vehicle is under or over height. *Note the saving* if you take off any cartop baggage or boat you can while riding the B.C. ferries, if it will allow you to stay at standard height! The ship has dayrooms with 2 or 4 berths. Prices vary with deck.

While the B.C. ferry dock in Prince Rupert adjacent to the Alaska ferry dock allows ships of both lines to be docked at the same time, if the southbound Alaska ferry is late, you may not be able to make same day connections there. The B. C. ferry sails promptly at 7:30 a.m. and you have to unload and clear Canadian Customs with a shipload of passengers. If you can spend a day in Prince Rupert and reserve accordingly, it will be a surer thing, especially with a vehicle. Northbound passengers arrive on the B.C. ferry the night before so the connection is easy, though you will have to stay ashore that night.

Most travelers with vehicles ride the B.C. ferries between the mainland and Vancouver Island, sailing Horseshoe Bay–Nanaimo, Tsawwassen–Nanaimo, Tsawwassen–Swartz Bay (near Victoria). Sailings are almost hourly in mid-summer from early morning to 9 p.m. or later first come-first served. Allow about C$50 for a standard car and driver, more for vehicles over 6'8" high or 20' long.

British Columbia resident seniors with identification receive discounts as do British Columbia handicapped residents who must travel with an attendant. For safety reasons, children under 12 are not allowed to ride the ferries without an adult.

Note that the B.C. ferries also have a very scenic route, "The Discovery Coast", from Port Hardy to Klemtu with stops at Ocean Falls, Bella Coola, Bella Bella, and Namu, giving access to hundreds of miles of kayaking and fishing.

**British Columbia Ferry Corporation,** 1112 Fort St., Victoria, BC, Canada V8V 4V2. Internet: http://www.bcferries.bc.ca At this very helpful web site, you can get schedules, make reservations, and even get current estimates of the number of sailings you'll have to wait at some terminals, for all the routes the system sails.

Phones:

| | |
|---|---|
| Vancouver | (604) 669-1211 |
| Victoria | (250) 386-3431 |
| Fax: | (250) 381-5452 |
| Port Hardy | (250) 949-6722 |
| Prince Rupert | (250) 624-9627 |

### Winter on The B.C. Ferries

Fares are based on 3 seasons—*peak* from June 1 through Oct. 17 *shoulder* April 30 to May 31 and Oct. 17 to winter dates, slightly reduced, and *low*, winter to early spring, about 40% off.

# Columbia

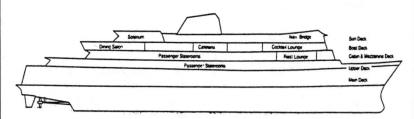

**INBOARD PROFILE**

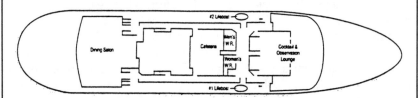

**BOAT DECK**
Cafeteria, main dining salon, cocktail lounge

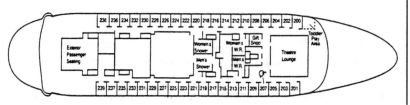

**CABIN DECK** 200-series staterooms

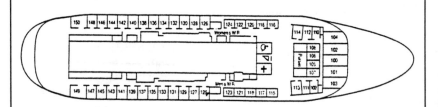

**UPPER DECK** 100-series staterooms

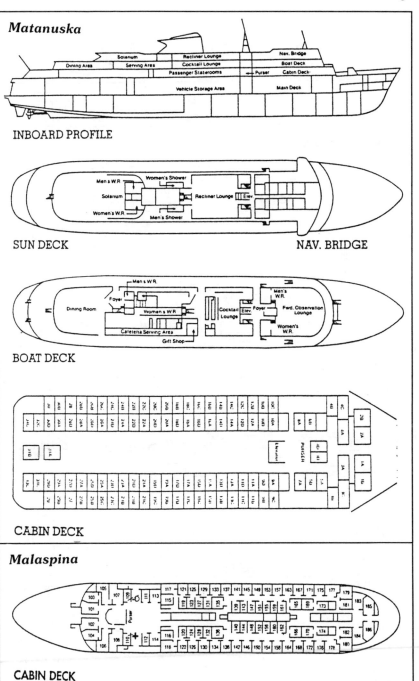

**Matanuska**

INBOARD PROFILE

SUN DECK            NAV. BRIDGE

BOAT DECK

CABIN DECK

**Malaspina**

CABIN DECK

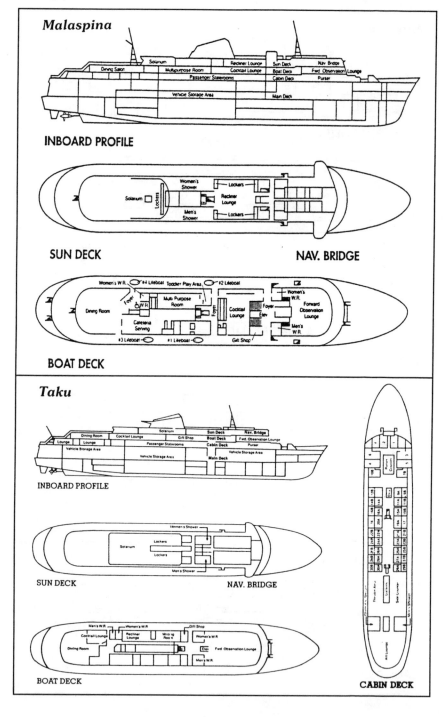

# Kennicott

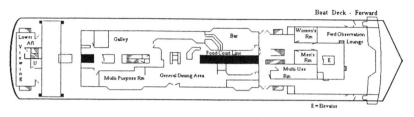

Lower Aft Viewing | U | Galley | Bar | Women's Rm | Fwd Observation Lounge | Men's Rm | Multi-Use Rm | Multi-Purpose Rm | General Dining Area | Food Court Line | E

E = Elevator

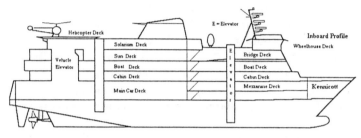

Helicopter Deck — Solarium Deck — Sun Deck — Boat Deck — Cabin Deck — Main Car Deck

Vehicle Elevator

E = Elevator

Inboard Profile

Wheelhouse Deck — Bridge Deck — Boat Deck — Cabin Deck — Mezzanine Deck

Kennicott

Bridge / Sun Deck - Forward

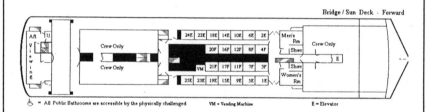

Aft Viewing | U | Crew Only | Crew Only | Men's Rm | Shwr | Crew Only | Women's Rm | E

24E 22E 18E 14E 10E 6E 2E
20F 16F 12F 8F 4F
VM 21F 17F 11F 7F 3F
25E 23E 19E 15E 9E 5E 1E

&#x267F; = All Public Bathrooms are accessible by the physically challenged.   VM = Vending Machine   E = Elevator

Cabin Deck - Forward

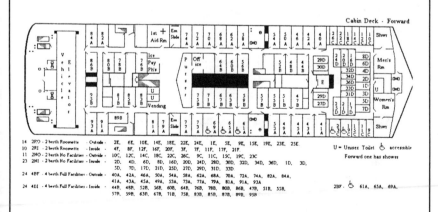

V e h i c l e   E l e v a t o r

1st Aid Rm · Em Slide · Ice · Pay Ph's · Off ice · Purser's · Vending · Em Slide · Men's Rm · Women's Rm · Shwr

| 14 | 2FO - 2 berth Roomette | - Outside - | 2E, 6E, 10E, 14E, 18E, 22E, 24E, 1E, 5E, 9E, 15E, 19E, 23E, 25E. | U = Unisex Toilet &#x267F; accessible |
| 10 | 2FI - 2 berth Roomette | - Inside - | 4F, 8F, 12F, 16F, 20F, 3F, 7F, 11F, 17F, 21F. | Forward one has shower |
| 11 | 2NO - 2 berth No Facilities | - Outside - | 10C, 12C, 14C, 18C, 22C, 26C, 9C, 11C, 15C, 19C, 23C | |
| 23 | 2NI - 2 berth No Facilities | - Inside - | 2D, 4D, 6D, 8D, 16D, 20D, 24D, 28D, 30D, 32D, 34D, 36D, 1D, 3D, 5D, 7D, 17D, 21D, 25D, 27D, 29D, 31D, 33D | |
| 24 | 4BF - 4 berth Full Facilities | - Outside - | 40A, 42A, 46A, 50A, 54A, 58A, 62A, 68A, 70A, 72A, 74A, 82A, 84A, 41A, 43A, 45A, 49A, 53A, 73A, 77A, 79A, 81A, 91A, 93A | |
| 24 | 4BI - 4 berth Full Facilities | - Inside - | 44B, 48B, 52B, 56B, 60B, 64B, 76B, 78B, 80B, 86B, 47B, 51B, 55B, 57B, 59B, 63B, 67B, 71B, 75B, 83B, 85B, 87B, 89B, 95B | 2BF &#x267F; 61A, 65A, 69A. |

31

Deck Diagrams

ings between Port Hardy and Prince Rupert have been Sat-
bound, Friday southbound, on the *Queen of Prince Rupert*. In
ear Christmas, there are additional sailings. Sailings are over-
h a short stop at Bella Bella. Staterooms are available at addi-
st. Call the numbers above for information, schedule changes, and
reservations.

### Information, Reservations

For reservations, schedules, and information: **Alaska Marine Highway**, P.O. Box 25535, Juneau, AK 99802. (907) 465-3941 or (800) 642-0066, any-where in the U.S. including Alaska. TDD (800) 764-3779. Fax (907) 277-4829. The Alaska Marine Highway Tour Desk at this number can also make reservations for excursions such as flightseeing over glaciers or tours to Glacier Bay. In Anchorage, (907) 272-7116.

The web site is http://www.dot.state.ak.us/external/amhs/home.html Here you can print out a schedule or request one, get fares for passen-gers, cabins, and vehicles from 10 to 70 feet long (including combined tow), latest promotional fares, print out a reservations form, and make reserva-tions (and even check the cafeteria menu and prices). The Ferry Schedule Search Engine on the home page is very helpful planning your choice of sailings.

Important! If you're meeting an arriving ferry to get on or pick up a pas-senger, it's wise *always* to call the terminal an hour ahead of its scheduled arrival to see what time it is actually arriving (in case it has been delayed by fog or tides). There's a phone number with a recording during closed hours in each town. Scheduled arrivals are given for a day or two ahead on the phone and on a notice board at each terminal.

**Alaska Division of Tourism**, P.O. Box E, Juneau, AK 99811. (907) 465-2010. Can send you their free annual *Alaska Travel Planner* with lots of info!

**AlaskaPass**, P.O. Box 351, Vashon, WA 98070. (800) 248-7598. (206) 463-6550, fax (206) 463-6777. Offers transportation passes good in both Alaska and Canada for buses, trains, B.C. and Alaska ferries, for 8, 15, 22, and 30 day trips May–September 15. If you will be on the go for most of your trip, these can save over $100 per person. web: www.alaskapass.com

## DRIVING THE ALASKA MARINE HIGHWAY— YOUR WAY

The Marine Highway is a well-designed system with thoroughly com-petent, experienced crews, running along an incredibly beautiful route. If you simply get on at one end and ride to the other, you will have a memo-rable trip. If you want to experience more of Southeastern Alaska, here is how you can do it:

The *Columbia.* docked at Skagway.

## Getting to the Ferry

From outside Southeastern Alaska, you can reach the ferries at the following locations.

BELLINGHAM, Washington: 90 miles north of Seattle on I-5. Airlines to Bellingham and via Bellingham Airporter from SeaTac. Highway connections with bus service. Amtrak has a daily train between Seattle and Vancouver, stopping in Bellingham northbound in the morning, southbound in the evening. Details in Bellingham section. Ferry sailings are weekly on Friday evenings, all year.

PRINCE RUPERT, B.C.: Airline, rail, and highway connections from interior Canada; airline from Vancouver; and B.C. ferry from Port Hardy on Vancouver Island. Ferries sail every other day in summer, less often in winter. In winter the ferry runs from Tsawwassen near Vancouver to Prince Rupert so you can choose whether or not to drive to Port Hardy. For accommodations in summer, especially at Port Hardy, be sure to get reservations in advance. (Note: we are publishing a guidebook to Vancouver Island, *Vancouver Island Traveler*, by Searby. To make the most of your time on the island, with all its choices for adventure, see information on the last pages of this book.)

From Horseshoe Bay near Vancouver, you can take the B.C. ferry, with or without your car, to Nanaimo near Victoria. You can then drive up Van-

The *Columbia's* baggage tug and carts haul walk-on passengers' baggage up to the terminal.

couver Island or ride the bus (**Pacific Coach Lines**, 710 Douglas St., Victoria, B.C., Canada. Phone (250) 287-7151) to Port Hardy at the north end. It's a 7-hour bus ride. For additional information, **British Columbia Ferry Corporation**, 1112 Fort St., Victoria, B.C., Canada V8V 4V2. Phones: Prince Rupert, (250) 624-9627, Port Hardy (250) 949-6722 Vancouver (604) 669-1211, Victoria (250) 386-3431. Schedule and fares are given in the 1999 season section. Reservations are a must in summer, especially if you bring a car. Rail information is in the Prince Rupert section.

STEWART/HYDER: Highway. Ferry *Aurora* meets the highway here on Tuesdays in summer 1999 at the head of Portland Canal, the most scenic route into or out of southern Southeast Alaska. Reservations for vehicles are a must as ship is small and doesn't come back for a week!

HAINES, ALASKA: Haines Highway, connects with the Alaska Highway, and bus service. Motorcoaches, bus: **Alaskon Express**, mid-May to mid-September. (800) 544-2206.

SKAGWAY, ALASKA: Highway and bus to Whitehorse, Yukon. White Pass and Yukon Railroad runs excursions daily from Skagway to Fraser, near White Pass summit in summer. In 1999 some trains go on to Bennett and Carcross (see Skagway chapter). The Klondike Highway connecting

# Time

North of the Alaska–Canada border in Dixon Entrance, your route is in the Alaska Time Zone, one hour west of the Pacific Time Zone. Blessed with a state government which doesn't believe in longitude, Alaska in 1983 persuaded the federal government to reduce its four time zones to two. The state is on Daylight Savings when the rest of the nation is.

All ferries operate on Alaska Time even when in Canada or Washington. You change time zones (set your watch back 1 hour) when you board the ship at Bellingham or Prince Rupert. From there you have a leisurely few days to get over jet lag!

During May, June, and July Southeast Alaska has very long hours of daylight though not the midnight sun that shines farther north. There is nearly an hour more daylight at the north end of Southeastern Alaska than at the south during these months. The situation is reversed in winter as daylight in Juneau is about seven hours a day. In summer the sun is up over 19 hours a day and much of the night is twilight.

| Location | Date | Sunrise | Sunset | Daylight Hours |
|----------|------|---------|--------|----------------|
| Juneau | June 20 | 3:51 a.m. | 10:09 p.m. | 18 |
| | Aug. 20 | 5:30 a.m. | 8:31 p.m. | 15 |
| | Dec. 20 | 8:46 a.m. | 3:07 p.m. | 6 |
| Prince Rupert | June 20 | 4:30 a.m. | 9:30 p.m. | 17 |
| | Aug. 20 | 6:00 a.m. | 8:00 p.m. | 14 |
| Seattle | June 20 | 5:00 a.m. | 9:00 p.m. | 16 |
| | Aug. 20 | 6:15 a.m. | 7:20 p.m. | 13 |

Approximate times of sunset and sunrise with hours of daylight.

to the Alaska Highway southeast of Whitehorse is open all year.

**Airlines**: **Alaska Airlines** (800) 426-0333 flies from Seattle and Anchorage to Ketchikan, Wrangell, Petersburg, Sitka, Juneau and Gustavus in Southeastern Alaska. Air taxi services connect to other towns.

Unlike flights on more competitive routes in the Lower 48 states, and even the route from Seattle to Anchorage, the flights serving Southeastern Alaska from Seattle and Anchorage feature some of the highest seat/mile costs in the country. There are discounted fares, especially during the off-season.

**Alaska Airlines** offers seniors 62 and over a 10% discount on any published fares. A companion of any age traveling with a senior also gets the 10% discount (ask for it, as they don't always tell you)!

If you're flying from the Pacific Northwest, you may find the 14-day advance purchase excursion fares requiring a Saturday night stay the best available rate, especially if you're a senior or traveling with one. Some now require 21 days advance purchase. Most are good for 30-day trips.

Many people fly to Juneau and use ferries for excursions throughout Southeast. *Suggestion:* for a very enjoyable week, you could fly from Seattle to Ketchikan, and ride the ferry to Skagway and back to Ketchikan in just over two days going direct both ways, or in three days if you go to Sitka on one leg. This would allow several days for stopovers in your choice of towns.

**Alaska Airlines** and the ferry system sometimes have a package fare allowing you to fly one way and ride the ferry the other.

**Stopovers:** if you want to stopover in towns along the route, you pay for each segment, only a few dollars more than if you didn't stop. For example, in 1999, an adult riding without stopovers from Bellingham to Skagway would pay $252 (not including meals, stateroom, or vehicle). Stopping over for as many days as you wish in Ketchikan and Juneau would add $18. Check the schedule when you are planning this to see which ferry you want to catch for the next leg. Make reservations for cabin or vehicle, if you will need them, before you leave the terminal if you have not done so already.

**Walk-on passengers**: It is easier to be flexible if you don't have a vehicle or a cabin, as there is usually space available on any of the ships for walk-on passengers. Get a reservation to or from Bellingham, perhaps in Juneau and Haines during fair weekend in the third week of August, and between Juneau and Petersburg on the weekend nearest May 17, the Little Norway Festival. You may weigh this convenience against the use you could make of a camper ashore. In general, there are few roads to drive

A DeHavilland Beaver and Cessnas on floats taxi out for takeoff going sightseeing and to a salmon bake near Juneau—one way to go beyond the airline or ship in Alaska.

on out of town, and these are short, and rental cars are usually available in the towns. If you bring your own car, you may spend time that you would prefer to spend sightseeing at ports in vehicle lineups waiting to load or reload.

**Vehicles**: Leaving your vehicle in Bellingham (next section) or Prince Rupert is one solution. Bringing a bicycle, very inexpensively, on the ferry, is another. Many people travel without vehicles, saving considerable cost on the ferry, and rent a car as needed where they stop over. There are car rentals in all mainline ports. You should reserve these by phone with credit card ahead of time as numbers are limited.

If you are traveling with a vehicle, you can plan stopovers ahead and reserve vehicle space for those segments of your trip. Once the cars are loaded on the car deck according to the ports where they will be unloaded, it is too late to change your mind. Note the required check-in times for vehicles at each port. Late arrival during loading can cost you your car deck reservation, putting your vehicle at the end of the standby line.

For vehicles sent on the ferries unaccompanied by a passenger and undriveable vehicles, you pay a surcharge of $10 within Alaska, $20 to or from Prince Rupert and Stewart/Hyder, and $50 to or from Bellingham. Loading and unloading are the shipper's responsibility.

U.S.-licensed vehicles may be left in Canada for as long as 45 days without a permit. In Prince Rupert they must be left in an authorized parking lot or at a private home where they can be parked off the street. They must be reported to the Inspector of Customs, either at his office in the Federal Building (Post Office at 2nd Avenue and 2nd street), to the right of the 2nd Ave. entrance or at the Alaska ferry office at the ferry dock before your departure.

Note that Alaska has a child restraint law for children under 12 in vehicles. They must be in approved child seats if too small to use seat belts. Canada has a similar law and requires all passengers to buckle up.

**Recreational Vehicles**

With increasing hotel rates, many people planning leisurely tours and stopovers bring camping vehicles or trailers. All campgrounds in Southeast Alaska will accommodate vehicles up to 24 feet in length; some can take longer ones. Most spaces are not drive-through, so you will have to maneuver. Most U.S. Forest Service and state campgrounds don't have hookups though most private trailer parks do. These are listed with the towns, as are dump stations and sources for ice, propane, and diesel.

During peak season, vehicle reservations to or from Bellingham require early applications and some luck. Reservations to or from Prince Rupert, B.C. are much easier to get. You can drive to Prince Rupert through interior Canada on paved roads, camping along the way, or ride the British Columbia ferry from Port Hardy at the north end of Vancouver Island.

The cost of taking a vehicle on the ferry increases rapidly with length over 21 feet. Check the ferry schedule for details. The length is the total length of deck space covered, including trailer hitch, bumper, trail-bike carried on the back, etc. The B.C. ferry has a hefty surcharge for vehicles over 20' long or over 7' high. There is a surcharge for vehicles over 8' wide on the Alaska ferry.

If you tow another vehicle, the fare is calculated for the total length of the unit, including towing bar. You can save if both vehicles are self-powered, *and* you have 2 drivers, *and* you ticket them separately, *and* you disconnect them before checking in. If you drive the vehicles separately, you accept that they may not be parked together on the car deck, and the possibility in peak season, especially if the vehicles are on standby, that one may ride the next ferry.

You will need to be able to back and maneuver the vehicle accurately. Seamen on the car deck will direct you, but you'll enjoy the trip more if you can do it easily. The length of overhang at the rear of the vehicle is important. While loading ramps are two-stage and can be adjusted, the change from horizontal car deck to steep ramp at low tide is considerable.

Gold panning demonstration on solarium deck of ferry bound for Skagway.

If you have more than a 2 foot overhang behind your rear wheels, you may want to add a protective bar there. If you have a motion sensor or burglar alarm on the vehicle, you should deactivate it so the ship's motion won't set it off.

You'll want to be sure your water and holding tanks seal tightly and check them regularly during the trip to be sure that recent travel on rough roads hasn't started leaks. Propane tanks will be inspected and sealed by ferry terminal staff before you board the ferry. Any spare fuel cans will be stored in the paint locker on the car deck after you board. Don't forget to pick them up when you leave.

If you carry perishables, including fish, on longer trips, do plan ahead. Your propane refrigerator will be off as the tank will be sealedwhen you check in. An electric refrigerator is OK if you have it on a separate battery so that running it won't make your RV battery too weak to start the vehicle. You will not be able to run the engine while it's parked on the car deck to recharge, nor will you be able to plug into the ship's power. For short trips, the refrigerator will stay cold. For longer trips, you may want to put a chunk of ice in it. The Ketchikan shopping center two blocks from the ferry is a good place to get more ice if your vehicle stays on the ship. Note that it's 36 hours non-stop from Ketchikan to Bellingham.

If you fill your gas tank just before getting on the ferry, any increase in temperature may make it overflow onto the car deck, creating a fire hazard. To avoid delay, you should be sure your vehicle is in good enough condition to get on and off the ship unassisted. Be sure all switches are off before you leave your vehicle.

Remember that Coast Guard regulations will not allow you to stay in your vehicle on the car deck when the ship is underway and you will not be able to cook in it even when the ship is docked. You will be able to go to the vehicle whenever the ship is in port and at scheduled car deck calls when it is more than 8 hours between ports. If you run out of medicine, diapers, etc., and can't wait until the next port or car deck call to go to your vehicle, you can ask at the purser's counter for an escort. It's easier to plan ahead and bring what you'll need when you leave the vehicle.

## On The Car Deck

A glance will tell you that the car deck is a working space, an equipment loading area. Eighteen wheel truck-van units maneuver in the small area along with cars, trailers, and RVs, with blind spots from the driver's view. In summer when the crew is trying not to leave standbys behind at ports, you'll think they deserve a Golden Shoe Horn Award for fitting the last few in.

Foot passengers leaving the ship may go to the car deck when the ship docks and the purser announces permission. The baggage cart is usually first off, so that's your chance to put your gear on it for the ride up the ramp. Another choice is to take your bags down to the cart at the port before the one where you're getting off (just before the ferry leaves).

If vehicles are moving when you're walking on or off, it's important to follow the crew's directions to get across the car deck and stay on the walkway of the loading ramp without stopping unnecessarily. Farewells and picture-taking are best done on the upper decks. If you're standing by your vehicle to see if you have to get off, the safest way is to sit in it. Standing where vehicles are unloading is dangerous for you and delays the unloading. When you drive a car off, the crew and your fellow passengers will appreciate your not starting it until a crew member tells you to, to avoid unnecessary exhaust fumes on the car deck. If you will need help loading or unloading, you should ask the purser.

## Staterooms

Staterooms are paid for separately from passage tickets. You can buy a passage and vehicle ticket for the whole distance that you will travel and then reserve cabin space, if it is available, for those segments on which you will need it. Four-berth cabins are generally easier to reserve than two-berth. Four-berth rooms have two lower and two upper bunks with ladders. The *Matanuska* has more two-berth cabins than the other ships. See deck diagrams at the back of this book for cabin layouts. Outside rooms

The *Columbia's* car deck, forward end with side door open.

face outside and have windows, for a slightly higher charge. The *Taku* has two staterooms with bathrooms designed for wheelchair use and all the other ships have at least one. If you need one, please request it when making your reservation.

For passengers on a hurried trip, staterooms offer a welcome rest. All cabins on the *Malaspina, Matanuska, Taku,* and *Columbia* have washbasin, shower, and toilet. The *Kennicott* also has two-berth cabins without showers and toilets and two-berth roomettes (similar to Amtrak's) without facilities or linen. It has five wheelchair-adapted cabins, both two and four-berth. All electric current is standard household, 110 volt. There is a closet and a ladder for reaching the upper bunk. Rooms are cleaned and made up before you enter, but are not remade daily by the stewards. You may request extra blankets and towel changes at the purser's counter.

Remember the alternatives to cabins—the recliner and forward lounges, and the solarium. A suggestion based on personal experience: being able to stretch out full length is more comfortable for a whole night than recliner chairs which don't recline very far. With a foam pad or air mattress and sleeping bag, sleeping on the deck, inside or out (if it's not raining or you're in the solarium) is comfortable. Except for the Bellingham–Ketchikan run, the time between ports is 10 hours or less.

## Baggage
A powered baggage cart will haul your baggage between the car deck and the terminal on shore. You are responsible for all other handling of it. If you are riding beyond the next port, you should remove your bag-

gage from the cart on the ship, for its safety at port stops and to leave space for others. While there is no limit on the amount of baggage you can bring in a vehicle, the baggage cart is for hand luggage only (not to exceed 100 pounds)—not for freight, household moving, boats or rafts (even disassembled). Clearly anyone who can paddle a boat or raft is more able to pack it onto the ship by hand than the arthritic oldster who has to carry his suitcase because the baggage cart is full. The crew will show you where to put canoes or kayaks safely. I recommend you pack only the amount you can easily carry at one time. You don't need many extra clothes—Alaskan living is simple. Don't forget raingear and binoculars.

A reminder: the baggage cart is usually the first off and last on at ports. If you're leaving the ship and want your baggage carried up to the terminal, you should go to the car deck to load the cart as soon as the purser says the car deck is open. Binoculars are good for close-up looks at eagles and other wildlife. You should bring these, and anything you will need en route, including medicines, cameras and film, to the upper decks before the ship leaves the dock.

## Children

As on any long trip, people traveling with children on the ferry should plan for their interests and safety. The trip can seem long for them, especially between Bellingham and Ketchikan where there is a day when the ship doesn't stop. There is no place on the ship to run that is not on someone else's ceiling. Quiet on the cabin deck is important to fellow passengers who may be trying to rest. The Forest Service naturalist may have some children's programs planned north of Prince Rupert. They'll enjoy walking with you around the decks looking for whales, eagles, and fishing boats. Games, books, coloring materials, sewing, knitting, according to age and interests would be worth bringing. One of those big doodle posters may last the whole trip.

Climbing on the ship's rail is **dangerous** as the water is very cold and a child might fall overboard without being seen. For their safety you should know where your children are all the time they are aboard. They can find the trip a real adventure if you explore the ship and scenery with them as well as providing other diversions. A play area for toddlers is in the cabin deck aft lounge of the *Taku*. The *Columbia, Kennicott, Matanuska,* and *Malaspina* have smaller play areas. Children should have rainwear and a pair of rubber boots.

Ashore, children can enjoy hiking, walking along the docks in fishing boat harbors, playing on beaches and in playgrounds, flying kites, fishing, berry picking, and wildlife watching. Some towns have fish hatcheries, totem parks, and eagle rehab centers where they can see the birds up

Child watches for whales and boats—safely.

Older children might enjoy being provided with a simple camera and film to make the trip really "theirs." They may have fun with inexpensive binoculars, a map of the route, and a diary. All ferries now have several video games.

Ashore, teens may enjoy playing hacky sack (even in the ferry terminal area), cycling, kayaking, hiking, beachcombing, pebble collecting, fishing, and berry picking. Summer recreation programs in towns may be a chance to meet local kids. They may enjoy touring museums and gift shops (if not for too long) and seeing native dances and summer melodramas.

Infants under 2 travel free; children 2–11 pay about 50% of adult fare.

### Seniors

The Alaska ferry system offers passage at 50% of the adult fare to seniors 65 and older between Alaska ports on the smaller ferries, the *LeConte, Aurora, Bartlett,* and *Tustumena,* except for restricted sailings as noted at the end of this section, May 1 though September 30. This rate covers passage only and does not include meals, rooms, or vehicle. From October 1 through April 30, seniors may travel on *all* ferries within Alaska at 50% of the adult fare and may make reservations.

If you plan to use one of the senior fares, carry your Medicare card and get the senior ticket for the portions of the trip where you will use it. Refunds are *not* given for the reduced rate after you have traveled on a regular adult ticket. In summer, for instance, you might book passage on the ferry from Bellingham to an Alaska port and then plan to use the smaller ferries for some trip segments or excursions.

Throughout Southeast Alaska many admissions and some campground fees are reduced. For reductions at **Forest Service** campgrounds you need a Golden Age card, which you can get from any national park or forest office. Most senior rates in British Columbia apply to B.C. residents only; exceptions are **Via Rail** and some airlines.

**Amtrak** offers seniors 62 and over 15% off any fare, including the train between Seattle and Vancouver that stops at Bellingham.

**Alaska Airlines** (800) 426-0333 has senior fares, usually 10% off any published fare, including advanced purchased fares, for anyone over 62. It also gives the 10% discount to a companion of any age traveling with a senior, if you ask.

**Elderhostel** offers programs during winter and spring on many round trips from Bellingham offering staterooms, instruction by specialists who travel with the group, and tours ashore in several places—all at very reasonable rates. The groups I've seen on the ferry seem to be having a wonderful time. These are open to people over 60 and the spouse or companion of a participant, regardless of age. Some Elderhostel programs in summer are shore-based, sometimes in Juneau and Sitka. For information, check the Elderhostel catalog in your local library or write **Elderhostel**, 80 Boylston Street, Suite 400, Boston, MA 02116-4899.

*Restricted sailings*: the following information applies to *both* senior citizens and handicapped individuals of any age. The pass privilege rate between Alaska ports has been extended to all year on the smaller ships only, the *LeConte, Aurora, Bartlett*, and *Tustumena*. Note that *Bartlett* doesn't have an elevator. Reduced rate travel is **not** allowed between May 1 and September 30 on the *Bartlett* or *Tustumena* between Valdez and Whittier or Seward or anytime on round trip sailings between Homer and Unalaska, Seldovia and Unalaska, or Kodiak and Unalaska on the same Aleutian Chain trip. These route restrictions apply to the Southwest System ferries only (see chapter at the end of this book).

### Handicapped

People of any age who have a certifiable physical or mental disability of 70% or more, may apply to the ferry system for a $25 one-year pass enabling them and an attendant (if required by a physician) to travel at 50% of the regular passenger fare, space available, between Alaska ports from October 1 to May 1 on all the ships and all year on the smaller ships. This covers basic passenger fare, but not stateroom, vehicle, or food. The ferry system furnishes an application form which requires a physician's statement. The completed form is reviewed by the ferry system and a pass may be issued. You should allow 6 weeks for this. Write Alaska Marine Highway System, Attn: Pass Desk, P.O. Box 25535, Juneau, AK 99802.

A boarded trail, with passing lanes for groups, crosses muskeg, a forested bog near Juneau.

All the ships (except the *Bartlett* in the Southwest region) now have elevators, and those with staterooms have at least one adapted for the handicapped (which you should request when making reservations). The four mainliners each have a restroom built for wheelchair use and a ramp into the forward observation lounge. A motorized rising chair (weight limit 400 lbs.) carries wheelchair passengers to the upper deck on the *Bartlett*. Wheelchair vans are aboard all ships to carry wheelchair passengers between the ship and the terminal.

Special diets are not provided on board though they can be heated in the microwaves on all vessels if you bring them. The stewards will refrigerate insulin if you request it. The ship's crew does not include a doctor or nurse, though all pursers have had first aid training and the ships have first aid supplies, including oxygen.

Onshore facilities for the handicapped are increasing. Most public buildings are now handicapped-accessible and some trails, including the Estuary Walk at Starrigavan Creek near Sitka, are boarded for wheelchair use. However, towns like Juneau and Ketchikan have some very steep streets.

## Pets

Pets must have valid health certificates signed by a veterinarian to enter Alaska. Pets must remain on the car deck in vehicles or in strong containers, provided by the owners. There is a surcharge of $10 for taking pets between Prince Rupert or Stewart/Hyder and any Alaskan port, and $25 between Bellingham and Alaska. At stops you may walk your pets ashore. Most travel times between ports are less than 8 hours, but Bellingham to Ketchikan can take over 36 hours and Petersburg to Sitka about 10 hours. Scheduled car deck calls will allow you to walk your pet on the car deck. Passengers are responsible for clean up, and a scooper is recommended. Tranquilizers may be advisable for nervous pets for their comfort and quiet. Barking, unfortunately, carries widely through the ship. Dogs really appreciate being walked at every port at any hour.

Riding the ferry can be great fun for you, but probably isn't enjoyable for animals. In World War II we were supposed to ask ourselves "Is this trip necessary?" to save gas. You might well ask yourself the same for the pet. If it must travel, plan for its comfort with adequate space, water, ventilation, and its usual food. Even if it doesn't really need to go ashore, it would certainly appreciate a pat and some encouragement at every car deck call or port—and you'll have a chance to spot any problem early. For its own safety, a pet should be leashed any time it's out on the car deck or ramp. If you have a bird in a cage, ask the purser for instructions.

## Sitka Run

The larger ships, northbound or southbound, go to Sitka at least once a week. The *LeConte* also sails there three times a week. It costs no more to go the extra distance when you are riding between Petersburg and Juneau, but it does take almost a day longer. The time will be well spent even if you don't stop off in Sitka, with narrow passages, great scenery and wildlife. To be sure of being on that run in daylight, check the schedule. The ship passes through Peril Strait, Sergius Narrows (where you can almost pick branches from the trees as you go by), and Olga and Neva Straits.

Leaving Sitka you follow the same route back out to Chatham Strait. Since the ship must wait 6 hours for slack tide at Sergius Narrows, you may have as much as 3 hours to spend in Sitka. The dock is 7 miles from town, but there usually is time for an optional bus tour or a trip downtown if it is daytime and no other ferries are using the dock. When the captain schedules departure time, the purser will announce if a bus tour is possible.

The bus tour passes all the Russian buildings in town, and stops at Sitka National Historic Park. A longer tour is given for people staying in Sitka.

To be sure of seeing the town, and of having more time to enjoy the museums and Russian buildings, you may want to stop over. Note that both the tour bus and the bus to town leave very shortly after docking,

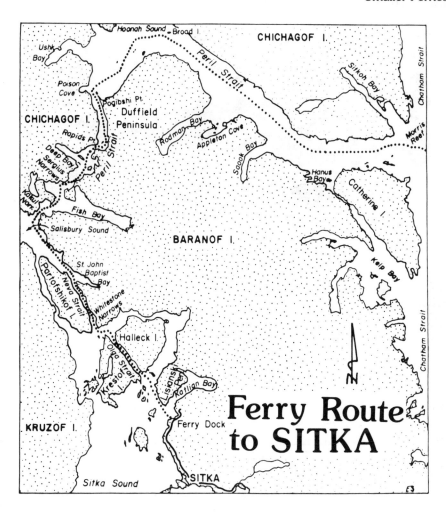

so board the buses quickly or you'll miss them. Taxis are expensive here.

## Smaller Ferries

You can see more of Southeastern Alaska by riding the *LeConte* and *Aurora* on their local routes. Based in Juneau, the *LeConte* serves the Tlingit villages of Hoonah, Angoon, and Kake, the fishing port of Pelican, and Tenakee Springs on Chichagof Island, in addition to mainline ports.

Most passengers on these ships ride their marine bus regularly to shop come into town, shop for 4 or 5 hours, and return home. Before Christmas it's like being on Santa's sled without the reindeer!

In summer these ships are generally less crowded and have a more relaxed, local atmosphere than the mainliners. If you have time and don't

Sergius Narrows, headed toward Sitka. Your ship turns right around the nearest buoy and then lines up between the three markers on the left and the rocky point on the right—very precisely!

need a stateroom, the *LeConte's* run from Juneau to Petersburg via Hoonah, Tenakee Springs, Angoon, Sitka, and Kake, will add another dimension to your trip.

Visiting a village for several days is a great way to get away from the tourist circuit and feel the tempo of real Alaska. You can enjoy fishing, hiking, kayaking, and birding as well as village life. The villages all have at least one hotel if you want to stop over. Some have rustic to deluxe fishing lodges with guided fishing. Reservations advised.

Pelican is an attractive fishing village beside scenic Lisianski Inlet on Chichagof Island, a one-day round trip from Juneau. In summer the *LeConte* goes twice a month.. The ship stays for an hour or more, allowing time to walk uptown on the boardwalk main street. En route scenery and, usually, whales make this a fine excursion from Juneau.

The *Aurora*, based in Ketchikan, goes to Hollis on Prince of Wales Island. Hollis connected by roads with Craig, Klawock, and some fine fishing and hunting areas. Prince of Wales Island has the most extensive road system in Southeast Alaska and lots to explore. There are no facilities except a waiting room at Hollis, but there is shuttle service to Craig and Klawock. Vehicles should have reservations.

The *Aurora* also goes weekly in summer to Hyder, actually docking at Stewart, B. C., where she can load vehicles up to 25 feet long. She stays about 3 hours, time enough to explore. The 9-hour trip up the scenic Portland Canal is a fine excursion. She leaves Ketchikan after midnight Monday night and arrives in Stewart Tuesday noon. She leaves Stewart Tuesday afternoon, arriving back in Ketchikan after midnight Tuesday night.

The *Aurora* also goes from Ketchikan to the Tsimshian village of Metlakatla on Annette Island. You may be able to reserve space in the only motel in Metlakatla to stay over. Metlakatla would be fun to explore. I'd bring a bike to ride the flat road out to Pt. Davidson.

The *LeConte* and *Aurora* have snack bars, and both ferries can carry limited numbers of cars. Several of their trips make good one or two day outings, even if you are not staying over.

## Photography

The Inside Passage is a great place for photography, whether you are professional or simply want a few nice shots to show friends back home. If this is your first trip, the following suggestions, based on what works for me, may help. The frequent rain and fog plus the ship's vibration make planning worthwhile. On any trip you'll improve your odds for good pictures by being very familiar with the camera, including loading film and rewinding, before you leave home. Bring all the film you think you'll need, plus a bit more. Shops along the way may be out of the film you use. If your camera is electronic, bring at least one set of spare batteries.

For color slides I use Fujichrome 100 or 200. I usually use a skylight filter, sometimes a polaroid. Particularly in summer, daylight hours are long, so I rarely have to shoot in twilight. For black and white photos in this book I use Tri-X shot at 400, usually with a yellow filter. For bright days, especially in British Columbia where there's a greater variety of trees, a greenish yellow filter (Hoya XO) is good for black and white film to show the different tree species.

My cameras are a Pentax ME body and a Pentax K-1000, one with black and white, the other with color film. I use a Pentax 50 mm lens and a Vivitar 70-210 macro zoom lens, switching them between the similar camera bodies—and usually remembering to change the filters. The zoom is a marvel for photography from a ship where one can't control the distance to a boat or glacier. Unless you're going to use incredibly fast film, 300 mm is probably as much as you can hold steady on a moving ship.

A short, beautiful hike leads to Fragrance Lake in Larabee State Park near Bellingham. Here the greenish yellow filter separates tree species even in black and white.

On shore, and sometimes when the engines are shut down at a dock, I use a Tokina 400 mm for wildlife. I use a Tokina 28 mm wide angle lens for deck shots, sea to mountaintop scenery, and in towns. On trips I take a changing bag for removing jammed film without losing the whole roll—rarely used but sometimes useful. Recently I've added an automatic point-and-shoot Canon with 35–70 zoom for color prints.

Keeping camera and film dry is all-important. Damp film jams easily in a camera. A rubber lens hood will keep raindrops off the lens or filter if it's not windy. In windy conditions with a telephoto lens, the hood may catch so much wind you have to remove it to hold the camera steady. I was able to keep working during an entire rainy afternoon in Petersburg by using a lens hood and tucking the camera in my rain parka whenever I wasn't shooting. I used a yellow filter to increase contrast. A good camera bag plus plastic bags helped.

On the ship, it's worth stepping out on deck for any picture you really want instead of shooting through windows. I dress warmly for the Narrows and stay out on deck (hypothermia in December!). The stern decks and several spots along the side decks on each ship are sheltered from the wind. From the stern you can photograph whatever comes up on either side, but there is more engine vibration. The side decks forward have far less vibration, important if you're using a telephoto. Photos this book were taken from both areas. Some spots on the stern deck more vibration than others. I try not to let my camera or any part of my upper body touch the ship while shooting. Tripods are great on shore but on a ship they pick up engine vibration you can't even feel.

An automatic exposure camera may be fooled by the commonly overcast sky into underexposing everything below. Learn your camera's ways before you go, and perhaps set it to give extra light to the film. Some of these suggestions also apply to VCRs. You'll want a wind shield to avoid noise on your microphone if you use it outside.

Good luck with your pictures and the weather!

### Exercise

For those who want to do more in fresh air than simply enjoy the scenery, plan brisk walking laps around the ships on deck, adding flights of outside ladders (stairs, to the non-sailor) where the open deck doesn't go all the way around. If you run on these, or play hacky-sack, it will be disturbing on someone's cabin or dining room ceiling—about 5 on the Richter scale. The cabin deck (lowest passenger deck) stern on all the ships is above the car deck. Running in place here is OK. Jumping would probably bother the people in the nearest cabins.

The ship offers many opportunities—but don't climb anything. The deck rails are about the height of a ballet barre. With the ship's wake, luminous at night, rushing by, you won't even miss the music if you're doing stretching exercises at the rail or on deck.

For hard core runners, planning a long run the day before and after the ferry trip may help, especially on the Bellingham–Ketchikan section where the ship doesn't stop. At most port stops there is a road leading away from town for good running if time permits. You should be back aboard the ship at least 15 minutes before announced departure as the ramp goes up *before* the departure moment. Otherwise you may share the feeling I had once, hundreds of miles from home in a sweaty T-shirt and running shorts, watching my ship pull out.

### The Narrows

The high points of any ferry trip are the narrows. Wrangell Narrows— the 21 miles just south of Petersburg, is a 46-turn slalom course for ships. In several places the channel is only 300 feet wide and 19 feet deep. Watching the precision and seamanship of your captain and crew is a thrill, night or day. At night the channel and range markers flash in red, green and white. Near Blind Slough, you can see 16 markers ahead, and it looks as if you are winding through a Christmas tree. In daylight, Wrangell Narrows and Sergius Narrows, near Sitka, offer your best chances of seeing

Humpback whales "bubble feeding", putting up a circle of bubbles to corral the fish they eat, near Juneau..

wildlife up close. These are eagle nesting areas where sometimes you'll also see deer or bears on the beach. Seals and sea lions haul out on some rocky islands. All the larger cruise ships miss these channels, going around the islands instead.

## Whales

You may spot whales, especially humpback and killer whales, at any time. Sometimes the mate on watch announces them on the ship's speaker. From the solarium, you may see whales come up behind the ship. Humpback whales tend to congregate in May and June near Juneau, Auke Bay, and near the south end of Douglas Island. You can usually see them July through September in Lower Stephens Passage, about 1.5 hours north of Petersburg. Passengers traveling through these areas in daylight may see as many as 40 humpback whales, often very close to the ship. On trips to Hoonah and Pelican with the *LeConte*, you'll nearly always see whales near Pt. Adolphus a few miles east of Hoonah. Often one or two whales will simply stay in a particular area for days, and you'll be lucky enough to see them.

Orcas are less predictable in Southeast Alaska—you may find them anywhere, especially if there are salmon runs or groups of seals nearby. Sometimes a pod even goes up Tongass Narrows, the water main street of Ketchikan! Robson Bight, near the north end of Vancouver Island, is a famous orca hangout in summer, and several boats run tours from Telegraph Cove on the island.

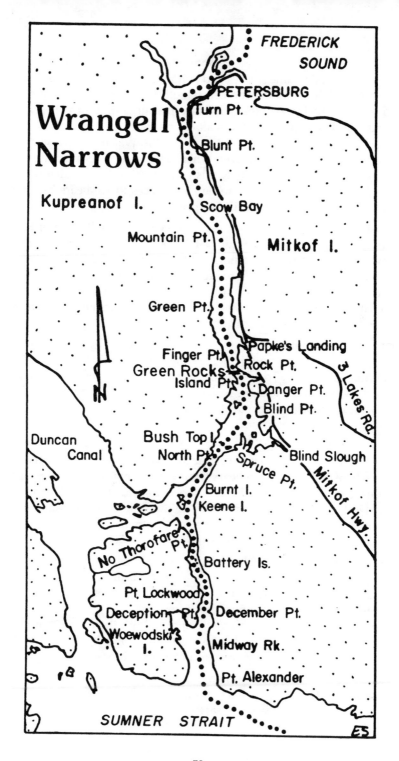

FREDERICK SOUND

Wrangell Narrows

Kupreanof I.

PETERSBURG

Turn Pt.

Blunt Pt.

Scow Bay

Mountain Pt.

Mitkof I.

Green Pt.

Papke's Landing

Finger Pt.

Rock Pt.

Green Rocks

Island Pt.

Danger Pt.

Blind Pt.

Bush Top I.

North Pt.

Blind Slough

Duncan Canal

Spruce Pt.

3 Lakes Rd.

Burnt I.

Keene I.

Mitkof Hwy.

No Thorofare Pt.

Battery Is.

Pt. Lockwood

Deception Pt.

December Pt.

Woewodski I.

Midway Rk.

Pt. Alexander

SUMNER STRAIT

ES

53

## Bears

Brown bears, the same species and irritability (caution!) as grizzly bears, live on Admiralty, Baranof, and Chichagof islands, as well as on the mainland. Black bears live on other islands, especially Prince of Wales, and on the mainland. You may see bears along the shore, particularly in spring, near skunk cabbage patches and stream mouths. Watching such spots from the ferry in the narrows, or even when docked at quiet places like Angoon, may let you see one safely. Fish streams and berry patches in season also attract bears. These can be hard places to see bears before you get too close. While you may like surprises, bears generally don't.

Most Alaska brown bear pictures are taken at McNeill River or Katmai on the Alaska Peninsula. In Southeast Alaska tideflats and stream mouths anywhere on Admiralty, Baranof, and Chichagof Islands during fish season offer the possibility if you're lucky and your lens is *long*. Brown bears are sometimes seen along fishing streams north of Juneau during salmon runs. The bears in and very near Juneau are black bears and their rare subspecies, the blue or glacier bear.

Pack Creek on northern Admiralty Island (reached by boat or plane) is famous for its bears although the ones there are usually females and cubs rather than big males. To protect the bears and avoid personal injury, the Forest Service has made some restrictions on where people may go, time of day, where food is allowed, etc. Peak season varies, but is usually July 10–August 20, when permits may be hard to reserve. The weeks just before or after that may have fewer people and just as many bears.

A viewing tower has been built near the creek. In the meadow area, visitors are kept 150 yards from bears fishing in the main creek unless a bear chooses to walk closer. You'll want binoculars and at least a 400 mm lens. Consideration for the bears and your fellow visitors will be appreciated. For current information and to get a visiting permit, call the Admiralty National Monument office in Juneau, 789-3111 or 586-8790.

At Anan Creek on the Cleveland Peninsula between Ketchikan and Wrangell, black bears and an occasional brown bear catch pink salmon in June and July. A viewing platform overlooks the area. Boat tours from Wrangell and air taxi tour operators from Ketchikan offer trips. The Forest Service is developing a plan which may limit the number of people going there. I recommend jet boat tours from Wrangell which offer more time at the creek, improving your odds of seeing bears.

More information on encounters with bears is in our "Having Fun in the Back Country" chapter later in this book. The Forest Service has an excellent brochure on bears and safety.

Female brown bear at Pack Creek.

Well-fed female black bear at Anan Creek near Wrangell eats only the brains and roe of the salmon she catches before tossing them aside for waiting gulls and eagles.

Volta, named for his disabling encounter with a power line, is a permanent resident at the Sitka Raptor Rehabilitation Center.

## Bald Eagles

Southeastern Alaska has the largest remaining U.S. population of bald eagles, some 15,000 birds. The majority of them live along the coast most of the year. They nest beside the ferry route, and you can easily see them on their nests along the narrows in early summer. Between mid-July and September, you will see some eagles, but fewer than at other times of the year, as they go up streams to follow spawning salmon. In fall and winter, thousands of them feed on the Chilkat River flats beside Haines Highway, Mile 19. You will often see them swooping down for fish near the ferry in the Narrows, especially in early evening. Docked at Prince Rupert, Ketchikan, and Petersburg, I've watched them in the harbor. Notice the difference in fishing skill and precision (also success) between mature eagles with white heads and younger eagles.

## Birding

Besides bald eagles there are hundreds of species of birds to watch, especially during spring and fall migration. Many ducks, geese, and swans fly through to nesting areas farther north. Petersburg harbor usually has a variety of waterfowl due to fish processing waste in the water. Here even birds you know from elsewhere may look different in their summer breeding plumage. Besides ducks and gulls, loons and great blue herons are common. A walk around the deck while the ship is docked may be the most rewarding bird walk of your trip! Channel markers here may be perches for 4-8 cormorants drying their feathers.

In winter, Blind Slough south of Petersburg, is home to swans and geese. There is a viewing blind. In both Petersburg and Wrangell you'll often see eagles perched in spruce trees along the street!

Near the Sitka dock, heading away from town, is the tidal marsh of Starrigavan Creek with ducks, geese, kingfishers, and a summer run of pink salmon, and the new Estuary Walk, a boarded wheelchair accessible trail across the marsh and creek. The trail around Sitka National Historical Park follows the beach where you may see harlequin ducks and other waterfowl. In Sitka, several boat operators offer tours to the seabird rookeries on St. Lazaria Island in Sitka Sound where you may see murres, cormorants, auklets, oystercatchers, puffins, and many others on their nests. July is the peak month.

The Raptor Rehabilitation Center at Sitka offers your best chance to see eagles, and possibly hawks and owls, up close and to learn about them. Admission charge. Guided tours include films of the rehabilitation and release of birds into the wild as well as demonstrations of the medical treatment given injured and ailing birds. Bring your camera or camcorder!

Auke Bay near Juneau is a good place to watch eagles, kingfishers, and herons, especially near the ferry dock. At Juneau Airport, starting from the end of Radcliffe Road is a road/path along the dike around the floatplane pond, bordering Mendenhall State Game Refuge. In summer Arctic terns nest along the dike and may dive at you to protect their nests. Canada geese are here all year. In spring you may see a dozen species of ducks and occasionally, swans. Once I stood on the path within 30 yards of four young trumpeter swans feeding in the pond! Besides the birds, this walk has great views of Mendenhall Glacier and expansive wetlands. Late afternoon light is magic here!

Glacier Bay is almost as well known for birds as for whales and glaciers. The tour boats from Glacier Bay Lodge go close to bird rookeries on the Marble Islands where you can see thousands of seabirds that come ashore only to nest. Even on shore around Bartlett Cove, there's a wide variety of waterfowl and forest birds. Park rangers lead daily nature walks to help you see and recognize more. I've seen many birds in June, but more species in July.

Haines is famous for eagles, and also has a growing population of nesting swans in summer. They may stay as long as they aren't approached closely. For birding suggestions, ask Chilkat State Park personnel.

Fish poster on Skagway dock shows local fish, important to know what you catch to stay within legal limits.

## Fishing

The water you are sailing through supports one of the world's richest fisheries. Depending on the season you may see commercial fishing boats trolling, seining, or gillnetting for any of the five kinds of salmon, tending crab or shrimp pots or fishing for halibut or cod. When you pass boats fishing, the ferry's officers often explain how the fishing gear works. Near the salmon fleet there's a large boat with a cargo boom and lights, the tender, which picks up fish from the fishing boats and hauls the load back to the cannery or cold storage plant so the boats can keep fishing. Some boats are equipped for more than one type of fishing so they can work more days a year. Fishing "openings," or open seasons are regulated by the Alaska Department of Fish and Game. They decide how many fish must be allowed to spawn and set the times, often in hours, that fishing is allowed in an area. When the opening is only for 24 or 36 hours, the boats and crews fish all night!

In season you can sportfish for salmon, halibut, red snapper, and Dolly Varden in salt water and trout and steelhead in creeks and lakes. Prince of Wales Island, west of Ketchikan, has great fresh and saltwater fishing and near miles of logging roads. Charter boat operators and guides are in every town. Often the sporting goods store personnel can tell you where there's a good spot you can fish from shore. A fishing license is required even for salt water. Non-resident licenses are available for 4 days ($10), 14 days ($30), and a year ($50). Get a tide table at any sporting goods store.

A 72-page book, *The Alaska Department of Fish & Game's Recreational Fishing Guide*, has maps and charts as well as descriptions for all significant fisheries in Alaska. You can find it in local bookstores or get it for $4 from: Alaska Dept. of Fish & Game, Public Communications, Box 3-2000, Juneau, AK 99811.

Fishing lodges can be reached by boat or plane (and, in some places, by car) from every town in Southeast. They offer package plans including meals, transportation, boats, and guides. Most will pack your fish for you to take home, and some will arrange for smoking it if you wish.

For more info: Fishing—Alaska Dept. of Fish & Game, Division of Sport Fish, PO Box 25526, Juneau, AK 99802. 465-4180. Hunting—Alaska Dept. of Fish & Game, Division of Wildlife Conservation, PO Box 25526, Juneau, AK 99802. 465-4190. Camping, hiking, cabins—Alaska Dept. of Natural Resources, Public Information Center, Box 107005, Anchorage, AK 99510. 762-2261.

## Kayaking

With respect for the cold water, strong tides, rain and cold, you can enjoy one of the world's finest sea kayaking areas. This is **not**, however, the place to make your first long kayak trip on your own. The rain and fog, very cold water, and changeable weather require experience or a very capable guide. Some people actually paddle from Seattle to Skagway in a summer, missing all those scenic inlets one has to pass to make such a schedule. More have discovered great shorter trips between towns and around islands like Revillagigedo, the island Ketchikan is on, or among the islands in Sitka Sound.

A look at the Tongass National Forest map should make any kayaker dream. Where they can, most kayakers use Forest Service cabins (next section) for a spot to dry out clothing and wait out weather. If you don't have a group for such a trip, shops like **Alaska Discovery** in Juneau have guides and can offer good local info. They offer day trips as well as longer ones.

A tide table is essential. Experienced kayakers have arrived with a schedule made out showing what time they wanted to be out of camp every morning on their route to have the tidal current with them instead of against them. A free 5 knots is not to be ignored!

You can bring your own kayak on top of a vehicle, or carry it onto the ferry where the crew will show you where to stow it. There's a small charge for carrying boats on the ferry, so you'll need to get a ticket for it if it's not on a vehicle. Note that it's possible to launch a kayak within

100 yards of any ferry dock in Southeast. Kayaks can be rented in Juneau at Alaska Discovery, or in Gustavus for paddling in Glacier Bay. Most larger ports now have someone renting kayaks and/or offering guided trips, some as short as a few hours. Folding boats and inflatables are usually not as efficient to paddle, but are much easier to transport, especially in floatplanes.

Prince of Wales Island, west of Ketchikan, has over 1000 miles of shoreline and miles of sheltered water on its west side reachable easily from Hydaburg, Craig, or the road system farther north. There are several deep inlets even on the east side of the island near the ferry dock at Hollis, but some of these have exposed headlands between. Carrying the kayak by ferry to Hollis on the island saves time and leaves you less vulnerable to the weather than attempting to paddle across Clarence Strait and its waves from Ketchikan.

Angoon is on Admiralty Island, at the mouth of Mitchell Bay, and at the west end of the Cross-Admiralty Canoe Route. Maps of the route are available from the Forest Service. Some portages are planked, and several Forest Service cabins can be reserved for $25 a night (more details at the end of this section). The *LeConte* takes you and your boat to Angoon and back without having to charter aircraft or larger boats. On the east side of Admiralty Island, reachable in good weather from Juneau, is Oliver Inlet, with a hand-cart on rails for the portage across to Seymour Canal.

Another interesting canoe trip possible, thanks to the *LeConte*, goes from Hoonah to Tenakee, with only a short portage (shorter at high tide) between Port Frederick and Tenakee Inlet. The rails on this portage have been improved, making boat hauling easier. For this trip you will want a tide table and some good judgment. Note that both of these canoe trips are on islands that have brown bears, and the portage is a bear trail.

Good kayaking is possible from Pelican, but it's awkward to get there and back, as ferry service is limited to one trip each month all year, two in summer. Charter aircraft do serve the area regularly. Lisianski Inlet is sheltered, and you can paddle from here to the coast and islands of West Chichagof or even down to Sitka. En route is the Forest Service cabin at White Sulphur Springs, a hot spring and favorite spot of those who've reached it.

Kake is a good starting point for a tour of the small offshore islands and coastlines of Kupreanof and Kuiu Islands. The bay between these islands has coves and islands enough to occupy boaters happily for a week in sheltered water, with Forest Service cabins on both shores to stay in. During waterfowl migration as well as summer, this would be a beautiful trip.

And of course there's Glacier Bay, where the day-tour boat will drop you off at designated places and pick you up there later or leave you to paddle for several days back down the bay to Bartlett Cove. Guided kayak tours for half-a-day to several days are offered by tour operators at Gustavus at the south end of Glacier Bay (see Glacier Bay chapter).

Guided kayak trips for half-day, whole day, or several days, are offered by guide services in Ketchikan, Petersburg, Juneau, Gustavus (in Glacier Bay), and Skagway—listed in the chapters for those towns.

## Beachcombing
Perhaps some can resist walking down a beach to see what's there, but I think they miss a lot. Most beaches you can get to here are rocky and so far back from open ocean that they aren't known for glass float balls. However the variety of rocks you can find, including jasper, make it fun. Prince of Wales Island, with over 1000 miles of shoreline, is popular with locals. Besides interesting beach pebbles, it has inland deposits of marble (from which the columns on Alaska's capitol came), rose quartz, and other minerals. Some are on claims or other private property; don't forget to check. Ask for suggestions. The expanding road system often reaches new spots. Of course watch road banks for interesting rocks.

The beach at Hoonah, north of the cannery and past the navigation marker, has fascinating rocks carried out of Glacier Bay by the ice that once filled it. Even the beach near the Haines ferry terminal has metamorphic rocks from both sides of the fault that makes Lutak Inlet. Juneau's mining start was due to its minerals. Many locals still pan gold in streams on weekends. Wrangell's ferry terminal is built on a black slate that's easy to carve (even with a screwdriver) into bas-relief scenes and figures. When oiled, the texture is like the argillite used by Haida Indians in their small totems.

At Hyder, pebbles along the road shoulder have spectacularly colored metallic ores. Be conservative with the weight of your collection if you're leaving the town by plane!

Often you can watch eagles fish and even feed their young in nests near the beach. If you find eagle feathers, be warned that it's illegal to possess them. Restricting this was the only way the government could keep people from killing eagles to sell their feathers.

The tidal animals and plants to watch, as well as a few polishable rocks for your tumbler at home, make a beach walk memorable.

## Shipboard Naturalist
Under an agreement between the U.S. Forest Service and the Alaska Marine Highway, there is a Forest Service or U.S. Fish & Wildlife Service naturalist aboard each of the larger ferries all summer, on trips north of

Mature bald eagles with white heads and immatures without scavenge on a beach near Klawock on Prince of Wales Island.

Starfish using its suction feet to pull open a mussle for food—a beach find that entertains adults as well as children. Warning: most such mussles carry paralytic shellfish poisoning and should not be eaten by people.

Prince Rupert. You are traveling the length of the Tongass National Forest, the largest national forest in the United States.

The naturalist offers nature programs aboard ship and sometimes ashore, answers your questions (or finds someone who can), and has a variety of handouts, films, and a lending library. For children the naturalist has reading and coloring materials, a wildlife checklist, and sometimes a special programs. All services are free. The programs vary with the weather, the facilities aboard the ships, your interests, and the different backgrounds of the naturalists. Programs are posted at the naturalist station in the forward lounge, and announced on the ship's speakers.

## Side Trips
Each town has charter planes and boats that can take you on scenic rides, and to out-of-the-way places such as Glacier Bay, Tracy Arm, the Juneau Icefields, the LeConte Glacier, and the Stikine River. Some charter boat operators are biologists and excellent nature guides who know where wildlife is now and can help you spot animals and nests. They are listed under the ports where they originate, and the visitors' bureaus in those towns will have the latest lists.

## Camping
Generally, in Alaska, federal and state campgrounds are scenic and have trees and more room between spaces than commercial ones, but have no hookups. They have firepits, tables, water, and toilets (sometimes pit rather than flush). Few have pull-through spaces. State park campgrounds cost $6–8, and an annual pass is $75. Day parking at state parks is $2, or $25 for an annual pass. U.S. Forest Service campgrounds in Alaska are mostly space available, usually $5–10.

If you camp without an RV in Southeast Alaska, you'll want a tent, cookstove, good raingear, insect repellent, and 50 feet of nylon line to throw over a branch to hoist your food out of reach of bears. While there aren't bears everywhere, you should *never* keep your food in your tent.

## Entrance fees/User fees
More federal facilities are charging admission, including the Alaska Public Lands Information Center in Ketchikan ($4) and the Mendenhall Glacier Visitor Center in Juneau ($3 adult, or $6 family). The Golden Age Passport for seniors 62 and over, the Golden Access card for handicapped, and the Golden Eagle Passport for all ages will reduce many fees. The Golden Eagle can only be obtained in Alaska in Anchorage and Fairbanks though you can get the others at any Forest Service or National Park Service office. If possible, get one before you come.

## U.S. Forest Service Cabins
If the Alaska you want to see has no roads or cars and makes few sounds

but waves, wind in the trees, and waterfalls, you may find a stay in a Forest Service cabin a rare and exciting experience. For a bit of the wilderness all to yourself for a few days, this is it, with a dry roof overhead! Some are near hot springs. Recently several state cabins have been added, usually operated by the Forest Service, with similar rates. Abandoned lighthouses may be added!

Most land (aside from the towns) between the Canadian border in the Portland Canal and Skagway is in the Tongass National Forest, 17 million acres. Scattered throughout the forest are 150 cabins that you can rent (by reservation) for $25–45 per night, for as long as a week, longer in winter. Note the $10 cancellation fee for any change in cabin or reservation. Changes made less than 14 days before the reservation also lose a night fee. The cabins sleep between four and eight people. Some are on the coast and others are near freshwater lakes (these have a skiff and oars provided by the Territorial Sportsmen). Very few cabins are reached by trails, more by boat, and the majority by floatplane, your main expense in using them.

Firewood, or an axe and maul is provided. You must bring your own food, cooking utensils, stove oil if needed, sleeping bags, foam pads, life jackets, tide table, insect repellent, good rain gear, and first aid kit. A small backpacking stove is useful if the cabin has a woodstove and green wood. By fall the woodpile consists of the knotted unsplittable pieces everyone else left. The Forest Service will send you an equipment list and a description of the cabin and its facilities if you ask. Garbage is to be packed out.

For your comfort and safety on the charter flight you'll probably use to reach the cabin, and to avoid looking like a total "cheechako", it's best not to expand on the list too much. Our pilot's comment, "You people are awfully optimistic about the carrying capacity of a Beaver," as we crammed five passengers, besides the pilot, a German Shepherd, two folding kayaks, and a mountain of personal gear into the flying workhorse. However, I would add to the list two mousetraps. Baiting them with peanut butter, I caught twelve mice the first two nights at one cabin.

If the cabin is in brown bear country (mainland or Admiralty, Baranof, or Chichagof Islands), you may want to take a heavy rifle or 12-gauge shotgun, if you know how to use it. Some guides now carry the more portable pepper spray gun (not allowed on airlines!). To avoid bear trouble for yourselves and those who come after you, don't teach the bears that humans are a source of food. Burn completely, or carry out with you, all garbage and containers. If the bears are to survive and we are to use the wilderness, we must all do this.

You will be on your own, with no road or phone for help, once the pilot leaves you until the day he picks you up. If the weather gets bad, he

Denver Glacier cabin near Skagway is retired White Pass caboose. The train drops you off there.

might be a few days late. Plan your gear carefully, and **be careful** so no one gets hurt. Know how to avoid and how to treat hypothermia. Wear lifejackets in the boat. Be extra careful with axes, fire, and while hiking. If no one stays at the cabin when you leave on day trips, you're wise to leave a note telling where you went and when you'll be back.

Some cabins are booked-up regularly, while others are rarely used. A few very popular cabins are reserved by lottery drawing from the reservation requests for certain dates. All cabins are shown and numbered on the Tongass National Forest map. Reservations are accepted no more than six months in advance. A table on the map lists the hunting and fishing available in each cabin's area. An Alaskan license is required, even for saltwater fishing. The table also shows how to get to the various cabins by trail, boat, or floatplane. Charter operators in each town can take you to a cabin and pick you up.

Cabins reached by Juneau's trail system must be shared 10 a.m.–5 p.m. with any hikers who want to dry out and warm up.

The flight services may be able to tell you who is using the cabin before or after you. If you can coordinate the flights so one party returns on the plane that brings the other in, you can all save money. This must be arranged ahead of time. Generally, an hour's charter will cover both trips, though a few cabins are farther. Cabins in both Alaskan national forests can be reserved with credit card by calling (800) 444-6777. From outside the U.S. (518) 885-3639. web: http://www.reserveusa.com For information and trip planning, write to:

| | |
|---|---|
| Sitka Ranger District | Chichagof and |
| 204 Siginaka Way | Baranof Islands |
| Sitka, AK 99835 | (907) 747-4220 |
| U.S. Forest Service Information Center | All other northern |
| 101 Egan Drive | areas, including Admiralty |
| Juneau, AK 99801 | Island and Yakutat |
| | (907) 586-8751 |
| Petersburg Ranger District | central area |
| Box 1328 | (907) 772-3871 |
| Petersburg, AK 99833 | |
| Wrangell Ranger District | central area |
| Box 51 | (907) 874-2323 |
| Wrangell, AK 99929 | |
| Southeast Alaska Visitor Center | Ketchikan area, Misty Fjords |
| 50 Main Street | Prince of Wales Is. |
| Ketchikan, AK 99901 | (907) 228-6214 |

These offices can send you a map of the forest, price $4, which is very helpful in planning your trip. It shows the entire Alaskan part of the ferry route and the location of cabins and campgrounds. They also sell detailed maps of the roads and other facilities in their districts—really useful for touring islands by car, boat, or on foot.

## Driving

Note that both Canada and Alaska require you to use seat belts and shoulder harness and to have the appropriate child seats for small children. British Columbia requires your headlights to be on at all times. Alaska requires headlights to be on at all times when you are driving on roads posted for 45 mph or higher. Both have very stiff penalties for driving under the influence. Drive carefully on gravel roads to avoid rock damage to your car or others and to keep traction on the gravel ball bearings. Logging trucks and ore trucks from mines always have the right-of-way.

## Reading

You may want to read *Discover Southeast By Backpack and Paddle*, by Margaret Piggott; *Milepost*, detailed annual; *Alaska's Southeast* by Sarah Eppenbach; *Birds of Alaska* by Bob Armstrong; *Camping Alaska and Canada's Yukon* and *Alaska, Off the Beaten Path* by Mike and Marilyn Miller. *Backpacking in Alaska* by Jim DuFresne (Lonely Planet). *Walking Southeast Alaska* by Andromeda Romano-Lax (Wilderness Press) describes easy walks starting near town centers throughout Southeast. *The Nature of Southeast Alaska*, by O'Clair, Armstrong, and Carstenson is an entertaining explanation of local ecology. *Alaska's Ocean Highways*, with text by Sherry Simpson and Mark Kelley's photos (almost all on sunny days), is a great souvenir of a ferry trip. Southeast Alaska bookstores, museums, and Forest Service visitor centers offer many books on native art and history and stories of Alaskan pioneers (even bears) that you won't find elsewhere.

### Holidays

July 4 is *the* big summer holiday in any Alaskan town. Alaskans celebrate the long summer daylight (it may not be quite dark for the fireworks) as well as our country's independence. Every port on the ferry route goes all out with parades, games, contests, barbecues, and fireworks. Ketchikan and Sitka have logging contests. Wrangell has very impressive fireworks for a small town. Everyone prays for no rain on the parade. Have fun with the Alaskans that day. If you're in Canada on July 1, join in the Canada Day celebration—or enjoy the combined holiday at Hyder and Stewart!

## Cruise Ships

This book emphasizes the ferry system because it's mainly for the traveler who wants to "see more, spend less." However, from mid-May until late in September many cruise ships travel through Southeast Alaska. Compared to the ferries, they offer more comfort, more service, finer food, more shipboard entertainment, more luxuries such as swimming pools and spas, and longer daytime stops at several ports. If you want a considerable amount of personal service and entertainment, you may prefer a cruise ship with its huge staff of stewards providing for your comfort.

Side trips may be part of the tour, or available as options— flightseeing, bus tours, guided walks, river rafting, and even sea kayaking. Depending on your interests, you may want to explore independently on your days ashore, adjusting your plans according to the weather. A day cruising in Glacier Bay or Tracy Arm is usually included. As ship traffic in Glacier Bay is controlled, several ships go instead to Tracy Arm or Endicott Arm, glaciated fiords south of Juneau.

Larger ships carry over 1000 passengers in floating resorts with pools, spas, entertainers, and gambling casinos. Recently ships that used to carry 300-700 passengers have gone elsewhere, replaced by ever-bigger liners. When several ships are in port on the same day, as they often are, downtown is a busy place. You have a wide choice of cruising style and route, sometimes offering very good values, especially in late spring and early summer.

The smaller ships in the second list pass through the Narrows on cruises between Ketchikan and Skagway. Without expansive lounges, pools, or hundreds of passengers and staff, these ships enter small bays and passages surrounded by up-close scenery and wildlife. They may anchor in scenic bays overnight where you can hear bird calls and watch eagles swoop to catch fish. Some will set you ashore with small boats for guided nature walks. Naturalists rather than professional entertainers may be aboard. You can fish from several ships or their boats. Most start within Southeast Alaska instead of Vancouver.

Routes and stops vary with the ships. Most offer rail, air, or bus connections for tours including Anchorage and Fairbanks. Your travel agent can make arrangements for you. Most sail from Vancouver, B.C., but may start or end in San Francisco or Los Angeles, especially in May and September. Early or late "positioning cruises" are often a bargain, but note better weather odds and longer daylight hours in May than September. Some offer longer cruises all the way to Anchorage or Seward, usually flying one direction. Most companies offer one-way or round trip cruises, so you can have 3–14 day trips. Itineraries shown here were listed at presstime, but you should call for changes.

## Cruise Ships in Southeast Alaska 1999 Season

**Carnival Cruise Lines**, P. O. Box 94000, Cranberry, NJ 08512. (800) CAR-NIVAL. *Jubilee*, 1486 passengers, Vancouver–Inside Passage–Seward. www.carnival.com

**Celebrity Cruises**, (800) 437-3111. *Mercury* and *Galaxy* , both 1870 passengers. Some sailings, Los Angeles–San Francisco–Inside Passage, Vancouver–Inside Passage–Seward. www. celebrity-cruises.com

**Crystal Cruises**, 2121 Avenue of the Stars, Ste. 200, Los Angeles, CA 90067. (800) 820-6663. *Crystal Harmony* , 940 passengers. San Francisco–Inside Passage.

**Holland-America Line/Westours, Inc.**, 300 Elliott Ave. West, Seattle, WA 98119. (800) 426-0327 and (206) 281-3535. Six ships. *Ryndam, Veendam, Statendam,* each 1266 passengers, *Nieuw Amsterdam, Noordam,* each 1214 passengers, *Westerdam,* 1494 passengers. Vancouver–Inside Passage and Vancouver–Seward. Offers combined land/sea trips including motorhome rental with planned itinerary. www.hollandamerica.com

**Norwegian Cruise Line**, 95 Merrick Way, Coral Gables, FL 33134. (800) 327-7030. *Norwegian Wind*, 1726 passengers, and *Norwegian Dynasty*, 800 passengers. Vancouver–Inside Passage-Seward. www.ncl.com

The Carnival Cruise Ship Line's *Mercury* visits a remote port.

The Alaska Sightseeing Cruise West's *Spirit of Discovery*, a small cruise ship, docks at Haines.

**Princess Cruises**, 10100 Santa Monica Blvd., Ste. 1800, Los Angeles, CA 90067. (800) PRINCESS. Six ships. *Sky Princess*, 1200 passengers, *Regal Princess* and *Crown Princess*, each 1590 passengers, *Sun Princess* , *Sea Princess*, and *Dawn Princess*, each 1950 passengers, will sail Vancouver–Inside Passage, Vancouver–Inside Passage–Seward, and San Francisco–Inside Passage. www.princesscruises.com

**Royal Caribbean Cruise Line**, 1050 Caribbean Way, Miami, FL 33132. (800)ALL-HERE. *Vision of The Seas* and *Rhapsody of the Seas*, each 2000 passengers, Vancouver–Inside Passage. www.royalcaribbean.com

**World Explorer Cruises**, 555 Montgomery St., San Francisco, CA 94111. (800) 854-3835. fax (415) 391-1145. *Universe Explorer*, 732 passengers, Vancouver–Inside Passage–Seward. www.WECruise.com

*Note:* the following firms offer tours with smaller ships to out-of-the-way areas, sometimes staying onshore in hotels. Most can land you on shore to explore secluded coves and beaches, often with naturalist guides.

**Alaska Sightseeing/Cruise West**, 4th and Battery Bldg., Suite 700, Seattle, WA 98121. (800) 426-7702. *Spirit of Discovery, and Spirit of Alaska*, 84 passengers, *Spirit of Endeavor*, 107 passengers, *Spirit of Columbia* and *Sheltered Seas*, each 80 passengers, *Spirit of '98*, 99 passengers, and *Spirit of Glacier Bay*, 54 passengers. Seattle–Inside Passage, and cruises within the Inside Passage from Juneau or Ketchikan, sometimes using hotels ashore. www.smallship.com

**Alaska Yacht Safaris**, (800) 325-6722). Luxury yachts, *Safari Quest*, 20 passengers, 120', and *Safari Spirit*, 12 passengers, 102'. Vancouver–Juneau, Sitka–Juneau. www.americansafaricruises.com

**Alaska's Glacier Bay Tours & Cruises**, 520 Pike St., Ste. 1610, Seattle, WA 98101. (800) 451-5952. *Executive Explorer*, 49 passengers, *Wilderness Adventurer*, 72 passengers, *Wilderness Discoverer*, 24 passengers, and *Wilderness Explorer*, 36 passengers. Seattle–Inside Passage and cruises within Inside Passage. www.glacierbaytours.com

**Clipper Cruise Line**, 7711 Bonhomme Ave., St. Louis, MO 63105. (800) 325-0010.*Yorktown Clipper*, 138 passengers. Seattle–Inside Passage and cruises within Inside Passage. www.clippercruise.com

**Discovery Voyages**, (800) 324-7602. *Discovery*, 12 passengers, Prince William Sound, College Fjord. www.discoveryvoyages.com

**Society Expeditions**, (800) 548-8669. *World Discoverer*, 138 passengers. Prince Rupert, BC–Inside Passage–Seward, Seward–Aleutians–Russia–Nome.

**Special Expeditions**, 720 5th Ave., New York, NY 10019. (800) 762-0003.

*Legend of the Seas* approches Haines.

*Sea Bird, Sea Lion,* each 70 passengers. Wildlife viewing trips in the Inside Passage to/from Juneau, and Sitka, Seattle.
www.specialexpeditions.com

Independent charter operators in Ketchikan, Petersburg, Sitka, and Juneau offer overnight or multi-day cruises with yacht and converted missionary boats, tugs, and fishing boats. Some cruises go to Misty Fiords, Glacier Bay, or around Admiralty Island. Some are scheduled so you don't have to charter the whole boat. Great food and individual attention with routes and schedules according to your interests are attractions. Frequently the owner is a biologist with years of experience in local wildlife. Check with the visitors' bureau in the port you'd like to start from.

With thanks to Mike Miller, Juneau, Alaska, author of *Alaska, Off The Beaten Path*, published by Globe Pequot Press, 1996.

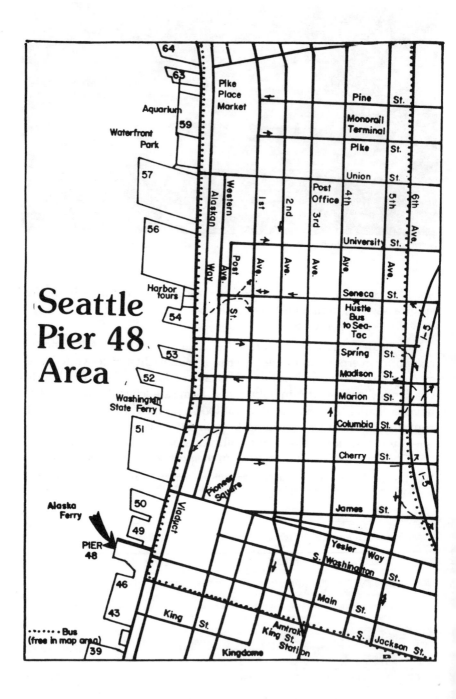

# SEATTLE

(Area code 206)

SEATTLE is a fascinating city with a good public transit system and lots to see. Do allow time for its sights on your Alaskan trip. Several guidebooks are available at Sea-Tac Airport and waterfront shops, including the Washington State ferry terminal at Pier 52.

Seattle's waterfront is where the Klondike gold-seekers once boarded ships for the Yukon, and ships loaded with those who had struck it rich, and those who hadn't, returned. Nearby is Pioneer Square, part of Klondike National Historic Park (along with Downtown Skagway, and the Chilkoot and White Passes). Some original buildings remain, and many of them are being restored. Art galleries, boutiques, restaurants, and bookstores occupy many old buildings. You may want to stroll around the historic square, and share the excitement that the men of '98 felt as they packed to sail for the North.

## Getting to Seattle's Waterfront and Downtown

FROM I-5, simply follow blue signs for ferries, directing you to Washington ferry terminals. The Madison Street interchange leads to the waterfront at Pier 52.

FROM SEA-TAC AIRPORT, the **Airporter**, airport limousine, takes you every 20 minutes to the Westin, Sheraton, Crowne Plaza, Four Seasons and other downtown hotels. Art galleries, boutiques, restaurants and bookstores are found throughout this area. From there you can walk about 10 blocks or take a taxi to the waterfront.

**Shuttle Express, 622-1424,** runs to and from Sea-Tac Airport to any destination between Tacoma and Everett. Van service, requires any airline ticket.

METRO TRANSIT (city bus) #174 runs regularly and cheaply between Sea-Tac and downtown. (206)553-3000.

RAIL—**Amtrak** station, 6 blocks, S. Jackson St. and 3rd Ave. S., on city bus routes with line to the waterfront. Goes once daily to Bellingham and Vancouver with new viewing cars, but limited baggage capacity.

BUS—**Greyhound**, 8th Avenue and Stewart. Greyhound goes to Vancouver and an affiliate continues to Prince Rupert.

TAXI—You can take any cab at a stand, not necessarily the first. Some serve certain areas of the city only. Since they have been deregulated, **Yellow**, 622-6500, and **Far West**, 622-1717, are the only ones which charge rates similar to the regulated fares. The others may charge as they choose. It's worth asking before getting in the cab.

## To See and Do

The Washington State ferry terminal for ferries to Bainbridge Island and Bremerton, Pier 52.

Some of the 200 parks in Seattle and King County displaying public art purchased by the city.

The Waterfront Trolley, running 1.6 miles from Chinatown/International District to Pier 70, has three 1927 Australian streetcars very much like the ones which plied this area in early days. They run every 20 to 30 minutes from 8 a.m. to 11 p.m. in summer and 8 a.m. to 6 p.m. in winter. Some have singing drivers. All are wheelchair accessible. They are fun!

Many waterfront gift shops, restaurants, crafts shops (including several on Pier 70).

The Seattle Aquarium, Pier 59. Excellent, featuring Puget Sound and nearby marine life. Open 10 a.m. daily to 7 p.m. in summer.

Omnidome, 3D photodrama, Pier 59.

Pike Place Market—across from the aquarium, with many shops on several levels. Fruits, vegetables, fish, gifts, antiques, and *much* more. Open 7 days a week in summer.

Waterfront parks next to the aquarium, fishing and shrimping.

Several art galleries and bookstores.

Argosy Tours, at Pier 54.

Cruises to Victoria on *Victoria Clipper I, II, III, and IV*, high speed catamarans that take walk-on passengers daily from Pier 69. 448-5000.

Kingdome Sports Arena, S. King St. and Occidental Ave. S. Tours 11 a.m., 1 p.m., 3 p.m.

Chinatown/International District. S. Main St. at 6th and 7th Avenues. Tours available.

The Coast Guard museum, Pier 36.

Klondike Gold Rush National Park, Seattle unit, 117 South Main Street. Free films and slide programs 9 a.m. to 5 p.m. daily, extended summer hours.

Underground Tours in Pioneer Square, guided tours of the old Seattle neighborhood built over by the present city.

The waterfront from S. Washington Street to Pier 67 is within the free zone for the bus system. The monorail, Pine and 5th, is a fast way to the Seattle Center, 1962 World's Fair site, and home of the Space Needle and Pacific Science Center.

Woodland Park Zoo, an easy bus ride from downtown, is one of the nation's most attractive zoos, featuring natural habitats and many breeding animals.

## Annual Events

Seattle Seafair. July-August. City-wide marine festival: regattas, hydroplane races, parades, sports events, exhibits, etc. Torchlight parade and hydroplane races weekend in August. Admission fee to best viewpoint, though most events can be seen from wider area.

Bumbershoot, Seattle Center. Outdoor/indoor festival of arts, music, and literature. Labor Day weekend.

Folklife Festival, Seattle Center. Outdoor music and crafts. Memorial Day Weekend. Free.

4th of July fireworks are spectacular here, over Elliott Bay. In some years there is also a display over Lake Union.

Pacific Northwest Arts and Crafts Fair, Bellevue Square (four miles east in Bellevue). Art exhibits, handicrafts. Late July. Free.

Arts and crafts fairs are held in the Seattle area almost continuously throughout the summer. The Visitors' Bureau has dates and locations.

Highland Games, traditional Scottish games and dances. Enumclaw Fairgrounds, southeast of Seattle. Late July.

ACCOMMODATIONS: Downtown lodgings range from deluxe to the YMCA, YWCA and youth hostel. On the highways north, east and south of Seattle, especially along Pacific Avenue near Sea-Tac Airport, and near Pike Place Market are moderate hotels, many from the national chains.

INFORMATION AVAILABLE: Seattle/King County Convention & Visitors' Bureau, mailing address: 520 Pike Street, Ste. 1300, Seattle, WA 98101. Visitor Information, 800 Convention Place, Galleria Level, Seattle, WA 98101. (206) 461-5800. Fax: (206)461-5855. Website: www.SeeSeattle.org 8:30 a.m.–5:00 p.m., Mon.–Fri., handicapped accessible, and TDD. Have excellent lodging guide listing B & Bs, hostels, budget hotels, as well as more expensive ones.

For Washington State information, call 1-800-544-1800.

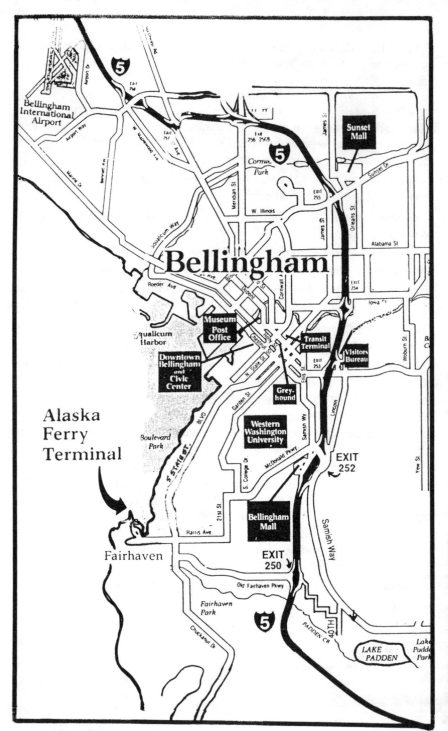

(Port of Bellingham)

Mural, one of several on Belingham walls extoll "The City of Subdued Excitement".

## BELLINGHAM

(Area Code 360, Zip Codes 98225, 226,227)

BELLINGHAM, Washington (pop. 61,240) is the southern terminal of the Alaska ferry. It's the county seat of rural Whatcom County, extending from the sea to the slopes of Mount Baker and to the Canadian boundary on the north. Seattle is 1.5 hours south (90 miles), Vancouver 1 hour north (54 miles) on Interstate 5.

The Port of Bellingham has built a new ferry terminal adjacent to the historic Fairhaven district on the south side of downtown. The terminal has a travel information center with very helpful people and a restaurant.

Bellingham is a regional shopping center with many parks, several lakes, a state university, and an international airport. The historic Fairhaven area offers restaurants, galleries, and sightseeing in restored brick buildings 1/2 mile from the terminal. It also has a supermarket, laundromat, propane, diesel, and ice (no dry ice). Bellingham's transit system provides 35¢ rides throughout Bellingham. Pet boarding is available. A lot for long term car and RV storage is across the street from the terminal. Call (360) 676-8445 or ask at the ferry ticket counter in the terminal.

Nearby mountains, fishing, skiing, 14 golf courses, many festivals at all seasons, museums, and beautiful countryside make this an area to explore.

Lynden, a few miles north, is a fascinating town featuring traditional Dutch shops and festivities, local and regional fairs.

Drive up to the Mt. Baker ski area in the Mt. Baker-Snoqualmie National Forest for a picnic and walk around to enjoy views of Mt. Shuksan, mountain forests, lakes, and glaciers. Bicyclists who get let off there can enjoy miles of scenic coasting back down the highway.

Enthusiastic shoppers can explore the range from gift shops and art galleries in Fairhaven and nearby towns to Bellisfair, the region's largest shopping mall near I-5 exit 256 and the Peace Arch outlet center near Blaine, 5 miles south of the Canadian border.

GETTING TO THE FERRY: from I-5, take Exit 250, follow signs 2 miles.

AIR: **From Sea-Tac Airport**, the **Bellingham/Sea-Tac Airporter** goes 4–6 times a day each way. On Fridays it stops twice each way at the Alaska ferry terminal, (800) BELLAIR. From Washington only, (800) 235-5247 or (360) 733-3600. Both **Horizon Airlines** (800) 547-9308 and **United Express** (800) 241-6522 fly into Bellingham from Seattle, a scenic 40 minute flight.

SHIP: Bellingham has daily seasonal passenger ferry service to and from the San Juan Islands and Victoria.

TRAIN: **Amtrak** has a daily Spanish Talgo train each direction between Seattle and Vancouver BC., stopping in Bellingham within walking distance of the ferry terminal. video and audio facilities at each seat. Northbound, it leaves Seattle at 7:15 a.m. arriving in Bellingham at 9:33 a.m. Southbound, it leaves Bellingham at 7:34 p.m. and arrives in Seattle at 9:15 p.m. Schedule may change during Daylight Saving Time. Adult $23 one-way, seniors over 62, $20.50. Children 2–15 with an adult, $14 (2 children per adult max). Children over 12 traveling alone, full fare. Children under 12 not allowed unaccompanied. Round trip fares lower, especially Mon–Thurs. Train has no baggage car, so baggage is limited to 2 hand-carried pieces. No bicycles or boats. Takes credit cards. Reservations mandatory. (800) USA-RAIL.

BUS: **Greyhound Bus Lines**, (360) 733-5251. Frequent service to Seattle and Vancouver. **Whatcom Transportation Authority** (city bus), (360) 676-RIDE. **Quick Coach**, (604) 244-3744 and (800) 665-2122. Daily service between Seattle, Bellingham, and Vancouver.

TAXI: **City Cab**, (360) 733-8294. **Yellow Cab**, (360) 734-TAXI.

CAR RENTAL: **Budget**, (360) 671-3800. **Hertz**, (360) 733-8336. **Avis**, (360) 676-8840. **National**, (360) 734-9220. **Enterprise,** (360) 733-4363.

VEHICLE PARKING: Long-term parking for vehicles in fenced lot across street from the ferry terminal. Pay at the ticket counter in the terminal.

Take time to explore the Whatcom Museum of History and Art inthe former city hall, built in 1892—historic landmark and cultural center with changing exhibits and children's activities.

Alaska Marine Highway System, (360) 676-8445. Daily $3.75, weekly $21 for standard cars up to 20 ft. long. Oversize vehicles occupying 2 spaces, $42 weekly.

TOURS: **Victoria-San Juan Cruises**, (800) 443-4552, offers daily trips May 16–October 4 from the Bellingham cruise terminal through the San Juan Islands, stopping at Roche Harbor, to Victoria on the 150 passenger luxury vessel, *Victoria Star*. You can stop over in Victoria on a tour package or make the round trip with a five hour layover in Victoria. Leaves Bellingham at 9 a.m., Victoria at 5 p.m. On return trip an all-you-can-eat salmon buffet is included. Adult $42 one way, $79 round trip, with $5 discount if prepaid reservation. Children age 6–17, $21 one way, $39.50 round trip.

**Island Shuttle Express**, (360) 671-1137, leaves Bellingham Cruise Terminal daily at 9:30 a.m., June through September, taking foot passengers to Orcas and San Juan Islands and whalewatching. **Island Mariner Cruises**, (360) 734-8866, offers whale watch and nature cruises. In cooperation with the Whatcom Museum of History and Art, it offers Bellingham Bay history cruises Thursday evenings, May through September. The

# Bellingham Accommodations

Bellingham/Whatcom County Convention & Visitors Bureau
904 Potter St. (I-5 Exit 253) Bellingham, WA 98226 360-671-3990 / 1-800-487-2032 (Voice Mail) / Fax: 360-647-7873

**Rates Code:**
A = Under $45/night/person;
B = $45-60; C = Over $60

**Amenities Code:**
R = Restaurant; L = Lounge;
E = Entertainment; J = Jacuzzi; S = Sauna;
OP = Outdoor Pool; IP = Indoor Pool

### HOTELS/MOTELS

| Name / Address / Phone | Rates | # of Rooms | Meeting Room Cap. | Restaurant/Brkfst | Lounge/Entertain. | Pool *Jacuzzi/Sauna | Television | Phone | Kitchenettes | Pets Allowed | Fitness Center | Credit Cards | Airport/Ferry Shuttle | Commercial Rates | Non-Smoking Rooms | Weekly/Long-Term | Notes |
|---|---|---|---|---|---|---|---|---|---|---|---|---|---|---|---|---|---|
| Bay City Motor Inn, 116 N. Samish Way — 1-800-538-8204 / 676-0332 | AB | 51 | 20 | near | | | • | • | | • | • | | • | • | | | |
| Bellingham Travelodge, 101 N. Samish Way — 1-800-732-1225 / 733-8280 | ABC | 56 | 55 | near | SJ | • | • | 1 | | | • | AF | • | • | | |
| Best Western Heritage Inn, 151 E. McLeod-Meridian Plaza — 1-800-528-1234 / 647-1912 | C | 104 | 75 | B | OP | • | • | • | | | • | AF | • | • | • | off-site apts. |
| Best Western Lakeway Inn, 714 Lakeway Drive — 1-800-528-1234 / 671-1011 | BC | 132 | 900 | BR | LE | IPSJ | • | • | | | • | AF | • | • | • | full brkfst. |
| Comfort Inn, 4282 Guide Meridian — 1-800-228-5150 / 738-1100 | BC | 85 | 24 | near | | IPSJ | • | • | | • | • | AF | • | • | • | |
| Days Inn, 125 Kellogg Road — 1-800-831-0187 / 671-6200 | BC | 70 | 45 | B | | OPJ | • | • | • | • | | • | | • | • | |
| Hampton Inn, 3985 Bennett Drive — 1-800-HAMPTON (426-7866) / 676-7700 | BC | 133 | 60 | B | | OP | • | • | | | • | AF | • | • | • | |
| Holiday Inn Express, 4160 Guide Meridian — 1-800-HOLIDAY(465-4329) / 671-4800 | BC | 101 | 15 | B | | IPJ | • | • | • | | | AF | • | • | • | |
| Motel 6, 3701 Byron St. — 671-4494 | A | 60 | | near | | OP | • | • | | • | • | | | | | |
| Quality Inn Baron Suites, 100 E. Kellogg Road — 1-800-221-2222 / 647-8000 | BC | 86 | 30-80 | B | | OPJ | • | • | • | • | • | | AF | • | • | |
| Ramada Inn, 215 N. Samish Way — 1-800-2RAMADA (272-6232) / 734-8830 | BC | 66 | 10 | near | | OP | • | • | | • | • | | | • | • | |
| Rodeway Inn, 3710 Meridian — 1-800-228-2000 / 738-6000 | AB | 75 | | near | | J | • | • | | • | • | | | • | • | |
| Shangri-la Motel, 611 Holly Street — 733-7050 | A | 20 | | near | | | • | • | 2 | • | | | • | • | • | |
| Travelers Inn, 3570 Meridian — 1-800-633-8300 / 671-4600 | AB | 124 | 40 | near | | OP | • | • | | • | | • | | • | • | |
| Val-U Inn, 805 Lakeway Drive — 1-800-443-7777 / 671-9600 | BC | 81 | 30 | B | | J | • | • | | | | AF | • | • | • | |

### BED AND BREAKFASTS

| Name / Address / Phone | Rates | # of Rooms | Meeting Room Cap. | Restaurant/Brkfst | Lounge/Entertain. | Pool *Jacuzzi/Sauna | Television | Phone | Kitchenettes | Pets Allowed | Fitness Center | Credit Cards | Airport/Ferry Shuttle | Commercial Rates | Non-Smoking Rooms | Weekly/Long-Term | Notes |
|---|---|---|---|---|---|---|---|---|---|---|---|---|---|---|---|---|---|
| A Secret Garden, 1807 Lakeway Drive — 1-800-671-5327 / 671-5327 | BC | 2 | 15 | B | | | • | • | | | • | AF | | • | | | |
| BABS Reservation Service, P.O. Box 5025 — 733-8642 | B | 3 B&B | | B | | | | | | | | | | | | |
| Big Trees, 4640 Fremont Street — 1-800-647-2850 | C | 2 | | B | | | | | • | | • | | | • | | |
| The Castle, 1103 15th Street — 676-0974 | BC | 2 | 15 | B | | | • | | | | | AF | | • | | |
| DeCann House, 2610 Eldridge Ave — 734-9172 | BC | 2 | | B | | | • | • | | | | | | • | • | |
| Fairhaven B&B, 1714 12th Street — 734-7243 | C | 2 | | B | J | • | • | • | | | | AF | | • | | game room |
| Marc-James Manor, 2925 Vining Street — 738-4919 | C | 1 | | B | JS | • | • | | | | | AF | | • | | |
| North Garden Inn, 1014 N. Garden — 1-800-922-6414 / 671-7828 | C | 10 | 10 | B | | | | | | | | AF | | • | • | |
| Schnauzer Crossing, 4421 Lakeway Drive — 734-2808 / 733-0055 | C | 3 | 12 | B | J | • | • | | | • | | | | • | | 1 Cottage |
| South Bay, 4095 South Bay Drive — 595-2086 | C | 5 | 30 | B | J | • | • | 1 | | • | | | | • | | |
| Stratford Manor B&B, 1416 Van Wyck Road — 715-8441 | C | 4 | | B | J | • | • | | | | • | | | | | |

## NON-MEMBER ACCOMMODATIONS

### BELLINGHAM

| | |
|---|---|
| Aloha Motel, 315 N. Samish Way | 733-4900 |
| Cascade Inn, 208 N. Samish Way | 733-2520 |
| Coachman Inn, 120 N. Samish Way | 671-9000 |
| Evergreen Motel, 1015 Samish Way | 734-7671 |
| Lions Inn Motel, 2419 Elm St. | 733-2330 |
| Mac's Motel, 1215 E. Maple | 734-7570 |
| Shamrock Motel, 4133 W. Maplewood | 676-1050 |
| Travelers Lodge, E. Holly & Railroad | 734-1900 |

visitors' bureau has a current list of fishing and nature charter boats.

WHERE TO STAY: Bellingham has over 30 hotels and bed and breakfasts, averaging $60. It also has a youth hostel. The Visitors Bureau has latest info, including accommodations in nearby towns, Ferndale, Blaine, and Lynden. We strongly recommend reservations, especially on weekends.

## Campgrounds

There are many campgrounds and RV parks in Whatcom County, especially in and near Ferndale and Lynden, north of Bellingham. The Visitors Bureau has a complete list. In the Bellingham area:

**Bellingham RV Park,** 3939 Bennett Dr., Bellingham, WA 98226. (360) 752-1224, (800) 372-1224. 56 sites self-contained or with full hookups. Toilets, showers, laundry. Pets allowed. Open year-round.

**Larabee State Park,** 245 Chuckanut Dr., Bellingham, WA 98226. (360) 676-2093. 53 standard sites, 8 walk-ins, all on first-come, first-serve basis without reservations, $10. 26 RV sites with utilities $15. 3 emergency sites and 67 picnic sites.. Group camp may be reserved but is available w/o reservation if not reserved by groups. $10 reservation fee plus $1/person/night. No RVs or trailers allowed in group camp. Shower, dump station. 7 miles from ferry with views of San Juan Islands, beaches, boat launch and hiking trails. *Note:* For information on all Washington State Parks, call (800) 233-0321. To reserve campsites in state parks, call (800) 452-5687.

**Sudden Valley,** Bellingham, WA 98226. (360) 734-6430, Ext. 335. 100 sites, 96 with hookups. Tent camping, shower, laundry, dump station. Lake access, fishing, boating, golf, tennis, pool, restaurant, store. $15 with hookups, $10 tent camp.

**Wildwood Resort,** 990 S. Lake Whatcom Blvd., Sedro Woolley, WA 98284. (360) 595-2311. 42 sites, 7 with hookups, tent camping, shower, dump station. Cabins, boats, kayaks, groceries, playground, swimming.

BAGGAGE STORAGE: No lockers in terminal.

INFORMATION AVAILABLE: **Bellingham/Whatcom County Convention & Visitors Bureau,** 904 Potter St., Bellingham, WA 98226. (360) 671-3990 and voice mail (800) 487-2032. Fax (360) 647-7873. From I-5, take Exit 253 to find very helpful people with lots of good, current info! E-mail: tourism@bellingham.org Web: www.bellingham.org

**Alaska Marine Highway** terminal office, (360) 676-8445. Toll Free, (800) 642-0066.

## Happenings

**Ski to Sea,** Memorial Day weekend. Five stage county-wide relay race from Mt. Baker to Bellingham Bay. Parade and festivities start the week before. Free.

**Deming Logging Show,** 2nd weekend in June. Traditional logging contests and barbecue, in Deming.

**Bellingham Festival of Music,** late July–early August, two weeks. Nightly performances with world class orchestra, chamber, jazz, and ethnic music. (360) 676-5997.

**Abbotsford Airshow,** usually first weekend in August. Just north of the border, less than an hour's drive from Bellingham, is the largest airshow in Western Canada. The RCAF Snowbirds are regulars. May become biennial, will be held in 1999.

**Puget Sound Antique Tractor & Machine Show,** Lynden. Antique tractor parade, pulling contests. Runs 4 days, including the weekend of the Abbotsford Airshow. A day at each is fun! What variety!

**Northwest Washington Fair,** mid-August. Agricultural fair with farm animals, crafts, music, and carnival in Lynden.

Check with the Visitors' Bureau and read the *Bellingham Herald* for other fairs, tractor pulls, and art shows. Several happen every weekend in summer and fall!

The oldest brick building in Washington state once served as Bellingham's city jail.

On a bright winter morning a tug pulls a bargeload of freight containers along Johnstone Strait.

# PORT HARDY

(Area Code 250; prices in Canadian $)

This town of 5000 on the north end of Vancouver Island is the southern end of the British Columbia ferry route to Prince Rupert. Fishing, scenic trails, and native Indian art are some of its attractions. It is 320 miles north of Victoria, about an 8-hour drive on a 2-lane road. Here, for the convenience of readers who may spend the night when connecting in either direction with the B.C. ferry, is a short list of relevant facilities.

Reservations for rooms or campsites are advised. A shipload of passengers headed in either direction fills the town. As an alternative, Port McNeill, 30 miles south of Port Hardy, has 2 hotels with a total of 98 rooms and a campground with 26 sites. Most have winter rates.

INFORMATION AVAILABLE: **Port Hardy & District Chamber of Commerce**, Box 249, Port Hardy, B.C. V0N 2P0. (250) 949-7622, fax 949-6653. Office at 7250 Market Street. e-mail: chamber@capescott.net **Vancouver Island North Visitors Association**, e-mail: vinva@capescott.net web: http: www.capescott.net/~vinva/

## Hotels

(15% tax added)

**Airport Inn**—4030 Byng Rd. Box 2039, Port Hardy, B.C. V0N 2P0. (250) 949-9434. Fax (250) 949-6533. 45 rooms, coffee shop, dining room, licensed lounge, beer & wine store. Adjacent to airport. Single $85, Double $95, Twin $105. Add'l. $7.50. Kitchen $10. Children under 12 free. E-mail: airportinn@capescott.net www.capescott.net/~airportinn/

**Glen Lyon Inn**—6435 Hardy Bay Road, Box 103, Port Hardy, B.C. V0N 2P0. 949-7115, fax 949-7415. 29 rooms, ocean view, restaurant, lounge, phone, cable TV, in room coffee. Boat launch and moorage adjacent. Wheelchair accessible. Pets allowed. Single/Double $88, Twin $98. e-mail: wshang@island.net

**North Shore Inn**—7370 Market St., Box 1888, Port Hardy, B.C. V0N 2P0. 949-8500, fax 949-8516. Full service hotel, 30 rooms, ocean view with balconies, phone, cable TV. Restaurant, lounge. Single $79, Double $93, Twin $103. Add'l. $10. Cot $10. Child under 12 free.

**Pioneer Inn**—Box 699, Port Hardy, B.C. V0N 2P0. 949-7271. (800) 663-8744. Adjacent to Quatse River in park-like setting. Kitchenettes, laundry, playground, restaurant. Single $75–94, Double $85–104. Add'l. 10. Kitchen $10. 25 Full service RV sites, $20. CAA/AAA approved. Website: www. travel.bc.ca

**Port Hardy Inn**—9040 Granville St., Box 1798, Port Hardy, B.C. V0N 2P0. 949-8525, fax 949-6248. Full service hotel, indoor pool. 85 rooms, wheelchair accessible, pets allowed $5. Single $96, Double $102, Twin $112. Add'l person $10. Multi-night discount.

**Quarterdeck Marina Resort**—6555 Hardy Bay Rd., Box 910 Port Hardy, B.C. V0N 2P0. 949-6551, fax 949-7777. New motel, 41 rooms. Single, $85, Double $95, Twin $105, Suites $110–135. Kitchen $10. Complete marine store, propane, ice, charts, marine fuel, laundromat, showers, docks. 60 ton Marine Travelift and repair yard. VHF Channel 73. Inner Harbour.

**Seagate Hotel**—8600 Granville St., Box 28, Port Hardy, B.C. V0N 2P0. 949-6348, fax 949-6347. 84 rooms, kitchenettes $10, restaurant. Single $85, Double/Twin $90–95. Add'l $10.

**Thunderbird Inn**—7050 Rupert St., Box 88, Port Hardy, B.C. V0N 2P0. 949-7767, fax 949-7740. 52 rooms, dining room, live entertainment, small pets allowed. Single $75, Double $85, Twin $85. Add'l $10.

## Campgrounds

**Quatse River Campground**—Box 1409, Port Hardy, B.C. V0N 2P0. 949-2395. 3 miles from BC ferries terminal, off Hwy. 19, 8400 Byng Rd. Laundry, showers, dump station. 62 sites, 41 with electrical and water hookups. Shaded sites, fishing. $14/site, up to 2 people, add'l $2/person. Elec. $4. Reservations recommended. E-mail: quatse@island.net

**Scotia Bay Resort**—Box 423, Port Hardy, B.C. V0N 2P0. 2 miles north of downtown Port Hardy through native reserve, 10 miles from ferry terminal. 949-6484, fax 949-8486.Skiff rentals, bathrooms, laundry. Tents $12, RV sites $20. Moorage $12 up to 20 ft. 75¢/ft. over 20 ft.

**Seven Hills Golf & Country Club**—Box 1710, Port Hardy, BC, V0N 2P0.

The native village of Bella Bella is on an island between Port Hardy and Prince Rupert. Some B.C. ferry trips stop here briefly.

Phone/fax 949-9818. 1 mile west of Hwy. 19 on rd. to Port Alice, on 9 hole golf course. Restaurant, central washroom, pro shop, rentals, driving range. For self-contained RVs, 10 grassy sites, water, elec. incl, $15.

**Stryker Electronics**—will have campground summer 1999. Phone 949-8022, fax 949-8077.

**Sunny Sanctuary Campground**—Box 552, Port Hardy, B.C. V0N 2P0. 949-8111. On Hwy. 19 near ferry. Adjacent to river and wildlife sanctuary. Full hookups, 30 amp elec., store, dump station, laundromat, tent areas. Free hot shower. Firewood, freezer facilities. Fire pits, pets allowed. RV and boat storage. Weekly & monthly rates. 80 sites. RVs $19 with full hookups.

**Wildwoods Campsite**—Box 801, Port Hardy, B.C. V0N 2P0. 949-6753. On road to ferry, nearest to terminal. Forested, with fireplaces, firewood, tables, beach access. Moorage. Pets allowed. 60 sites. Hot showers. $15 per vehicle, incl. hookups. May 1–October 1.

## Car Parking & Storage

**Sunny Sanctuary Campground**, listed under campgrounds.

**Wildwood Campsite**, listed under campgrounds.

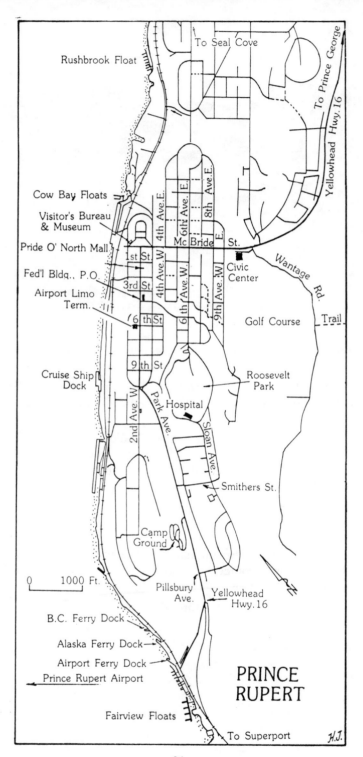

Rushbrook Float

To Seal Cove

To Prince George

Yellowhead Hwy. 16

Cow Bay Floats

Visitor's Bureau & Museum

Pride O' North Mall

4th Ave. E.

6th Ave. E.

8th Ave. E.

Mc Bride St.

Fed'l Bldg., P.O.

1st St.

4th Ave. W.

6th Ave. W.

9th Ave. W.

Civic Center

Wantage Rd.

Airport Limo Term.

3rd St.

6th St

Golf Course

Trail

9th St

Cruise Ship Dock

2nd Ave. W.

Park Ave.

Roosevelt Park

Hospital

Sloan Ave.

Smithers St.

Camp Ground

0    1000 Ft.

Pillsbury Ave.

Yellowhead Hwy. 16

B.C. Ferry Dock

Alaska Ferry Dock

Airport Ferry Dock

Prince Rupert Airport

PRINCE RUPERT

Fairview Floats

To Superport

H.J.

86

Totem at entrance of carving shed next to visitor center and museum.

# PRINCE RUPERT

(Area code 250, prices in Canadian $)

PRINCE RUPERT (pop. 17,500) is Canada's northernmost ice-free port, the third largest naturally deep harbor in the world. It is a lumbering and fishing center (mainly for halibut and salmon), and a transportation hub. Here the Yellowhead Highway and the Canadian Railroad from the interior meet passenger ships and freighters from all over the world. It is the main trading center for the Canadian coast north of Vancouver. The British Columbia ferry from Port Hardy and the Alaska ferry arrive here several times a week in summer. The B.C. ferry has ferry service to the Queen Charlotte Islands at Skidegate. It is worth taking time to explore Prince Rupert and enjoy the views over its harbor. Bald eagles dive beside the fishing boats and deer walk along the railroad tracks near the ferry terminal.

## To See and Do

See 25 totems standing throughout the town

Enjoy the view of the harbor from Roosevelt Park.

Visit Kwinitsa Station Railway Museum across from Via Rail on the waterfront. Donations.

Visit the North Pacific Cannery Museum in Port Edward, living museum in historic cannery building. Demonstration of net-mending and rope-making some days. Shows, tours. Adult $6, youth $3. Children under 6 free. 628-3538.

Explore the waterfront of this busy port.

Take a city walking tour (maps available at Infocentre).

Take some of many tours available through the Infocentre, including walking tours of town, archeology tour of harbor by boat.

See and photograph Chatham Village Longhouse, adjacent to Pacific Mariners Memorial Park. Visit the Museum of Northern British Columbia in the Chatham Village Longhouse. Native art and wildlife exhibits are featured. The Museum offers guided archeology/harbor tours in season. Open 9 a.m.–8 p.m., Mon.–Sat., 9 a.m.–5 p.m. Sun., mid-May through Labour Day. Off season, 9 a.m.–5 p.m., closed Sunday. Admission, $5 Adult, $2 Student, $1 Child age 6–12. Children under 6 and members free. 624-3207.

Visit the Pacific Mariners Memorial Park, adjacent to Chatham Village Longhouse, overlooking the harbor. It features a statue of a mariner looking out to sea and a shrine around a Japanese fishing dinghy which drifted across the Pacific Ocean after its owner died. The boat's owner was from Prince Rupert's sister city, Owase, Japan. Bricks commemorating mariners lost at sea are on walls around the statue.

Visit the Firehall Museum in the present firehall 2 doors up 1st Avenue from the Longhouse. Donations.

Explore the Cow Bay revitalization area on Cow Bay Road near the harbor, with gift shop, restaurants, pub, B & B, and more!

Watch reversing Butze Rapids from the highway. Best time is on an ebbing tide, 1 1/2 hour after summer high tide, shown in the telephone book. (1/2 hour in winter)

Ride harbor tours, with trips to Venn Passage and Metlakatla.

Hike the trails on Mt. Hays, at your own risk, with caution.

Enjoy the beautiful parks and gardens throughout the city, including the sunken garden behind the Court Building and Mariners Memorial Park

A DeHavilland Beaver on floats taxis out of Seal Cove to fly freight and passengers to a logging camp or village.

next to Chatham Longhouse.

Fish from boat, shore, or in the Skeena River—with B.C. license in freshwater, Canadian federal license in saltwater. Check at fish and game or sporting goods stores to learn where and when the closures are.

Pick wild berries in summer (get suggestions from Infocentre).

Take a B.C. ferry side trip to the Queen Charlotte Islands with or without your car. Call the Infocentre or B.C. Ferries for schedules and information. The only public transportation on the Queen Charlotte Islands is taxis. Helicopters take sightseers to former village sites on Indian reserves.

Play golf on Prince Rupert's golf course or watch one of the summer tournaments. In this climate players often wear rubber boots. The course has an unusual hazard—ravens sometimes steal the balls!

World War II historians or veterans of war in the Aleutians will find bunkers on shore, some visible from the ferry and some covered with undergrowth. Thousands of U.S. troops came by train to Prince Rupert and went from here to the Aleutians by ship. Several buildings near Seal Cove housed some of them. Roosevelt Park and a plaque near the hospital across from the park commemorate the action.

EARLY MORNING COFFEE SHOPS for those early arrivals! **Prince Rupert Hotel**, 2nd Ave. West & 6th Street. **Raffles Inn**, 1080 3rd Ave. West.

**Best Western Highliner Inn**, 815 1st Ave. West, 6 a.m. **Crest Motor Hotel**, 222 1st Ave. West, 5:30 a.m. **Moby Dick Motor Inn**, 935 2nd Ave. West, 6 a.m., and **McDonald's**, 99 11th Ave. East, open at 7 a.m. daily. **Tim Horton's**, 5 a.m.–1 a.m. A Chevron station and 24-hour convenience store are at 400 2nd Ave. West. **7-11** store/gas station open 24 hours at 250 2nd Avenue West.

INFORMATION AVAILABLE at **Prince Rupert Infocentre**,100 1st Ave. West, 9 a.m.8 p.m. daily mid-May to Labour Day. Off season 9 a.m.–5 p.m., closed Sunday. Very helpful people. (250) 624-5637. Toll free, Canada and U. S., (800) 667-1994, fax 627-8009. Box 669, Prince Rupert, B.C. V8J 3S1 Canada Web: city.prince_rupert.bc.ca E-mail: prtravel@citytel.net The infocentre is at the west end of McBride, north of the courthouse. They have the latest lists of B&Bs, art galleries, shopping and hiking trails.

If you haven't yet acquired a free copy of the current Tourism British Columbia *Accommodation Guide,* this is a good place to get one. It lists hotels and useful info for every B.C. town and village. As a small fee is charged for listing, you will find some hotels not listed. The prices stated for rooms show the low and high season rates. The higher number for each room is its price in summer. **Super Natural British Columbia** has an information and reservation service for the whole province with toll-free phone for North America, (800) 663-6000.

## Transportation

FERRY: **Alaska Marine Highway**, May, 3–6 ships/week; June, July, August, September, 6 ships/week. Winter, 2–3 ships/week. Drivers should look over terminal area in daylight. Alaska Ferry Office, Box 457, Prince Rupert, B.C. V8J 3R4 Canada. (250) 627-1744. (800) 642-0066 in the U.S. and Canada.

**B.C. Ferries** run from Port Hardy at the north end of Vancouver Island in summer. Box 697, Prince Rupert, B.C. V8J 3S1. (250) 624-9627, 28, 29. Reservations: **British Columbia Ferry Corporation**, 1112 Fort St., Victoria, B.C. V8V 4V2. (250) 386-3431, fax (250) 381-5432.  www.bcferries.bc.ca

In summer 1999 the B.C. ferries will run all daylight cruises between Port Hardy and Prince Rupert, with all departures at 7:30 a.m. and all arrivals about 10:30 p.m., with a stop at Bella Bella on some runs.

| Schedule: | Lv Port Hardy | Lv Prince Rupert |
| --- | --- | --- |
| June | odd days | even days |
| July | odd days | even days |
| August | even days | odd days |
| September | odd days | even days |

About half of the trips stop at Bella Bella for a few minutes.

**Queen Charlotte Islands**: From June through September, the *Queen of Prince Rupert* makes 4–6 round trips weekly between Prince Rupert and Skidegate in the Queen Charlottes. Fall through spring, fewer sailings weekly each direction. Sailing time 8 hours (Hecate Strait can be rough). Adult passenger $24, car $90. Low season is September 28–June 1, when fares are at least 10% off those in peak season.

Cabins can be reserved as dayrooms or for overnight sailings. Some sailings from Skidegate to Prince Rupert, arriving at about 6 a.m. on Friday and Saturday mornings in summer connect with ferry sailings to Port Hardy leaving at 7:30 a.m.

From the end of September to May, the *Queen of the North* sails a weekly round trip between Port Hardy and Prince Rupert and between Prince Rupert and the Queen Charlottes 3 times a week.

BUS: **Greyhound Bus Lines** (Canadian Coachways), 106–6th St., Prince Rupert, V8J 3L7. 624-5090, twice daily, with connections at Prince George to Vancouver. **Farwest Bus Lines**, 624-6400, and **Haida Coach Lines**, 624-6236, local only, bus tours.

TAXI: **Skeena Taxi**, 624-2185.

CAR RENTAL: **Budget**, 627-7400, and **Tilden**, 624-5318, are in Rupert Square Shopping Mall, near the Canadian Airlines terminal, 500–2nd Ave. West, Prince Rupert, B.C. V8J 3T6.

RAIL: **Via Rail**, Waterfront at foot of 2nd St., Prince Rupert, 627-7589. Train service to Prince George several times weekly. Reservations office in Winnipeg is open Mon. 10:30–7:30, Tues. closed, Wed., Fri., Sun. open 7:30-4:30, Thurs. and Sat. 7:30-4:30. For reservations call toll free in British Columbia (800) 561-8630 in Canada, (800) 561-3949 from the U.S., or see a travel agent. The fares between Prince Rupert and Prince George were being revised at presstime. The train leaves Prince Rupert at 8 a.m. Wed., Fri., Sun. It arrives in Prince Rupert on Mon., Thurs., Sun., at 3:40 p.m. Sometimes, by prior arrangement, the train will stop for passengers at the ferry dock en route to Prince George.

AIR: **Canadian Airlines International (CAI)**, (250) 624-9181, to and from Vancouver, Rupert Square. 500 2nd Ave. West, Prince Rupert, V8J 3T6. Three flights daily in summer. **Air B.C.** offers regular flights between Prince Rupert and Vancouver. For schedule and fares, call 624-4554. Note: airport ferry to CAI and Air B.C. flights leaves dock near Alaska and B.C. ferries, but passengers must check in at airline office downtown and ride out to the ferry. Do allow time for this! Airport ferry fare: Adult $11 one-way, seniors and children $7. Round trip with same day return, $18. Pilots and boaters note: there are now 11 ferry sailings a day to Digby Island to serve those not on scheduled flights. 624-3355.

**Harbour Air**, Seal Cove, 627-1341, also serves Queen Charlotte Islands and coastal communities. Scheduled flights 3 times a week to Ketchikan in summer.

**Inland Air**, Seal Cove, 627-1351. Serves Queen Charlotte Islands and other coastal communities.

Helicopters: **Alpen Helicopters**, Seal Cove. 627-4354. Tours and charters.

**Vancouver Island Helicopters**, Seal Cove, 624-2792. No passenger service to Queen Charlotte Islands.

TOURS: Bus tours and service to interior points available from bus lines listed above. A full list of tours is available at the Infocentre.

## Car and Baggage Storage

**Park Avenue Corner Store and Gas Bar**, outdoor. 1665 Park Ave. 624-3201. $2.50–6 per day. Will pick up and drop off passengers to ferries Mon.–Sat. in summer, Mon.–Fri. in winter. **Parkside Resort Motel**, outdoor. 101 11th Ave. E. 624-9131, fax 627-8457. $3/day. **Philpott Evitt & Company Ltd.**, indoor. 101-500 2nd Ave. W. 624-2101. Vehicles under 20 ft., $4/day. Over 20 ft., $6. Monthly rate, $4/ft. **Rupert Towing**, 101 Shawatlans Rd., Prince Rupert Industrial Site. 624-2722. Rate negotiable, about $2. **Pacific Inn**, 909 3rd Ave. W., 627-1711. Cars only, $4/day, $25/week, $85/mo. **Totem Lodge Motel**, outdoor. 1335 Park Ave., 624-6761. Cars only, $3/day, with priority to hotel guests.

BAGGAGE STORAGE at B.C. Ferry office (check for hours). Most hotels allow storage on day of departure for patrons.

## Suggestion

For reasons possibly known to themselves, the U.S. and Canadian mails frequently take 3 weeks to get airmail between the U.S. and Prince Rupert. We advise using the telephone or fax freely to make reservations or get information here. You can call **Super Natural British Columbia**, (800) 663-6000, for travel information and lodging reservations.

## Hotels

Prices in Canadian dollars. Room tax is 6% up to $49, 8% above that. Reservations advised in summer. Most have lower off season rates.

**Aleeda Motel**—900 3rd Avenue West, Prince Rupert, BC, V8J 1M8. 627-1367. Quiet, Clean, 31 rooms, phone, TV. Non-smoking units available. Single $53, Double $65, Twin $70. Add'l, $6/person, kitchenette $6.

**Anchor Inn**—1600 Park Avenue, Prince Rupert, BC, V8J 4P7. 627-8522, fax 624-8137. 46 rooms with private bath. TV, phone. Two rooms wheelchair accessible. Single $69, Double $79.

**Highliner Inn**—815 1st Avenue West, Prince Rupert, BC, V8J 1B3. 624-

Entrance to the Court House on McBride Street.

9060, fax 627-7759. Reservations: (800) 668-3115. Restaurant, lounge, banquet facilities, wheelchair accessible, non-smoking rooms, ocean view, balconies with all rooms. Single/Double $120, Twin $125. Add'l $10. web: www.floriangroup.com

**Coast Prince Rupert Hotel**—118 6th Street, Prince Rupert, BC,V8J 3L7. 624-6711, or (800) 663-1144 (Canada & US), fax 624-3288. Has 92 rooms, harbor view, dining room, lounge, cabaret, wheelchair accessible, pets allowed, satellite TV. Single $95, Double $115, Twin $125. Add'l $10.

**Crest Hotel**—222 1st Avenue West, Prince Rupert. Mail: Box 277, Prince Rupert, BC, V8J 3P6. 624-6771, (800) 663-8150, fax 627-ROOM. 100 rooms, harbor views, restaurant, coffee shop, cocktail lounge, TV, pets allowed. Fishing charters. Single/Double $139–149, Twin $159–169. Ocean view rooms add'l $10. Day rooms. Cot/crib available. Web: www.cresthotel.bc.ca E-mail: infocresthotel.bc.ca

**Inn On The Harbour**—720 1st Avenue West, Prince Rupert, BC, V8J 3V6. 624-9107, (800) 663-8155, fax 627-8232. Has 50 rooms, harbor view, continental breakfast, phone, satellite TV, sauna. Single $65, Double $72, Twin $77. Add'l $8.

**Moby Dick Inn**—935 2nd Avenue West, Prince Rupert, BC V8J 1H8. 624-6961, fax 627-3760. Sauna and whirlpool. Restaurant, banquet facility, coin-op laundry. Near B.C. and Alaska ferries. Single $69, Double/Twin

$79. Add'l $10. Pets welcome.

**Neptune Motor Inn**—1051 Chamberlin (Yellowhead Centre on Hwy. 16). Prince Rupert, BC V8J 4J5. 627-1377. Toll free in B.C. (800) 772-0802, fax 627-7500. Has 39 units. Restaurant, cable TV, pets allowed. Wheelchair accessible. Kitchenettes. Single $50, Double $56, Twin $60. Add'l $5. Kitchen $6.

**Ocean View Hotel**—950 1st Avenue West, Prince Rupert, BC V8J 1A9. 624-6259. Restored older hotel. Pub downstairs with ocean view. 55 rooms (some with bath, TV). Shared bath, single $30, double $45. Private bath, $70–125.

**Pacific Inn**—909 3rd Avenue West, Prince Rupert, BC V8J 1M9. 627-1711, or (800) 663-2831 in B.C., (888) 663-1999 in North America, fax 627-3831. Has 77 rooms, restaurant, lounge, cable TV. Single $79, Double/Twin $85. Children under 12 free. Add'l $10. Senior rate 10%.

**Parkside Resort Motel**—3 miles, 101-11th Avenue East, Prince Rupert, BC V8J 2W2. 624-9131, fax 627-8547. Has 34 rooms (18 with kitchen), phone, complimentary coffee, satellite TV, pets allowed. Single $49, Double $52, Twin $55. Kitchen $6. Weekly rates, senior and family rates. Camper, trailer parking, and5 campsites with hookups, $18. Car storage $4/day.

**Pioneer Rooms**—167-3rd Avenue East, Prince Rupert, BC V8J 1K4. 624-2334. Hostel in historic building "with colourful past," not with CYH. Popular with backpackers, clean. Guest cooking area, backyard barbecue. Baggage storage. Single, double, twin rooms, $15–$20 per person.

**Raffles Inn**—1080 3rd Avenue West, Prince Rupert, BC V8J 1N1. 624-9161, or (800) 663-3207 in B.C., fax 624-8249. 50 rooms with phone, TV, restaurant, lounge. Coin-op laundry. Single/Double/Twin $50. Add'l, $6/person. $5 cot. Special backpacker rates.

**Totem Lodge Motel**—1335 Park Avenue, Prince Rupert, BC V8J 1K3. 624-6761, (800) 550-0178, fax 624-3831. 31 units, phone, TV, car storage, coin-op laundry. Single $75, Double $79, Twin $85. Add'l $8. Kitchen $7. Rollaway bed $8. Car storage $3.

## Bed & Breakfasts

**Caroline's Home Comfort B & B**, 1441-2nd Ave. West, 624-3635. **Eagle Bluff B & B**—201 Cow Bay Rd, Prince Rupert, B.C. V8J 1A2. 627-4955. **Raindrop B & B**, 2121 Graham Ave., 624-5564. **Rose's B & B**— 943 1st Ave. West, Prince Rupert, V8J 1B4. 624-5539. **Andrea's Place B & B**, 315 4th Ave. East, 624-3666. **Snuggle Inn**, 152 Raven Crescent, 624-6370, 624-9735. **Service Park Guest House**, 445-4th Ave. West, 624-6068.

## Campground

**Park Ave. Campground**—1/2 mile from ferry, 1 mile from downtown, on Highway 16, 1750 Park Ave., Box 612, Prince Rupert, BC V8J 3R5. 624-5861, (800) 667-1994, fax 627-5105. Visitor information. Has 97 sites with and without hookups. Tenting area, playground, pay phone, coin laundry, mail drop, showers, flush toilets, full hook-ups, dump station, firewood. Wheelchair accessible. Visa and MC accepted. $18.50 full serviced site, $13.50 unserviced site, tenting $10.50. Rates are for 2 people. $1/$2 per Add'l. child/adult. Reservations recommended in summer, with credit card or 1 night's deposit. e-mail: prinfo@citytel.net

There are other campgrounds along the highway and river east of Prince Rupert, but no others in town.

## Facilities

LAUNDROMAT—**King Koin**, 743-2nd Ave. W. **Maytag**, 226 7th St.

ICE—any gas station. **Park Avenue Corner Store** across from campground. **Safeway**. Dry Ice—**Chevron Town Pantry**, open 24 hours.

PROPANE—**Farwest Fuels**, 225-2nd Ave. West. **ICG Propane**, 170 George Hills (near Cow Bay). **Park Avenue Shell**, 1665 Park Ave. **Valley Oxygen**, 139 George Hills Way.

DIESEL—**Park Avenue Shell**, 1665 Park Ave.

DUMP STATIONS—**Campground** and **Park Avenue Corner Store**, 1665 Park Ave., across from campground.

CARWASH—**Total Wash**, 3rd Ave. West between Aleeda Motel and Beacon Motors.

HOSPITAL—**Prince Rupert Regional**, 1305 Summit Ave., 624-2171.

PETS—**Veterinary Services**, 975 Chamberlin, 627-1161. Boarding $4-6.25/day. **SPCA**, 2200 Seal Cove Circle, 624-2859. $4-6.50/day. Male cats must be neutered. Will board ferrets.

## Boats

CHARTERS: For current information on boat charters, ask at **Infocentre**. 624-5637 or (800) 667-1994.

PUBLIC FLOATS, FUEL. **Fairview Public Floats** just south of ferry dock. Fishing boat traffic is heavy here during summer. **Cow Bay Floats**, north of Atlin Fish Co., fuel. **Rushbrook Public Floats**, north of downtown and fish canneries. Can be reached on land by going north on 3rd Ave. past Court House, taking second left. Launching ramp. Fuel at Cow Bay. **Government Harbour**, Bayview Drive in Port Edward, 20 miles from Prince Rupert. 628-3211.

## Happenings—1999

| | |
|---|---|
| Year-round | Bingo at Rupert Bingo Centre. |
| | Bowling, at Totem Lanes Bowling Centre,. |
| | Art exhibits changed monthly at the Prince Rupert Museum Art Gallery. |
| | Performances at Performing Arts Centre |
| May 2–8 | B.C. Annual Jazz Dance Competition & Gala |
| June 10–13 | Seafest. Parade, Children's events. Land and water events. Native Cultural Days. |
| June 12–13 | Ladies' Jubilee Golf Tournament. Call 627-2000 for info on all golf events. |
| June 19–20 | Men's Jubilee Golf Tournament |
| June 26–27 | Seniors Mixed Jubilee Golf Tournament |
| July 1 | Canada Day Celebrations. |
| July | Cow Bay Days, fun events, mini-golf, street dance 1-800-677-1994 for dates |
| August | Seashore Fishing Derby 624-2000 for dates |
| September | Terry Fox Run (entrants get pledges for cancer research) |
| September 18–19 | Duffers Golf Tournament |
| October 31 | Halloween Party |
| November TBA | Fishermen's Bonspiel, curling |
| December 4–5 | Winterfest '99 |

The latest list of things to see and do is available at the Infocentre. Prince Rupert is a cultural center! Throughout the year and particularly in summer, there are music, dance, and drama performances with local and touring artists.

### Canadian Customs and Regulations

**Vehicles** can be left in Canada for up to 45 days without a permit, under supervision in a lot, not on street. Report leaving car to Customs, Room 105, Federal Building, or at Alaska ferry terminal. When driving in Canada, especially the Yukon, carry proof of adequate liability insurance, at least $200,000. Seat belts must be used and children under 6 or under 40 lbs. must be in infant or child seats. The Yukon requires headlights on day or night. Blood alcohol levels over .08% are illegal in Canada, and penalties are severe.

Carry **money** sufficient to pass through Canada by your planned route and method of travel, allowing for emergencies, to avoid being refused entry to Canada.

**Personal identification** is required for everyone, including infants, proving residence and citizenship. A passport is best and may speed your way through immigration in either direction, but a certified, not just notarized, copy of your birth certificate will do. A driver's license is no longer adequate.

**Firearms.** Handguns are not permitted into Canada. Rifles and shotguns for personal use are allowed. If they will be in B.C. for a week or longer, you need a $1 permit, available from the RCMP or Fish & Wildlife. Some sports stores may sell the permits.

**Pets** (cats and dogs), over 3 years of age, must have proof of rabies vaccination within past 36 months. Health certificate advised, within 30 days of trip.

**Pilots.** Canadian Customs now have 24-hour service, free of charge, at Digby Island Airport, Prince Rupert. For others, including boats and floatplanes, customs inspections free at Seal Cove between 7 a.m. and 10 p.m. in summer. After hours, by reservation made during above hours, the charge is $50. Winter hours are 7 a.m.–4:30 p.m.

**Boats.** Pleasure craft have free clearance 7 a.m.–10 p.m. daily. Overtime charges apply at other hours.

## Goods and Services Tax (GST)

Canada's national sales tax is 7%, some of which may be rebated to non-residents of Canada. Keep your receipts. If your purchases of short term accommodations and most goods you remove from Canada within 60 days total over C$100, you may claim a rebate within one year. If your rebate is $500 or less, you may present your receipts for rebate at a duty free shop in Canada (usually near the border). For an application or information, write Revenue Canada, Customs and Excise, Visitors' Rebate Program, Ottawa, Canada K1A 1J5. Phone (613) 991-3346.

Most provinces have a provincial sales tax which is not refundable. British Columbia's sales tax is 7%. The provincial hotel room tax is 8%, and some cities also charge a local 2% tax.

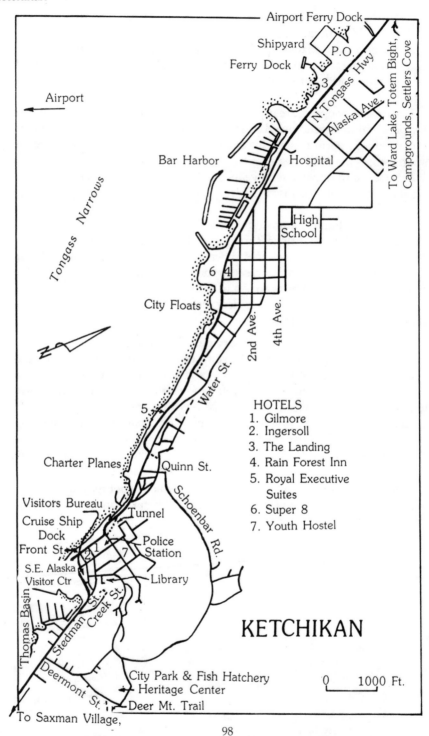

Airport Ferry Dock
Shipyard
P.O.
Ferry Dock
3
N. Tongass Hwy
Alaska Ave.
To Ward Lake, Totem Bight, Campgrounds, Settlers Cove

Airport

Bar Harbor
Hospital

High School

Tongass Narrows

6 4

City Floats

2nd Ave.
4th Ave.

Water St.

5

HOTELS
1. Gilmore
2. Ingersoll
3. The Landing
4. Rain Forest Inn
5. Royal Executive Suites
6. Super 8
7. Youth Hostel

Charter Planes
Quinn St.

Schoenbar Rd.

Visitors Bureau
Cruise Ship Dock
Front St.
Tunnel
Police Station
2 1
7
S.E. Alaska Visitor Ctr
Library

Thomas Basin
Stedman St.
Creek St.

KETCHIKAN

Deermont St.
City Park & Fish Hatchery
Heritage Center
Deer Mt. Trail

0     1000 Ft.

To Saxman Village,

Ketchikan's charming Creek Street was the infamous red-light district in the town's lusty frontier days. Today the "madame's" house is a museum. Although its population is less than 15,000, it is Alaska's fourth largest city, and boasts the world's largest collection of totems. Just two and a half miles away from the ferry terminal, it is well worth a walking tour or less energetic visitors can utilize the taxi service or Gray Line Tours to visit the totem parks.

## KETCHIKAN
(Area code 907, Zip code 99901)

KETCHIKAN (pop. 14,600) is the fourth largest city in Alaska and the commercial center for most of Southeastern Alaska. Early Indians settled here. Later, salmon canneries and sawmills were built, and copper, gold, and other minerals were discovered nearby. In 1954 the Ketchikan Pulp

Company mill was built at Ward Cove, just north of town, closed in 1997. From Ketchikan, planes and boats work in all directions, supplying logging camps, fishing resorts, and settlements on other islands.

The town, like most in Southeastern Alaska, is linear, never more than 10 blocks wide, but several miles long. Tongass, the main street, is built on pilings that take it out over the water in several places. Some of the cross "streets" are really wooden steps climbing the steep hillside.

The largest collection of totems anywhere in the world is found here in three locations: at Totem Bight State Park, 7.5 miles north of the ferry dock. Saxman Native Village, 4.5 miles south of the ferry dock, and the Totem Heritage Center, 601 Deermount Street, 4 miles south of the dock.

The ferry terminal is 2.5 miles north of downtown Ketchikan.

## To See and Do

Take a walking tour of Ketchikan. Maps available at ferry terminal and Visitors Bureau on downtown dock. Covers all the sights within walking distance of downtown. The public bus stop on Tongass Ave. in front of the ferry terminal parking lot, has buses every half hour to downtown.

Take a taxi tour, including totem parks if you wish. **Alaska Cab** charters cabs for $42/hr. for 1–6 people.

**Gray Line** offers sightseeing tours from hotels and from the ferry parking lot during longer ferry stops.

Visit totem parks. **Saxman Village**, 4.6 miles from ferry, Mile 2.3 S Tongass Highway. **Totem Bight**, totems and ceremonial house, 7.6 miles, Mile 9.9 N. Tongass Highway.

**Totem Heritage Center Museum**, 4 miles, 601 Deermount St., 8 a.m–5 p.m. daily May 15 through September. Tues–Fri 1–5 p.m. October through May 14. Adults, $4 admission, children 12 and under, free.

See **Deer Mountain Tribal Hatchery and Eagle Center** with observation platforms and signs and videos explaining the life cycle of salmon. Watch salmon climbing the fish ladder in mid to late August. Across City Park from Totem Heritage Center. Open daily 8:30 a.m.–4:30 p.m. May 15–September 30. Adults $5.95. Note combined rate with Totem Center, $7.95. Both have tours conducted by native guides.

See the **Tongass Historical Museum**, 2.4 miles, Dock St., adjacent to the library. Pioneer and native artifacts, minerals, shells. $1 admission.

Tour **Dolly's House**, 2.4 miles, Creek St. This residence of Ketchikan's last "madame" has been opened as a museum, with other Creek Street houses in this professional district. Summer hours, 9 a.m.–5 p.m. $2.50.

Visit boat harbors and the waterfront. Nearest to ferry dock is Bar Harbor, about 1 mile, with most types of fishing and pleasure boats. Much of this can be seen during a regular ferry stop if you have at least an hour on shore—walk briskly, and keep track of the time. This is a good chance to see all types of fishing gear close-up, talk to fishermen, and see jellyfish and sea anemones under floats.

Ward Lake Recreation Area, 5.8 miles from ferry, turn off at Mile 6.8 N. Tongass Highway. Nature and hiking trails, picnic area, and campgrounds. A good place to explore and learn about a temperate rainforest. Canoeing tours offered by **Alaska Travel Adventures**, 789-0052 (Juneau)

**Southeast Alaska Visitor Center:** 50 Main St., 228-6214, Fax: 228-6234. Enjoy world-class exhibits and award-winning audio-visual programs. Enjoy Tsimshian, Haida and Tlingit totem poles, stroll through a rainforest room, discover a native fish camp scene, learn about Southeast Alaska's ecosystems, and listen to people who work in the timber, fishing, mining and tourism industries. Seven exhibit rooms. Bookshop with many hard-to-find books and pamphlets on nature, native people and Southeast Alaska. The center is one block from the cruise ship dock in downtown Ketchikan. Open daily from 8:00 a.m.–5:00 p.m. May–September. Admission $4, May–September, discount with Golden Age card. www.ktn.net/usfs/ketchikan/

Hike trails to top of Deer Mountain (from Deermount) for spectacular view over town, waterways and islands. Perseverance and Talbot lakes, and White River. Maps available from Forest Service in Visitor Center.

Ride the *Aurora* on her local runs to Metlakatla and Hollis. Hollis has no facilities, but offers road access to Craig, Klawock, Hydaburg, and Thorne Bay. Check the ferry schedule.

Ride the *Aurora* on her cruise up Portland Canal to Hyder and back on alternate Tuesdays, or ride one way and fly the other with a local air taxi. Ask the ferry terminal if one is offering a package rate. Portland Canal is a long fiord marking the U.S. and Canadian boundary which early explorers hoped would be a Northwest Passage. Rock walls over 1000 feet high rise on both sides, broken by the occasional waterfall. At its end are the villages of Stewart, B.C. and Hyder, Alaska with glimpses of icefields and hanging glaciers above.

See Misty Fjords National Monument via tour boat from Ketchikan. Ketchikan Visitors Bureau has information at its building on the city dock. All air charter companies make flightseeing excursions May–September.

Fish or kayak in Misty Fjords using Forest Service cabins or camping out. Transportation via air and *M/V Misty Fjords* daily, high speed catamaran seating 92 passengers. **Alaska Cruises**, Box 7814, Ketchikan, AK

99901. 225-6044 or (800) 228-1905, fax 225-8636. www.ptialaska.net/ ~akcruise E-mail: akcruise@ptialaska.net

Cruise/fly with boat one-way and flight the other to Misty Fjords. Tues., Thurs., Sat.. and Sun. June 1–Aug. 31, plus some dates in May and Sept. **Alaska Cruises**, address and phones above.

Tour the recently explored El Capitan Caves on northern Prince of Wales Island, accessible only by plane or boat, with permission of the U.S. Forest Service. Caves have limestone formations, native artifacts, and hints of life during the Ice Ages. **Taquan Air Service**, 225-8800, offers charter flights from Ketchikan via floatplane. Arrangements must be made with Forest Service for guide. Not recommended for children under 8.

Fish from shore or boat. Mountain Point, 8.5 miles from ferry, is a favorite fishing spot for pink salmon, from mid-June on. There's a boat launching ramp and parking area. Residents can tell you the current hot spots. Fishing is *the* local sport here. Charter a boat, rent one, or bring your own. Do respect the tides, currents, weather, and cold water. Traffic, especially in Tongass Narrows, is heavy with ships, tugs and barges, boats, and floatplanes. The Visitors Bureau has a current list of charter operators. Fishing license info is listed for Ketchikan under Facilities.

Enjoy miles of sheltered water for boating or kayaking. Apply the cautions above, but enjoy easy access to such areas as Behm Canal, the passage around Revillagigedo Island, Ketchikan's island.

Drive "out the road" as Alaskans describe towns where all the roads have ends, to picnic, hike, birdwatch, beachcomb—north to Settlers Cove at the end of Tongass Highway, or turn off at Ward Cove for 10 miles, passing Ward Lake, Harriet Hunt Lake, and White River to end at a bay.

Pick berries in season—July, August, September for blueberries, red huckleberries, salmon berries. The big clearcut above the north end of town is a huge berry patch. It's less than half a mile straight up the hill from the ferry terminal.

## Transportation

FERRY: Runs daily in summer; fewer sailings in winter. Dock and terminal are at Mile 2.3 N. Tongass Highway (north of town). Airport ferry dock 1/2 mile farther north, serves the ferry to Ketchikan Airport (across the Narrows on Gravina Island).

BUS: North end of the line is at the ferry parking lot, 3501 Tongass. 225-6182 and 6181 for schedule info. Buses run from here to the center of town, and south to Tatsuda's Market, every half-hour 6:45 a.m.–6:45 p.m. Mon.–Sat. $1. Senior and child fares.

TAXI: **Alaska Cab**, 225-2133. **Yellow Taxi**, 225-5555. **Sourdough Cab**, 225-

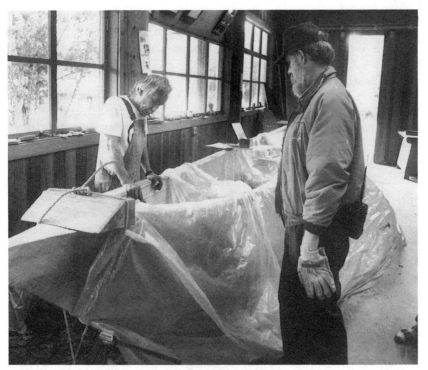

Master carver Nathan Jackson at Saxman Totem Park discusses nearly finished canoe with guide Ken Mix.

5544.

CAR RENTAL: At airport and in town, **Alaska Car Rental**, 225-5000. Excellent service. **Practical Rent-A-Car**, 225-8778. Service varies.

AIR: **Alaska Airlines** has daily jet flights between Ketchikan Airport and Seattle, Anchorage, Juneau, Sitka, Wrangell, and Petersburg. 800-426-0333.

The airport is served twice hourly by 5-minute ferry from its dock 1/2 mile north of ferry terminal, $2.50. Be sure to allow time for the airport ferry in making connections. It departs from Ketchikan at 15 and 45 minutes past each hour. The uphill walk from ferry to airport terminal is two blocks. The airport shuttle, for a higher charge, stops at hotels and delivers you to the terminal door. 225-5429.

AIR CHARTERS: **Taquan Air Service**, 1600 Ketchikan Int'l. Airport, and at 1007 Water St. (near cruise ship docks), Ketchikan, AK 99901. 225-8800 and (800) 770-8800. Scheduled service to several outlying towns. Offers flightseeing tours by floatplane to Misty Fjords and Anan Creek where black bears catch fish, overnight package tours to lodges, and a round trip to Alaska's only Indian reservation at Metlakatla with self-guiding tour brochure for $38/person, several flights daily.

**Island Wings Air Service**, 1935 Tongass Ave., Mail: PO Box 7432, Ketchikan, AK 99901. 225-2444 and 888-854-2444. Flightseeing, guided wilderness hikes, tours.

**ProMech Air**, 1515 Tongass Ave., Ketchikan, AK 99901. 225-3845. These charter services are based along the waterfront, and their takeoffs and landings provide much of the action in the harbor. Some also have bases on the airport. All can fly you into fishing resorts, Forest Service cabins, and virtually any place in Southeastern Alaska.

## Tours

BUS TOURS: around Ketchikan and to totem parks, museums, and fish hatchery. Most operate mid-May to late September. **Alaska Sightseeing**, summer number, 225-2740. **Blue Spot Tours**, 225-4081. **Cape Fox Tours**, 225-5163. **City Tour**, in English or German, 225-9465. **Classic Tours**, 225-3091 (in restored 1955 Chevy with retired high school teacher). **Gray Line of Alaska**, 225-5930. **Seahorse Ventures**, 225-5713, by horse-drawn trolley. **Dolly's Trolleys** (motorized streetcar), 247-8625.

KAYAK TOURS: **Outdoor Alaska**, 225-6044. **Southeast Exposure**, 225-8829. These companies offer half-day tours of Ketchikan's waterfront and Tongass Narrows as well as multi-day trips to the backcountry.

DIVING TOURS: **Alaska Diving Service**, 4845 N. Tongass Ave., Ketchikan, AK 99901. 225-4667, fax 225-5667. Instruction, rentals, tours.

INFORMATION AVAILABLE at **Ketchikan Visitors Bureau** on the downtown dock. Very helpful people. 131 Front St., Ketchikan, AK 99901. Call: 225-6166. To request free activity planner: (800) 770-2200 US & Canada, fax: 225-4250. E-mail, kvb@ktn.net. Web site, www.visit-ketchikan.com **Chamber of Commerce**, Box 5957, Ketchikan, AK 99901. Call: 225-3184. **Alaska Fish and Game** office downtown, 225-2859, recorded info 225-0475. The **Southeast Alaska Visitor Center** is between the cruise ship dock and Thomas Basin, with information on the Ketchikan area and public lands in Southeast Alaska. 228-6214, fax: 228-6234.

BAGGAGE STORAGE available at hotels, for patrons, on day of departure (check with individual hotels).

## Hotels

(plus 11.5% room and sales tax in city limits, 6% outside. )

**Alaskan Home Fishing Lodge**—11 miles from ferry, 11380 Alderwood St. N., Ketchikan, AK 99901. 225-6919, (800) 876-0925. 5 rooms incl. suite. Package rates at ocean view lodge include meals, spa, boat, guide, gear, cleaning and freezing your fish. Rental cars, courtesy van. Brochure and video available. In summer reserves rooms without package no more than 30 days ahead, Single from $55, Double from $75 including full breakfast.

**Alaska Rain Forest Inn**—1/2 mile from ferry. 2311 Hemlock, Ketchikan, AK 99901. 225-7246. Seven rooms, some available on per bunk, dormitory basis. Restaurants nearby. Clean. Open all year. $35 in dorm. $52 private room, single or double. $6 add'l adult. Often full during summer season. Fully equipped vacation apartments within walking distance.

**Best Western Landing**—across the street from ferry dock, 3434 Tongass, Ketchikan, AK 99901. 225-5166, fax 225-6900. 76 rooms/suite, restaurant, lounge, TV. 2 conference rooms. Ample parking. Freezer space for your fish. Courtesy van. Single/Double $115, QQ $138, Suite $150. e-mail: landing@ktn.net  web: www.landinghotel.com

**Clover Pass Resort**—13 miles from ferry, Mile 15, North Tongass. Box 7322, Ketchikan, AK 99901. 247-2234. Lodge, cabins, restaurant, lounge, marina, boat rentals and supplies, fishing information and charters. Boat moorage. Package tours for three to eight days include cabin, boat, motor, fuel, bait, rod and reel, breakfast, lunch, dinner, fish packing boxes, transportation to and from Ketchikan. $970–2240 for 3-8 days. Deluxe package includes chartered boat with guide. Trailers and campers $20 for 2 people. Add'l, $2/person. Season runs from April 2 to October 1.

**George Inlet Lodge**—15 miles from ferry, Mile 12, S. Tongass, Box 7356, Ketchikan, AK 99901. 225-6077, fax 225-0801. 10 deluxe rooms in restored cannery building moved 90 miles on raft from Hidden Inlet cannery, now on shore of George Inlet with creek. Restaurant, lounge. Fishing packages, boat rental. Single $75, Double $85. Open all year. Winter rates. e-mail: george@ktn.net

**Gilmore Hotel**—2.2 miles from ferry (downtown), 326 Front St., Ketchikan, AK 99901. 225-9423, fax 225-7442. (800) 275-9423. 38 rooms, color TV, phones, Annabelle's Keg & Chowder House in building. Courtesy van, call on arrival. Single/Double/Twin $82. Add'l. $5. Higher rate for waterfront view. Small pets allowed, $40 cash deposit or credit card guarantee. web: www.gilmorehotel.com

**Ingersoll Hotel**—2.3 miles from ferry (downtown corner of Front and Mission), 303 Mission St., Ketchikan, AK 99901. 225-2124 or (800) 478-2124, fax 247-8530. 58 rooms. Single $79, Double $89, including coffee.

**New York Hotel**—3 miles from ferry, next to Creek Street, 207 Stedman St. Ketchikan, AK 99901. 225-0246. Built in 1925, restored hotel with 8 rooms furnished in period style, sitting area, some with view, cable TV, phone, queen beds, full baths. Continental breakfast, local phone calls included. Single $69, Double $79.

**Super 8 Motel**—1/2 mile from ferry, 2151 Sea Level Drive, Ketchikan, AK 99901. 225-9088 or (800) 800-8000, fax 225-1072. 82 rooms. Pets ($25 deposit), guest laundry, 10% VIP member discount. Courtesy van. Single, 99.88, double $107.88.

**The Cedars Lodge**—1471 Tongass Ave., Box 8331, Ketchikan, AK 99901. 225-1900 and (800) 813-4363, fax 225-8604. e-mail is cedars@pti.alaska.net 13 rooms, jacuzzis, waterfront views. Rooms $110 single/double, $140 with jacuzzi. Suite with jacuzzi, $215. Fishing packages in summer. Rooms only reserved less than 30 days ahead.

**The Narrows Inn**—1.5 miles north of ferry dock, 4871 N. Tongass Hwy., Box 8660, Ketchikan, AK 99901. 247-2600 or (888) 686-2600, fax 247-2602. Overlooks Tongass Narrows. 43 rooms, 3 handicapped-equipped, phones with modem/fax capability, cable TV, smoking and non-smoking rooms. Restaurant, lounge, free shuttle service 6 a.m.–11 p.m. to ferry, town, airport ferry. Marina with moorage. Fishing packages and charters. Continental breakfast included. Standard rooms, Single $95, Double $105. Ocean-view rooms with balcony, Single $115, Double $119. Winter, weekly rates. web: www.visit.ktn.net/yes e-mail: narrows@ktn.net

**Salmon Falls Resort**—15 miles from ferry on N. Tongass Highway. Box 5420, Ketchikan, AK 99901. 225-2752 or (800) 247-905, fax 225-8604. E-mail bvwhite@plialaska.net. Restaurant, lounge, conference room. Fishing package rates includes room, meals, airport transfers, guided fishing, fishing gear and bait, and fish processing. Room only, single $115, double $147.

**Westmark Cape Fox Lodge**—800 Venetia Way, Ketchikan, AK 99901. 225-8001 or (800) 544-0970, fax 225-8286. On hill above city with funicular down to Creek Street. 70 rooms, 2 suites, restaurant, conference rooms. Wheelchair-accessible. Courtesy van from airport and ferry terminal. Single/Double $159 with mountain view, $169 with water view.

**Youth Hostel**—First Methodist Church, 400 Main, Box 8515, Ketchikan, AK 99901. 225-3319. Bring sleeping bag to use in male and female dormitories. Register 6 p.m.–11 p.m. $7, with AYH pass (available at hostel), $10 for non-members. Open Memorial Day to Labor Day.

### Bed & Breakfasts

Bed & breakfasts are increasing rapidly throughout Alaska, and our readers enjoy them. Prices usually range from $60 to $90 depending on season and facilities. Each town's visitors bureau has a list of the homes in that town, individual or organized under an association. Additional b&bs in most towns don't belong to the visitors bureaus and may not be listed, except in the phone book. Some homes are open all year, while others operate seasonally. Do ask whether the room has private or shared bath if that is important to you. To save space and the book weight you

Enthusiastic youngsters enjoy the pie-eating contest at Ketchikan's annual Blueberry Arts Festival.

carry, I usually list associations and local visitors bureaus rather than individual homes. I do the same for fishing charters in larger towns where there are many, constantly changing.

**Bed & Breakfast Association—INNside Passage Chapter**, Box 22800, Juneau AK 99802. 789-8822, fax 5869861.

**Ketchikan Reservation Service: Bed & Breakfast Lodging**, 412 D-1 Loop Rd., Ketchikan AK 99901. Phone/fax (907) 247-5337, toll-free (800) 987-5337. www.ktn.net/krs e-mail: krs@ktn.net Has suites and apartments as well as b&bs.

**Ketchikan Visitors Bureau**, 225-6166, (800) 770-2200, has a current list of over 15 individual bed & breakfasts, some in town, some surrounded by forest, and some on the waterfront. Fishing charters, skiff rentals, and airport/ferry transfers may be offered.

FLY-IN RESORTS: Near Ketchikan, offer a variety of rustic to modern facilities, and excellent fishing. Included are: **Yes Bay Lodge**, 225-3845, and **Unuk River Post**, P.O. Box 5065, Ketchikan, AK 99901. On Prince of Wales Island (some described in that section), some reached by ferry and bus as well as plane are: **Boardwalk Wilderness Lodge**, (800) 372-9382, **Coffman Cove Wilderness Lodge**, 329-2249, fax 329-2260, **Fireweed Lodge**, 755-2930, **Gold Coast Lodge**, 225-8375, (800) 333-5992, **Haida Way Lodge**, 826-3268, **Silver King Lodge**, 225-4965, **Sportsman's Cove Lodge**, (800) 962-

7889, **Whale Pass Resort**, (800) 531-9643, **Waterfall Resort**, 225-9461, ( 800) 544-5125, **Whale's Resort**, 846-5300, (800) 846-5300, **Log Cabin Resort & RV Park**, 755-2205, (800) 544-2205, **McFarland's Floatel**, 828-3335. Information available from air charter services and **Ketchikan Visitors Bureau**, 225-6166.

## Campgrounds
(7 day limit)

**Signal Creek**—5.2 miles from the ferry, Mile .7 on Ward Lake Road, on the shore of Ward Lake. 24 units. Firewood, toilets, water, tables. $8. Open May 1–mid-September.

**3 C's Campground**—5.4 miles from ferry, Mile 1 on Ward Lake Road. Water, firewood, grates, tables, toilets. 4 units. $8. Open April 1 through September.

**Last Chance Campground**—7.2 miles from ferry, on Ward Lake Road. Firewood, water, tables, grates, toilets. 19 units. $10. Open June 1 through mid-September. The U. S. Forest Service campgrounds have no hookups.

**Settlers Cove**—16 miles from ferry, Mile 18.2 North Tongass Highway. State campground. Adjacent parking, with overnight parking allowed. Picnic area, beach, fishing, swimming, firewood, tables, grates, toilets, water. No hookups. Super view. Good berry picking in August. 12 units, $8.

**Clover Pass**—private campground, RV hookups, laundry, dump station, 12 miles from ferry, $20/night for 2 people, add'l $2. P.O. Box 7322, Ketchikan, AK 99901. 247-2234 and (800) 410-2324.

## Facilities

LAUNDROMATS: **The "Mat,"** 989 Stedman, 225-0628. **Highliner Laundromat**, 2703 Tongass, 225-5308.

SWIMMING POOL: Ketchikan High School. Scheduled open hours. Sauna. 225-2010.

HOSPITAL: **Ketchikan General** 3100 Tongass, 225-5171.

DIESEL: **Gas At Last** 655 Stedman. **Petro Marine** S. Tongass Hwy.

PROPANE: **Petro Marine** S. Tongass Hwy. **Amerigas**, N. Tongass Hwy.

DUMP STATION: **Public Works Warehouse,** 3291 Tongass Ave., 2 blocks north of ferry terminal. 24 hours/day, 7 days/week, all year. Free.

ICE: All supermarkets.

PETS: Vet **Dr. Vern R. Starks**, mile 4, North Tongass. Mail: Rt. 1, Box 863, Ketchikan, AK 99901. 225-6051. Pet boarding and dog grooming: **Gail Oaksmith** 225-6393, and **Debbie Turner**, 225-6786. Boarding: **Claudia Brooks** (at vet clinic).

FISHING GEAR REPAIR: **Butch's Rod & Reel Repair,** 225-5155, 225-4656.

FISHING LICENSES: Required even for salt water fishing, are available at **The Outfitter,** 3232 Tongass Ave., at **Plaza Sports** in the Plaza Port West Mall, and at **Tongass Trading Company** on the downtown dock. Nonresident licenses, 1-day $10, 3-day $15, 14-day $30, and year $50.

## Boat Rentals

**Clover Pass Resort**—Rentals, supplies, launching. Resort and campground. P.O. Box 7322, Ketchikan, AK 99901. 247-2234. **Knudson Cove Marina**—Rentals, supplies, launching. Full service marina. 407 Knudson Cove Road, Ketchikan, AK 99901. 247-8500. **Mountain Point Charter and Boat Rental**—Rental skiffs and boats, gear. 5660 S. Tongass, Ketchikan, AK 99901. 225-1793 or (800) 634-6878, fax 225-7994.

KAYAK RENTALS—**Alaska Cruises,** 225-6044. **Southeast Exposure,** 225-8829.

## Charters

**Alaska Cruises,** P.O. Box 7814, Ketchikan, AK 99901. 225-6044. Sightseeing, canoe and kayak transportation trips to Misty Fiords. Licensed for 92 people. Cruise/fly $198. Cruise both ways, $145.

**Ketchikan Charter Boats, Inc.,** P.O. Box 9076, Ketchikan, AK 99901. 225-7291. Fleet of independent, licensed skippers and boats.

**Ketchikan Sportfishing,** P.O. Box 7896, Ketchikan, AK 99901. 225-3293, 225-9505. Day & overnight charters. Books for 40 boats, 22 to 54 feet.

**Ketchikan Visitors Bureau,** 225-6166, and (800) 770-2200, in office on the downtown dock, has a current list of individual charter boats with local owner/guides.

## Happenings

**Ketchikan Frontier Revue,** rollicking musical revue of Ketchikan's wilder early days, 45 minutes, at the Westmark Cape Fox Lodge, 7:30 p.m. Fridays, mid-May to mid-September $15.

**Fish Pirate's Daughter,** classic melodrama of early Ketchikan life, performed at 7 p.m. and 8:45 p.m. Fridays, July 9–30, 1999. Main Street Theatre at Main & Dock. $10. 225-4792

**Ketchikan King Salmon Derby,** Memorial Day weekend and following weekends. Prizes and fish are big. Chamber of Commerce, P.O. Box 5957, Ketchikan, AK 99901. 225-3184.

**Killer Whale Halibut Derby,** mid-May through Labor Day.

**4th of July** celebration is Ketchikan's big holiday, with parade at 11 a.m. followed by a logging show with contests at the ballpark. Fireworks over the channel at night and many other events.

**Blueberry Arts Festival**, second weekend in August, August 7, 1999, with crafts show, art exhibits, blueberry pies, scones, tarts, and other creations, pie eating contest, and games in basement and lower floor of state office building. Fun run, bed race, dance. 225-2211.

**Great Alaskan Sportfishing Championship**. September. 225-0309.

**Christmas Festival of Lights**, Friday after Thanksgiving. Community lights up, Santa arrives by helicopter. 225-3184.

**Winter Arts Festival**, November, Saturday after Thanksgiving. 225-2211.

**Festival of the North**, February, month-long. Mid-winter celebration with variety of performing & visual arts events including drama, ballet, literary readings, piano & jazz programs, and art walk. 225-2211.

### Ferry Tales

A traveler standing in the *Malaspina* solarium looked ahead and announced to his girl "There's another glacier coming up." Without rising, she asked, "Is it just your basic glacier?"

Two Michigan women, headed south on the ferry, talked about the Alaska Highway they had driven up—the usual about the holes, gravel, and transport trucks. "And those miles of too-close-together trees. Why, we have better trees than that in our backyard!"

A bearded sourdough in wool shirt and black felt hat was riding the ferry back to his home on the Haines Highway. "I sit up on my hill looking down on that bend in the road and I can't see what all those folks are in such a hurry for. When I get out on the road with my horse and wagon, we only go 4 miles an hour, but you wouldn't believe all the things we see. Wheels, hubcaps,—and you know those wire screens they put over their lights to keep the rocks off? Folks out my way all made rabbit hutches out of 'em."

Ketchikan's Ferry Terminal is a busy place. It serves not just the town but the resorts, camps and settlements of the area.

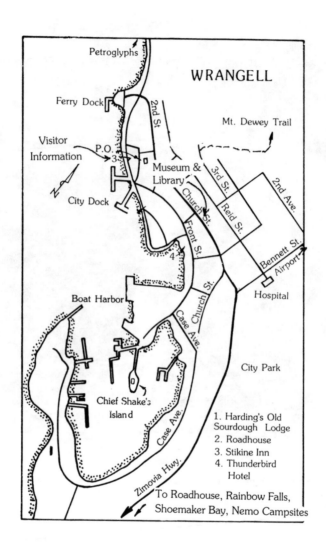

WRANGELL

Petroglyphs

Ferry Dock

Mt. Dewey Trail

Visitor Information

P.O.

Museum & Library

City Dock

1. Harding's Old Sourdough Lodge
2. Roadhouse
3. Stikine Inn
4. Thunderbird Hotel

Boat Harbor

Chief Shake's Island

City Park

Hospital

Bennett St.
Airport

Zimovia Hwy.

To Roadhouse, Rainbow Falls, Shoemaker Bay, Nemo Campsites

Bird petroglyph photographed after being wet with sea water. Crop out the dry rock and you have a good photo souvenir without wearing the prehistoric carving by rubbing.

# WRANGELL

(Area code 907, Zip code 99929)

AT THE MOUTH of the Stikine River, Wrangell (pop. 2,543) is the only town in southeastern Alaska to have flown three flags. The Russians built Fort St. Dionysius here in 1834 to guard the mouth of the Stikine against the Hudson's Bay Company trappers hunting sea otters. Later the British leased most of the area, calling their post Fort Stikine. Under the American flag, Wrangell, named for Russian Baron Von Wrangell, became the jump-off point for gold miners headed up the Stikine to the Klondike and Cassiar Mountains. Today Wrangell depends on fishing, processing of shrimp, fish, and crab, wood products, and tourism.

Its attractions include excellent fishing, totem parks, a good museum, petroglyphs, and a variety of minerals, including the garnets sold by local children at the ferry and cruise ship docks.

## To See and Do

Visit Chief Shakes Island, one mile (a brisk 15 minute walk each way from ferry), in the boat harbor. You will find a good collection of totems and a ceremonial house. Normally locked, it is open in summer when tour ships are in, or on request in IRA Council office. 874-3747. Donations.

Tour the museum, four blocks up 2nd St. (the main street leading away from the ferry dock) next to the high school. Artifacts from Wrangell's early days, Tlingit art and tools, fishing, and mounted game specimens. Summer hour, Mon.–Fri. 10–5, Sat., Sun. 1–4. Open for cruise ships. Winter hours: Mon.–Fri. 10–12 and 1–4. Closed Tuesdays. Open Sat. 1–4 or by appointment. Wrangell Museum, Box 1050, Wrangell, AK 99929. 874-3770. Admission $2, children under 16 free.

See the Wrangell Art Gallery adjacent, open same times as museum.

Take the Wrangell walking tour of sights, totems, etc. Map available at hotels and information centers.

See the new Totem Park on Front St. across from City Market. The totems were recently carved in Wrangell.

See petroglyphs carved by prehistoric natives. The nearest is on the library lawn. At least 20 more are carved in black argillite rock on the point about 1/2 mile north of the dock at Petroglyph Beach. From a sign on the road, walk down a boarded path to the beach. A few yards to your right you will see scattered black rocks with designs and faces carved on them. You are encouraged to take home a memory by taking photos.

Photo Hints: If you pour water (sea water is OK) over the carving and wait a minute, the carving shows up well for photos. Side lighting is very important. Maximum shadows early in the morning or late evening bring out the design. You can make night shots with artificial side lighting.

These are prehistoric artifacts—please treat them with respect. Some may be 2,000 years old. Never chalk, paint, or in any way alter the art. Many people have made rubbings with rice paper and crayons, so many that the carvings are being worn away. Unless you are something of an artist, you'll get much better results with photos and save the petroglyphs too.

Hike the Rainbow Falls trail. The maintained trail begins at Mile 4.7 Zimovia Highway.

Fish in the harbor, up the Stikine River, or in surrounding waters with guide or rented boat. Hunt in season for moose, bear, deer, mountain goats. Licenses and info at **Angerman's**, **Ottesen's True Value**, **Sentry Hardware & Marine**.

Hike up Mt. Dewey for great view over harbor, 1 mile trail, starts at 3rd Street. Trail is well marked and maintained.

Charter a boat up the Stikine River for animal and bird watching. This is a major migratory flyway in spring and fall where birds stop to rest

Young entrepreneurs peddle garnets to travelers at the ferry dock in Wrangell.

and feed.

Charter a plane to fly over the Stikine River to LeConte Glacier.

Watch black bears catch salmon at Anan Creek 30 miles south of Wrangell. Get there by boat or floatplane. Viewing platform. Day trip or reserve USFS cabin a mile away. July and August are peak months.

Play golf on Muskeg Meadows, the rustic 9-hole course and driving range recently built near the airport by Wrangell Golf Association. No green fee, equipment rentals available at Angerman's. Lloyd Hartshorn, 874-3989.

Meet local children (the Garnet Ledge mine was given to the Boy Scouts allowing Wrangell children to mine garnets) at the cruise ship and ferry docks and see or buy the garnets they have gathered. Their salesmanship is often hilarious.

Buy local garnets at Wrangell Museum or from children at the ferry terminal parking lot when the ferry is in during summer. Permits to collect garnets are available for a nominal fee at the museum. Garnet Ledge is 7.5 miles from Wrangell by boat.

Note the small flattened pieces of dark-grey slate near the ferry terminal building. These are similar to the argillite used in Haida carvings and can be carved. Experienced carvers easily make bas-relief scenes and figures even with a screwdriver.

The Wrangell ferry stop is usually only 1/2 hour southbound, 1 hour northbound, but it can be longer depending on the tide in Wrangell Narrows. The Zimovia Highway (called 2nd St. there) starts at the ferry dock.

INFORMATION AVAILABLE at the museum, 2nd St., **Wrangell Chamber of Commerce Visitor Center**, Box 49, Wrangell, AK 99929. 874-3901, 800-FOR-WRGL. Office is on the corner of the Stikine Inn Bldg. **U.S. Forest Service**, Box 51, Wrangell, AK 99929. 874-2323, fax 874-7595. Office at 525 Bennett Street has info on USFS cabins, trails, Anan Creek Wildlife Observatory, Wrangell Island road maps. Recreation cabins can be rented using toll-free (877) 444-6777 or web www.reserveusa.com

### Transportation

FERRY: Runs daily in summer, fewer sailings in winter. Recorded message on schedule, 874-3711. Information on office hours, 874-2021. Reservations 800-642-0066.

AIR: **Alaska Airlines** daily, year-round. 800-426-0333.

AIR CHARTER SERVICES: **Sunrise Aviation**, 874-2319, (800) 874-2311. **Taquan Air Service**, 874-8800, (800) 770-8800. **Temsco Helicopters**, 874-2010.

AVIATION FUEL: **Delta Western**, 874-2388, has 100 octane and jet fuel at their float in the harbor and in 2 tankers parked with **Sunrise Aviation** at the airport. Regular service Mon.–Fri. 8–5. $20 service charge after hours (24 hours service).

BUS: There is no scheduled bus service.

BUS TOURS: Bus tours are available from **Allweather Tours**, the owners of **The Roadhouse**, 874-2336. They also run shorter narrated tours when ships wait for tides. Salmon bakes on request. **Rain Walker Expeditions**, 874-2549, town bus tours and naturalist-guided walks.

BOAT CHARTERS (some are also licensed guides, may rent kayaks & canoes): **Alaska Peak & Seas**, 874-2454. **Alaska Tugboat Tours**, 874-3101, 888-488-4386. **Alaska Vista**, 874-2429, 874-3006. **Alaska Waters, Inc.**, 874-2378, (800) 347-4462. **Allweather Industries**, 874-2335. **Aqua Sports Enterprises**, 874-3061. **Belinda V Charters**, 874-2870. **Boat House**, 874-3813, 874-2554. **Breakaway Adventures**, 874-2488. **Coastal Island Charters**, 874-2014. **Marlin's Fly Fishing & Tackle**, 874-2590. **Natchik Charters**, 874-

2747. **Shamanz Charters**, 874-2249. **Silver Fox Charters**, 874-3054. **Silver Wind Charters**, 874-3168. **Slipper Skipper Charters**, 874-3958. **Stickeen Wilderness Adventures**, 874-2085, 874-3455, (800) 874-2085. **Tenacious Charters**, 874-3723. **Treasure Island Charters**, 874-3624. Timber Wolf Charters, 874-2893. Note: Anan Creek is so far that even a jet boat takes over an hour one-way. A slower boat could be a long ride in the rain.

MARINE/RIVER TRANSPORTERS—can transport and drop off people who want to fish, hunt, stay on outlying islands or up the Stikine River. Some can haul freight—**Buness Diving**, 874-3122, **Aqua Sports**, 874-3061, 874-3811, **Emde Charter Service**, (Wed, Thurs, Fri only) 874-3501, **Ellis Marine**, 874-3178, **Kurtti Marine**, 874-3849.

TAXI: **Star Cab**, 874-3622, 874-3511. **Porky's**, 874-3603.

CAR RENTAL: **Practical Rent-a-Car**, at the airport. 874-3975. Late model cars in excellent condition.

BAGGAGE STORAGE at hotels, for patrons, on day of departure.

CUSTOMS: Wrangell has customs service, with office in trailer at Wrangell Airport. 874-3415 and 874-2762.

## Hotels
(7% tax additional plus $3 per room)

**Hardings Old Sourdough Lodge**—1 mile, Shustak Point south side of harbor. Box 1062, Wrangell, AK 99929. 874-3613, fax 874-3455. (800) 874-3613. Courtesy transportation to/from ferry or airport. 18 rooms, coin-op laundry, TV, sauna/jacuzzi/steam bath. Handicapped-accessible suite. Fishing, hunting, wildlife viewing trips, including Anan Creek, with package rates. Packs fish for guests. Bed and breakfast, continental breakfast, Single $75, Double $95. B&B with full logger's breakfast, Single $85, Double $105. Deluxe suite for up to 6 people, with jacuzzi. Open all year. web: www.akgetaway.com

**The Roadhouse**—4 miles from ferry, Zimovia Highway, across from the boat harbor at Shoemaker Bay, Box 1199, Wrangell, AK 99929. 874-2335. Fax 874-3104. 10 rooms with pvt. bath, courtesy car, restaurant, lounge, salmon bakes, sightseeing tours (Allweather Tours), raft trips, fishing, and hunting charters. Pets allowed. Open all year. Single $65, Double $72. Caters to river rafters on Stikine.

**Stikine Inn**—1 block on Front St., Box 990, Wrangell, AK 99929. 874-3388, fax 874-3923. Toll free number 1-888-874-3388. 34 rooms with telephone, restaurant, gift/art gallery. Open all year. Single $70, Double $75. Twin, $85. Suites with microwave & refrigerator $100. Children under 12 free. E-mail: inn@stikine.comt Web: www.stikine.com

**Thunderbird Hotel**—6 blocks, 223 Front St., Box 110, Wrangell, AK

99929. 874-3322. Courtesy coffee, laundromat, TV. Restaurant next door. Single/double $55, Twin $65.

**Grand View Bed & Breakfast**—2 Mile Zimovia Hwy. 874-3225. 4 rooms with private bath and entrance. $75–105. e-mail: bakerj@seapack.net

**Harbor House**—8 blocks, 645 Shakes St., Box 2027, Wrangell, AK 99929. Phone/fax 874-3084. Overlooks boat harbor and Chief Shakes Island.3 rooms with shared bath and 2 suites with pvt. bath, full kitchen, balcony, sun room, for up to 9. Rooms, $65 double, suites $110 for 2. Breakfast optional, $5.

**Rooney's Roost**—26 McKinnon St., Box 552, Wrangell, AK 99929. 874-2026. Rooms with private bath, $55. Non-smoking, no drugs or alcohol.

The Visitors Bureau has a list that includes any other B&Bs opening in Wrangell.

**Wrangell Hostel**—4 blocks, 220 Church St., Box 439 Wrangell, AK 99929. 874-3534. First Presbyterian Church. Has showers, sleeping mats, kitchen facilities. Bring sleeping bag or blankets, food. Open June through August, 5 p.m.–8 a.m. $10/night. Closes labor Day.

## Campgrounds

**City Park**—Tent camping only. 24 hour limit, free. Mile 1.7 Zimovia Highway. Restrooms, flush toilets, sinks. Free.

**Nemo Point campsites**—entry kiosk off Forest Hwy. 16, 14 miles south of Wrangell, high above shore. 6 sites, parking, tables, fire grills, wood. Free, no reservations.

**Shoemaker Bay**—29 RV campsites, $8/night. Picnic tables, firepits, water available, but no hookups. Can be reserved in advance, City Hall, 874-2381, Mon.–Fri., 9–5. Tent sites free. Mile 4.5 Zimovia Highway. Near new boat harbor. Tennis court, dump station, boat launching ramp.

## Facilities

ICE—**Benjamin's** and **City Market**.

LAUNDROMAT—**Thunderbird Hotel**—5 blocks from ferry, on Front St. 12 washers, dryers. **Panhandle Trailer Court**, Zimovia Highway. 10 washers, 5 large dryers.

DUMP STATION—Near Front St. and Case Ave., next to Brig Bar. Note orange door on ground. Water available. Shoemaker Bay.

HOSPITAL—**Wrangell General**, Bennett St. near Zimovia Hwy. 874-3356.

## Boats

**Harding Boat Rentals**, 16' glass boat, 140 Mercury, 4 hp kicker, $250/day. Also a 16' Zodiak, 15 hp, $50/day. 874-3613 and (800) 874-3613.

The ferry dock at Wrangell in the rising morning mist.

Charters can be arranged to Garnet Ledge, Stikine River, Anan Creek, and for fishing. See list under boat tours and check latest list at **Wrangell Museum**, 874-3770 or at the **Wrangell Visitors Information Center** on the corner of the Stikine Inn Bldg., 874-3901.

Transient moorage available at boat harbors downtown and at Shoemaker Bay, about 4 miles south of town. Fuel, **Union** and **Chevron**, at waterfront in downtown harbor.

### Happenings

**Tent City Winter Festival**—celebrating gold rush in 1890s. First weekend in February. Fun, food, games.

**Garnet Festival**—third week of April, spring arrival, family fun, arts festival, eagle and bird activities, golf tournament.

**Salmon Derby**—Last two weeks of May and first two weeks of June. Wrangell Chamber of Commerce, (800) 367-9745.

**Fourth of July festival**—Logging contests, Queen contest, drawing for big prizes, food and games, boats, parade at 11 a.m., evening fireworks. Wrangell puts on some of the finest fireworks I've seen.

**Christmas Tree Lighting/Midnight Madness**, first Friday, December.

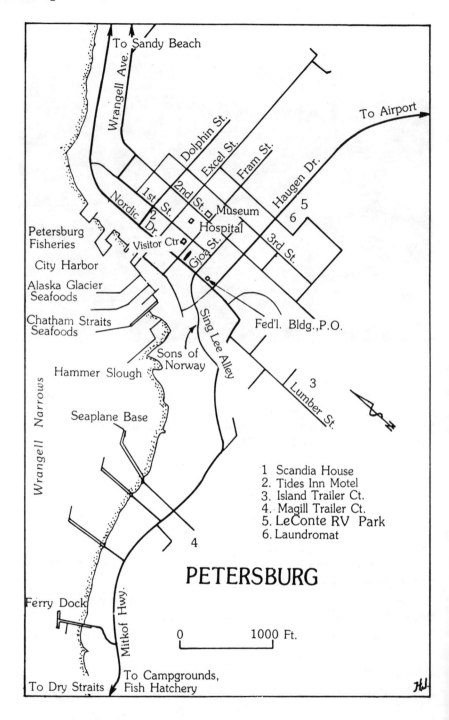

To Sandy Beach

To Airport

Wrangell Ave.

Dolphin St.

Excel St.

Fram St.

Haugen Dr.

Nordic Dr.

1st St.

2nd St.

Museum

Hospital

5

6

Petersburg Fisheries

Visitor Ctr

Gjoa St.

3rd St.

City Harbor

Alaska Glacier Seafoods

Chatham Straits Seafoods

Fed'l. Bldg.,P.O.

Hammer Slough

Sons of Norway

Sing Lee Alley

Wrangell Narrows

Seaplane Base

3

Lumber St.

1  Scandia House
2. Tides Inn Motel
3. Island Trailer Ct.
4. Magill Trailer Ct.
5. LeConte RV Park
6. Laundromat

4

**PETERSBURG**

Ferry Dock

Mitkof Hwy.

0          1000 Ft.

To Dry Straits

To Campgrounds, Fish Hatchery

View north along Wrangell Narrows and Petersburg's waterfront to glaciers and Canadian boundary peaks.

# PETERSBURG
(Area Code 907, Zip Code 99833)

Petersburg (pop. 3,350) was named for its founder, Peter Buschmann who, with his wife and eight children, moved here in 1897. The similarity of the geography to his native Norway, the mountain peaks, the fiords, availability of good timber for building, abundant ice from nearby LeConte Glacier, a good natural harbor, and its position in the center of the world's richest fishing grounds made this an ideal site for his new home. Today it is the main fish processing port in Southeast Alaska, with four canneries, a cold storage plant, and a fish meal plant that reduces scrap. In season they handle five kinds of salmon, crab, shrimp, halibut, herring and black cod and various exotics like sea cucumbers.

Many people in Petersburg are of Norwegian descent, and they are proud of their ancestry. The Norwegian character is evident in the town's houses, gardens, and boats. On the third weekend of May, Petersburg celebrates a "Little Norway" festival, with Viking boats and Norwegian dancing, lots of terrific food, costumes, street booths, games, and competitions.

## To See and Do

Visit Clausen Memorial Museum, 1 mile, 203 Fram Street at 2nd. Open daily 9:30–4:30 in summer through September. Winter hours are Wed, and

Sat, 12:30–4:30 and by appointment. It has a section on fish and fishing (including the world's largest king salmon, 126.5 pounds), the Cape Decision Lighthouse lens, Norwegian costumes, and other historical items.

Walk self-guided tours along waterfront and Hammer Slough in town. Great photography possible. Take a 5 mile loop walk via Sandy Beach. A city map is available at the **Visitor Information Center** at First and Fram Streets.

Ask about interpretive programs at the **Visitor Information Center** at First & Fram, or just chat with the staff and pick up a few brochures. The Visitor Information Center is a partnership between the U.S. Forest Service and the Chamber of Commerce. 772-4636.

Walk on floats in fishing boat harbor, children with an adult and wearing a lifejacket. Children can borrow lifejackets from the Harbormaste.

Tour the shrimp cannery and fish hatchery with the **Tongass Traveler**. **See Alaska** offers tours of Tonka Seafoods, a small specialty cannery. **Tides Motel** and **Visitor Information Center** have info. Special tours on request.

Watch salmon at Falls Creek Fish Ladder, 10 miles, at Mile 10.8 Mitkof Highway. Allows spawning salmon to pass falls into good spawning waters above.

Tour Crystal Lake Fish Hatchery, 16.5 miles, Mile 17.5 Mitkof Highway. This modern hatchery raises both salmon and trout. Employees will explain the operation. Fish are sent from here to much of Southeast Alaska. Open 8 a.m.–4 p.m., weekdays.

Take a self-guided tour of Mitkof Island. A map is available at the Forest Service office in Federal Building, Main Street and Haugen Drive or at the Visitor Information Center, $4. You can see 25 points of interest, inlcuding different stages of regrowth. Also a good view of Wrangell Narrows. Berry picking in season.

Hike out to Hill, Crane, and Sand Lakes on Three Lakes Trail, a boardwalk, built by the Youth Conservation Corps. There's good berry picking in several areas, and the lakes have a skiff for trout fishing.

Fish in Scow Bay, Blind Slough, Frederick Sound, and streams. If you fish in the Narrows, beware of tidal currents and the suction and force of ship wakes. Do not get in the way of ships, tugs, and ferries.

Watch wildlife. In the Narrows, along the Mitkof Highway, and on the logging roads, you may see bald eagles (this is a nesting area), otters, porpoises, bear, deer, and porcupines. Eagles often fish beside the ferry dock and perch in trees near the waterfront in town. Cormorants, loons, terns, and several species of gulls fish in the harbor. Watch sea lions in boat harbor. North of town, on the shore of Frederick Sound, you may see humpback whales in summer as well as icebergs from LeConte Glacier. The road around the north end of the island has recently been extended and will eventually connect with the Mitkof Highway to encircle the island.

Drive out the Mitkof Highway to enjoy scenery, picnic on rocky beaches, launch a canoe or kayak in quiet water, and fish from shore. It's a refreshing experience and a fine activity for children.

Note that some of the best birdwatching on the ferry route is from the ferry decks while it's docked here. You can watch gulls, ducks of many kinds, loons, and great blue herons if you step out on deck. Southbound, watch for cormorants perched on the channel markers just after the ship leaves the dock.

Enjoy Blind Slough Recreation Area. 16.5 miles from ferry, Mile 17.5 Mitkof Highway. Swimming, picnic area, daytime use only.

From the wildlife viewing blind at Blind Slough, watch wintering swans, migrating waterfowl in spring and fall, a variety of birds and an occasional bear in summer.

Hike through the old growth forest of the Ohmer Creek Nature Trail, Mile 21, Mitkof Highway.

Hike to Raven's Roost on mountain behind town, about 4 miles each way. Camping possible on upper part. Overnight shelter available by reservation, $25, from U.S. Forest Service in Federal Building or from the Visitor Information Center. Trail starts from road to airport.

See the LeConte Glacier by charter plane, helicopter, boat, or kayak.

Mountaineering for experienced, well-equipped climbing teams. Petersburg is the jump-off point for Devil's Thumb and other major peaks on the mainland.

INFORMATION AVAILABLE at the **Visitor Information Center**, corner of First and Fram Streets, Box 649, Petersburg, AK 99833. 772-3646 phone/fax. E-mail: pcoc@alaska.net **Chamber of Commerce** and **U.S. Forest Service** information desk, 772-3871, are in same building. The **Harbormaster** is on Harbor Way. 772-4688.

## Transportation

FERRY: Runs daily in summer, fewer sailings in winter. Dock is near the south edge of town, .9 miles from the Federal Building.

BUS: None

TAXI: **City Cab**, 772-3003.

CAR RENTAL: **Avis Car Rental**, Box 1048, Petersburg, AK 99833 at Tides

Inn, 772-44288. **All Star Rental**, 772-4281, Scandia House. Some travelers rent a car to get to out of town campgrounds.

BICYCLE RENTAL: **Northern Bikes—Tours & Rentals**, Box 461, Petersburg 99833. 772-3777. Mountain bike rentals and tours.

TOURS: Boat and floatplane tours to LeConte Glacier (sail among icebergs in the fiord). Get the latest list at the **Visitor Information Center**, 772-4636. Reservations can be made through the tour or charter operators or through **Viking Travel**, 772-3818.

Mitkof Island tours: **See Alaska Land and Water Charters**, 772-4656. Guided town and island tours according to your tastes. **Tongass Traveller**, 772-4837. Guided island tours feature shrimp cannery (with samples) and fish hatchery.

**Viking Travel Agency**, Box 787, Petersburg, AK 99833. 772-3818, (800) 327-2571, has a list of boats for tours, including fishing en route to the glacier. Day to day availability varies with seasonal fishing openings. Bus tours of Petersburg and fish ladder and fish hatchery arranged.

AIR: **Alaska Airlines** has daily jet service, year-round. (800) 426-0333.

AIR CHARTERS: Charter service and flight to Kake: **Temsco Helicopter**, Box 829, Petersburg, AK 99833. 772-4780. **Pacific Wing Charters**, Box 1560, Petersburg, AK 99833. 772-4258. **Nordic Air**, Box 1292, Petersburg, AK 99833. 772-3535. **Kupreanof Flying Service**, Box 867, Petersburg, AK 99833. 772-3396. **Taquan Air Service**, 772-8800.

BAGGAGE STORAGE by arrangement with hotels.

## Hotels
(10% city sales tax + bed tax)

**Green Rocks Lodge**—12 miles from ferry, 10.5 Mi. Mitkof Hwy. Box 110, Petersburg, AK 99833. 772-7625 and 772-4343. Cabins and dock very near Green Rocks, the tightest turn in Wrangell Narrows. Fishing package for up to 4 people includes cabin, meals, skiff and fuel, fishing gear, raingear, airport/ferry transfers, 4 days, $550/person, 6 days, $875/person. Guided fishing available.

**Scandia House** —1 mile from ferry, downtown, Nordic Drive between Fram and Gjoa. Box 689, Petersburg, AK 99833. 772-4281 and (800) 665-8433. Scandinavian decor. 33 rooms with private bath, with/without view, some with kitchenettes. Courtesy van from airport and ferry. Complimentary muffins, juice, and coffee. Single $80–165, Double $90–175. Add'l $10. Boat and car rentals.

**Tides Inn Motel**—1.3 miles from ferry, 1st St. corner of Dolphin St., Box 1048, Petersburg, AK 99833. 772-4288, fax 772-4286. 46 rooms, queen-size beds, conference room, courtesy refreshments, phone, color TV with movie channel. Wheelchair-accessible. Single $70, Double $85. Kitchenette, no extra charge. Can issue fishing and hunting licenses 24 hours/day. Avis cars.

**Bed & Breakfasts**—**Visitor Information Center**, 772-4636, has lists, including lodges and bed & breakfasts outside of Petersburg along Wrangell Narrows. **Alaska Bed & Breakfast Association**, 586-2959, has listings in Petersburg.

**Broom Hus Bed & Breakfast**, 772-3459. **Harbor Day B&B**, 772-3971. **Mitkof Island B&B**, 772-3800. **Mountain Point B&B**, 772-4669. **Nordic House B&B**, 772-3673. **Sea Breeze B&B**, 772-3279. **Water's Edge B&B**, (800) TO-THE-SEA, 772-3736. Several have kitchenettes, some on the waterfront.

## Campgrounds

**Ohmer Creek Campground**—21 miles from ferry, Mile 22 Mitkof Highway. Drinking water provided. 10 sites for tents or RVs up to 35' length. Barrier-free trail. Small fee. 14 day maximum.

**Green's Camp**—26 miles from ferry, Mile 26.8 Mitkof Hwy. Unimproved site on state land. Road to it is washed out 1/4 mile away; you can walk in. Boat launching at Banana Pt. Bring water. Free.

**Tent City**—3 miles from ferry, out Haugen Dr. past airport. 50 tent pads. Purpose is housing cannery workers. Not family-oriented. Restrooms, sinks, firepits, wood, picnic tables. No vehicles permitted. Daily $5, monthly $125. Pay at Parks & Recreation, 12 S. Nordic St., 772-3392, or manager on-site.

**Twin Creeks**—6 miles from ferry, 7.5 Mi. Mitkof Hwy. P.O. Box 90-B, Petersburg, AK 99833. 772-3244. 20 spaces with full and partial hookups, bathhouse, laundromat, dump station, convenience store, fish cleaning station. $18/night.

**LeConte RV Park**—1.2 miles from ferry, 4th & Haugen Streets, P.O. Box 1548, Petersburg, AK 99833. 772-4680. Full hookups for 13 vehicles to 35', 5 elec. only sites. Laundromat with showers, restrooms. $16.50/day.

**Northern Lights RV**—1.5 miles from ferry, 2.5 Mi. Mitkof Hwy. P.O. Box 1637, Petersburg, AK 99833. 772-3345. Full hookups. $19.06 with city tax.

## Boats

RENTALS: **Scandia House**, 772-4281. **Tongass Marine**, 772-3705.

CHARTERS: Check with the **Visitor Information Center** for charter boat listing—fishing, sightseeing, glacier tours, whalewatching, also Stikine River trips for hot springs, birdwatching, river fishing.

HARBOR: Moorage available for boats to 140'. See Harbormaster. Restrooms, grids to handle boats up to 200 tons, water and electricity, public showers, and hot water. **Harbormaster's Office**, Box 1047, Petersburg 99833. 772-4688. Channel 16 VHF and CB Channel 9.

**Petersburg Shipwrights**, boat pull out and grid. 772-3596.

## Facilities

LAUNDROMATS: **Glacier Laundry & Dry Cleaning**, 311 N. Nordic Drive, near the corner of Excel Street. 772-4400. **LeConte RV Park**, 4th & Haugen. 772-4680.

PROPANE: **Petersburg Bottled Gas,** Box 818, Petersburg, AK 99833. 772-4270.

DIESEL: **Union Oil** on Union Oil dock. 772-4219.

AVIATION FUEL: **Temsco Helicopters,** 772-3728.

DUMP STATION: **SE Island Fuel Station**, one block north of ferry terminal. 772-3740. **LeConte RV Park**, 4th & Haugen. 772-4680.

ICE: **The Trading Union, Inc.** general store. **Hammer & Wikan, Inc.**, general store. All liquor stores.

HOSPITAL: 13 beds with limited medical capabilities. Two doctors, six emergency medical technicians, city operated ambulance, two dentists, one chiropractor. 772-4291, or 772-9246.

SWIMMING POOL: **Roundtree Swimming Pool**, behind Petersburg Elementary School on 3rd Street. Charge for swim, lower for shower and locker only. Call for open times, 772-3392.

COMMUNITY GYM: 2 racquetball courts, wallyball nets (correct), weight room, open gym, showers, lockers. 772-4224.

VET: **Jane Egger**, Box 328, Petersburg, AK 99833. 772-3191.

FISH SMOKING, PROCESSING: these companies will smoke, process and ship your fish. Also have smoked fish for sale. **Coastal Cold Storage**, Box 307, Petersburg, AK 99833. 772-4177. **Tonka Seafoods, Inc.**, Box 1420, Petersburg, AK 99833. 772-3662, fax 772-3663. Have no-fat salmon sausage, tours of plant.

## Happenings

Petersburg celebrated its centennial in 1998, 100 years since it was offically incorporated as a city.

**Little Norway festival**, May 13–16, 1999, celebrating Norwegian Independence Day (May 17), Petersburg's *big* festival. You need a reservation for rooms or a sleeping bag, perhaps with tent.

**Annual Chamber of Commerce Salmon Derby**, Memorial Day weekend. Cash and prizes for largest salmon.

**Canned Salmon Classic,** June 1 through August 15. Contest to guess

The ferry passes Petersburg in the fog. It is settled by descendants of Norwegian pioneers.

the number of cans of salmon canned by Petersburg canneries during the season. First prize, $2500. Supports college scholarship fund. 772-3646.

**Fourth of July** enthusiastically celebrated by visitors and residents. 3 days of street booths, logging and fishing competitions, street games, races, fireworks display over the Narrows.

**Octoberfest**, Month of activities, art show. Most activities above are sponsored by the Petersburg Arts Council, 772-4573, 772-3334..

**Seafood Fest & Humpy 500 Go-cart Race**, third Saturday in October. Food, crafts, games, and live entertainment with fishy theme. Canned Salmon Classic winners announced.

**Octoberfest Artshare**, fourth Saturday in October. Arts and crafts fair, quilt show and auction. Sponsored by the Muskeg Maliers, 772-3576.

**Christmas Tree Lighting Ceremony**, first Friday in December. Lighting and music starting the Christmas season.

**Julebukking**, Christmas Eve. In Norwegian tradition, shoppers tour downtown where merchants offer food and drink in thanks for their business that year.

### Ferry Tale

Most Alaskans are used to the classic questions about what stamps and money we use, and how high above sea level we are. (The answer, looking over the side, "about 50 feet"). One traveler asked me "Do you get down to the United States very often?"

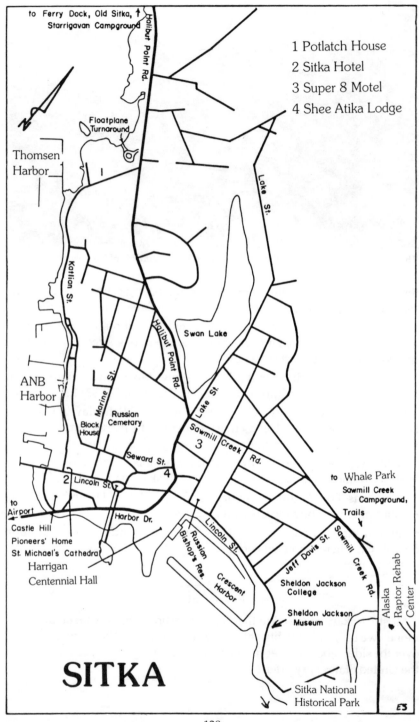

to Ferry Dock, Old Sitka,
Starrigavan Campground

Halibut Point Rd.

1 Potlatch House
2 Sitka Hotel
3 Super 8 Motel
4 Shee Atika Lodge

Floatplane
Turnaround

Thomsen
Harbor

Lake St.

Katlian St.

Swan Lake

ANB
Harbor

Marine St.

Halibut Point Rd.

Russian
Cemetery

Block
House

Lake St.

Sawmill Creek Rd.

3

Seward St.

4

to Whale Park
Sawmill Creek
Campground,
Trails

2 Lincoln St.

to
Airport

Harbor Dr.

Lincoln St.

Castle Hill
Pioneers' Home
St. Michael's Cathedral

Harrigan
Centennial Hall

Russian
Bishop's Res.

Crescent
Harbor

Jeff Davis St.

Sawmill Creek Rd.

Alaska Raptor Rehab Center

Sheldon Jackson
College

Sheldon Jackson
Museum

SITKA

Sitka National
Historical Park

E3

St. Michael's Cathedral, rebuilt after a fire with the original carved doors and Russian icons brought by sailing ship from Russia.

## SITKA

(Area Code 907, Zip Code 99835)

Sitka (pop 8,700) was the site of the first Russian settlement in Southeast Alaska, established by Baranof in 1799. Originally built just north of where the ferry terminal now stands, it was destroyed by Tlingit Indians. A new fort and town were built at the present townsite. For years Sitka was the European cultural center of the Pacific. It had the first shipyard and built the first steam-driven vessel in the Pacific. American, Spanish, and British ships came here to trade with the Russians for otter pelts. When the United States bought Alaska from the Russians in 1867, the changeover took place in Sitka. Her Russian heritage, her historic sites and buildings, the Sheldon Jackson Museum (with its excellent Indian collection), and the Sitka National Historical Park make a stopover here very rewarding. Main economic activities are fishing and fish processing, national interest, education, tourism, and health care.

### To See And Do

(Ferry dock is 7.1 miles north of town)

Tour Sitka National Historical Park about 7.4 miles from the ferry. See its program on Sitka's history and Tlingit culture. Visit workshops teaching Tlingit arts and watch artists weaving, carving and demonstrating other native arts. This is the site of the Tlingit fort and "Battle of Sitka." Walk forest and beach paths with totems. Picnic area. Park is open 5 a.m.–10 p.m. in summer. Visitor center is open 8 a.m.–5 p.m, daily in summer, M–F in winter.

See the state museum at Sheldon Jackson College, 7 miles from ferry. It has large collection of artifacts from all the Alaska native cultures. Summer hours: 8 a.m.–5 p.m., daily. Winter hours: 10 a.m.–4 p.m., Tues.–Sat. Admission, $3.

Visit the Harrigan Centennial Hall's wildlife exhibit and the Isabel Miller Museum of Sitka history. Summer hours, 8 a.m–6 p.m. daily. Winter hours, Tues.–Sat., 10 a.m–4 p.m.

Tour the Russian Bishop's House and Fort Site. Open 9 a.m.–1 p.m., 2 p.m. –5 p.m. daily, May– September. Open to tours by reservation in winter. 747-6281.

See the New Archangel Dancers in a program of Russian folk dances at Harrigan Centennial Hall, downtown. Sitka women in authentic costumes have danced their energetic and beautiful performances for many years. Check there for times of programs. Admission charge. Summer only.

Tour St. Michael's Cathedral, 7.1 miles from ferry, at center of town. This is a Russian Orthodox cathedral, replica of the original which burned in 1966. The icons, doors, and other items were saved from the original. Open 7:30 a.m.–5:30 p.m. cruise ship days, 1:30–5:30 p.m. non-cruise ship days. Winter hours Mon.–Sat. 1:30 p.m.–5:30 p.m. Check with Father Eugene, 747-8120. $1 donations accepted..

Sitka Lutheran Church is across from St. Michael's on the site of the Lutheran church, first on the west coast of North America. The first pastor of this church later founded the public school system in Finland. Artifacts from the 1840s include the organ, pulpit, and communion rail. Free.

Castle Hill, overlooking Sitka harbor, was an early Tlingit stronghold. Baranof later built his "Castle" and other buildings there after the Tlingits eliminated his first settlement at Old Sitka. On October 18, 1867, Russia transferred Alaska to the United States on Castle Hill, where the ceremony is reenacted annually on Alaska Day. Children, as well as adults, enjoy the view and several cannon placed on the hilltop. Recent excavation has located many artifacts.

Sitka Pioneers' Home is a state home for older Alaskans, built in 1934 on the former Russian parade ground. Visitors are welcome—residents have great stories. The gift shop sells crafts made by the residents. In front is a bronze statue of a pioneer, William "Skagway Bill" Fonda.

Walk or take a bus tour to Sitka's historical sites. Walking distances be-

Tourism is important to Sitka, and its entrepreneurs include this child selling sand dollar shells in front of the Russian Bishop's House.

tween these sites are short and take only a few minutes each. These include: Castle Hill, the Russian cemetery, the Lutheran-Finnish cemetery, Russian blockhouse, Russian cannons, Russian Bishop's Residence, the Tilson Building (log building from 1837), Pioneer's Home, Sitka Nat'l. Cemetery (veterans).

On Sitka Tours' bus tour you will see the Sitka National Historical Park, Sheldon Jackson Museum, Isabel Miller Museum, St. Michael's Cathedral, Old Sitka, Castle Hill, and the Russian Bishop's House. Some tours include admission to the New Archangel Dancers. Some tours go to the Raptor Rehabilitation Center. Stops vary with time of day.

If you fly in or out of Sitka by wheeled plane or airliners, you will visit Fort Ray, the name for all the World War II facilities including the airport on Japonski Island across the causeway from Sitka. The Coast Guard base provides search and rescue service for most of Southeast Alaska's waters. The causeway offers a good view of harbor boats and floatplanes.

Watch pink salmon and a few kings and cohos migrate up Starrigavin Creek along road .5 mile north of ferry terminal, late July through September. Eagles usually in trees. Good walk for the children or pets. Another good viewing spot is the Indian River in the Sitka National Historical Park.

Drive up Harbor Mt. Road (2-wheel drive OK in summer) to its end at the trailhead next to a World War II airplane spotting station. At an over-look just before the end of the road are picnic tables, restrooms, and spec-tacular views over the harbor and up Neva Strait.

Hike local trails, including Mt. Verstovia (past Russian charcoal pits, and through 130-year-old clearcut) and Harbor Mt. trail (for an easily acces-sible look at alpine tundra, and a good view of the Sitka area).

Other trails include the Gavan Hill Trail from town and the level In-dian River Trail at Sitka National Historical Park, and at Halibut Point. See the U.S. Forest Service booklet, *Sitka Trails*. Remember this is brown bear country!

Visit Old Sitka, .5 mile north of the ferry dock. This is the site of the first Russian settlement started in 1799, destroyed by the Tlingits in 1802. Interpretive panels, the Forest & Muskeg Trail (fully accessible), and a pub-lic boat launch.

Boat tour Sitka Sound. Special tours to watch sea otters. Charter a boat to visit bird refuge islands with rookeries of nesting seabirds.

Fly over Mt. Edgecumbe, Southeast Alaska's only dormant volcano. You can reach the top by trail from the beach on Kruzof Island if you go by boat or plane.

Fish from boat or shore. Inquire locally about hot spots.

Visit Southeast Alaska's first Raptor Rehabilitation Center in Sitka. Tak-ing in sick and injured eagles, hawks, and owls, staff treats and releases about 50% of the birds. Birds that can't be restored to survive in the wild are often sent to zoos or breeding centers, some in the Lower 48. The cen-ter offers your best chance to see and photograph eagles close-up. It's off Sawmill Creek Rd., on Indian Creek, about 1.5 miles from town. 747-8662. Guided tours including demonstration of treatment and feeding are given in the morning during summer when cruise ships are in. Open 8 a.m.–5 p.m. daily in summer for guided tours. Admission $10. Gift shop has great posters, photographs, T-shirts. Check for scheduled open houses in the winter.

INFORMATION AVAILABLE from the **Sitka Convention & Visitors Bu-reau**, Box 1226, Sitka, AK 99835. 747-5940, fax: 747-3739. Visitor informa-tion desk in Harrigan Centennial Hall, staffed by volunteers, and in the Visitors Bureau Office at 303 Lincoln. Open daily. Publishes a Vacation Planner annually. e-mail: scvb@sitka.org web: www.sitka.org. *Sitka Sen-tinel*, 112 Barracks St., Sitka, AK 99835, 747-3219, publishes an annual tour-ism guide to the Sitka area as well as the weekly paper.

The **U.S. Forest Service** office is in the Totem Square Building, one block from the center of town. **Sitka Ranger District**, 201 Katlian St., Ste. 109,

Sitka, AK 99835. 747-4220. They have information on USFS cabins which may be reserved in advance andcan be reached by plane or boat from Sitka. A booklet, *Sitka Trails*, is available with maps and information about the trails from town up nearby mountains, plus many useful brochures.

**Sitka National Historical Park**. Box 738, Sitka, AK 99835. 747-6281, also has information. **Alaska State Division of Parks**, 3803 Halibut Point Road, Box 142, Sitka, AK 99835. 747-6279. The National Park Service's web site is www.nps.gov You can search by park or themes to get Sitka info.

## Transportation

FERRY: **Alaska Marine Highway**. Four ships/week (both northbound and southbound) in summer; three in winter. Dock is 7.1 miles north of town.

BUS: **Sitka Tours**, 747-8443. Buses meet ferry for ride downtown. Leave very shortly after ship docks. $2.50 one-way.

TAXI: **Arrowhead Taxi**, 747-8888. **Sitka Cab**, 747-5001. Inquire about rates. Car rental may be cheaper if you need more than two rides.

CAR RENTALS: **A & A Auto Rental**, 747-8228. **Avis**, 966-2404. **All Star**, 966-2552 and (800) 722-6927. **Advantage Car Rental**, 747-7557.

TOURS: **Sitka Tours**, Box 1001, Sitka, AK 99835. 747-8443, fax 747-7510. Historical tour lasts 3 hours. Complete tour includes a visit to the Raptor Rehabilitation Center and the New Archangel Dancers. Morning and afternoon tours daily in summer with pick-ups at all hotels.

Ferry stopover tour is two hours, $10 adults, $5 child, when the ferry arrives at a reasonable hour and is in port long enough. Stops at Nat'l. Historical Park, Isabel Miller Museum, St. Michael's Cathedral, plus short shopping time.

**Sitka Tribal Enterprises**, 456 Katlian St., Sitka, AK 99835. 747-7290. Tour Sitka from the Alaska native perspective. Scenic drive, 1 hour, $10/person. Comprehensive 2.5 hour tour includes stops at Sitka National Historical Park and Sheldon Jackson Museum and a 30 min. Tlingit dance performance. Adult $28, Child $18. Native natural history walking tour, 1.45 hours, includes Sheldon Jackson Sage Building (marine display). Adult $18, Child $10.

**Sitka Walking Tours**, Jane Eidler, Box 1673, Sitka, AK 99835. 747-5354. Guided tour of Sitka, 1 1/2 hours. Adults $9, Children $4.

BOAT TOURS: **Allen Marine Tours**, Box 1049, Sitka, AK 99835, 747-8100. $49/adult, $30/child. Two-hour tour. Reservations advised. Call for information about other available tours.

Small boat nature tours, some with very knowledgeable guides and even hydrophones for listening to whales, offer your best photo opportunities.

They are quiet, can get close to shore, and don't have crowds blocking your view. **Alaska Adventures Unlimited**, 747-5576, (800) 770-5576. Fax 747-5910. Offers variety of fishing, wildlife tours, cabins on an island off Sitka. **Sitka's Secrets**, 747-5089, offers wildlife viewing and photography with biologist guides (birders note).

AIR: **Alaska Airlines**, daily service to Seattle, Anchorage, Juneau, Ketchikan, Petersburg. (800) 426-0333. Get reservations early in summer as some flights fill with passengers on cruise-fly package tours with cruise ships. Shuttle bus serves the airport to/from downtown hotels for airline flights.

AIR CHARTERS: **Taquan Air**, Box 371, Sitka, AK 99835. 747-8636. **Mountain Aviation**, at Sitka Airport. Box 2487, Sitka, AK 99835. 966-2288.

BAGGAGE STORAGE in hotels, for patrons only, on day of departure and in Harrigan Centennial Hall.

## Hotels
(rates plus 4% hotel tax and 5% sales tax)
Seniors with Medicare cards are exempt from tax.

**Cascade Inn**—4.5 miles from ferry. 2035 Halibut Point Rd., Sitka, AK 99835. 747-6804, fax 747-6572. 10 rooms facing Sitka Sound, one handicapped accessible. Non-smoking rooms. Phone, cable TV with VCR. Restaurant, laundry. Convenience store adjacent. No pets. Single/Double $100. Kitchenettes $125.

**Sitka Harborview Inn** (formerly Potlatch House)—5.5 miles from ferry. 713 Katlian St., Sitka, AK 99835. 747-8611, fax 747-5810. Reservations: (800) 354-6017. 35 units, some with kitchens. Lunch & dinner restaurant, lounge. Phones, cable TV. No pets. Courtesy van service. Laundry, freezer. Single $82, Double $90.

**Sitka Hotel**—7 miles from ferry. 118 Lincoln St., Sitka, AK 99835. 747-3288, fax 747-8499. 57 rooms, downtown. Victorian decor completely renovated. Phone, cable TV. Restaurant, lounge, free parking. Coin-op laundry. Some rooms handicapped accessible. Shared bath, Single $50, Double $55. Private bath, Single $65, Double $70. Child under 12 free. e-mail: sitkah@ptialask.net   web: www.sitkahotel.com

**Super 8 Motel**—7 miles from ferry. 404 Sawmill Creek Blvd., Sitka, AK 99835. 747-8804. (800) 800-8000. 35 rooms. Complimentary morning coffee. Jacuzzi, laundromat. Car/room package available. Pets with deposit. Honors Super 8 VIP cards. Single $100, Double $108.

**Westmark Shee Atika**—7 miles from ferry. 330 Seward St., Sitka, AK 99835. 747-6241, fax 747-5486. (800) 544-0970 in U.S. including Alaska and Hawaii.  www.westmarkhotels.com 101 rooms, dining room, bar. Wheelchair accessible. No pets. Town view, Single/Double $129. Harbor view, Single/Double $139.

**Youth Hostel**—United Methodist Church, Edgecumbe and Kimsham Streets. Mail: Box 2645, Sitka, AK 99835. 747-8661. Open June 1–August 31. Check in 6–10 p.m. Out by 8:00 a.m. $9 with AYH card, $12 without. Sleeping bags required. Kitchen available.

## Bed & Breakfasts

**Sitka Convention & Visitors Bureau**, Box 1226, Sitka, AK 99835, 747-5940, has current list, including some on nearby islands reached by boat as well as nearby fishing lodges. **Alaska Bed & Breakfast**, 586-2959, fax 463-6788, based in Juneau, has Sitka listings.

A sampling of the 20+ B & Bs in Sitka includes **Alaska Ocean View**, 747-8310, **Creeks Edge** 747-6484, **Helga's** 747-5497 (waterfront, new building, with kitchens or fridges), **Karras** 747-3978, **Mountain View** 747-8966. All of these have 3 or more rooms—most others have 1 or 2. These people are very helpful with information and arranging tours.

*Special Restaurants:* **The Channel Club**, Halibut Pt. Rd, 747-9916, may have the best salad bar in Alaska, with at least 20 kinds, cold and hot. Well known for steaks and seafood. Reservations essential. **Twin Dragon** on Katlian St. downtown, has good, reasonably-priced Chinese food.

## Campgrounds

**Starrigavan Campground**—.7 miles north of ferry dock. 30 spaces with trees near creek. Fills fast when ferry arrives. Picnic tables, firepits, toilets, water. Estuary Loop suited to RVs. Bayside Loop suited more for tenters. $8, 14 day limit. Open May 1 through mid-September. *Note:* access gates closed and locked 10 p.m.–7 a.m. daily during camping season. (USFS)

**Sawmill Creek**—13 miles from ferry, off Sawmill Creek Road, near the pulp mill. Take spur road 1.4 miles. 11 sites, few sites suitable for RVs. Picnic tables, firepits, toilets. No water or garbage services. Free. 14 day limit. (USFS)

**Sealing Cove**—8 miles from ferry on Japonski Island, next to Sealing Cove Boat Harbor. 26 RV sites, no reservations. Water and electrical hookups. Limit 15 nights. $16.80 plus tax per night. 747-3439. Open May 1–October 1. (City & Borough of Sitka)

**Sportsman's Campground**—1 block toward Sitka from ferry dock. 8 RV sites, water and electrical hookups. Indoor shooting range, skeet shooting. Reservations, 747-6033. $18 plus tax per night (Sitka Sportsman's Association).

## Boats

Information on fishing charters and charters to offshore bird rookeries and sea otter areas with skippers licensed by the Coast Guard is available at Harrigan Centennial Hall and from Sitka Tours. Boat fuel at three fuel docks in Sitka Channel near Thompson Harbor. Boats can be moored overnight at certain stalls on floats in Thompson Harbor. Contact the Harbormaster, VHF Channel 16 or call 747-3294.

KAYAK RENTALS: **Alaska Adventures**, Box 6244, Sitka, AK 99835. 747-8996. **Bidarka Boats**, Box 2158, Sitka, AK 99835. **Sea Trek Charters & Kayak Rentals,** 747-8295, (800) 747-8295. **Sitka Sound Ocean Adventures**, P.O. Box 1242, Sitka, AK 99835. 747-6375. Sitka Sound has miles of sheltered water and islands. Enjoy guided tours, or, if you're experienced in kayaks and cold water, rent kayaks and go exploring with friends (not alone).

## Facilities

LAUNDROMAT: **Duds & Suds**, 908 Halibut Point Rd. 747-5050. Showers. Open 8 a.m.–8 p.m. **Super 8 Laundromat**, 404 Sawmill Creek Rd.

PROPANE: **Service Transfer**, 321 Lincoln St. 747-3276. **Texaco Station**, 613 Katlian Ave. 747-8460.

DIESEL: **Sitka Fuels** on Katlian St. **White Pass Alaska**, 747-3414.

ICE at canneries on Katlian St. and at supermarkets.

DUMP STATIONS: **Wastewater Treatment Plant**, Japonski Island. Big grey building on airport side of Sealing Cove, 966-2256.

OUTBOARD MOTOR REPAIR: across from ferry terminal at **Southeast Marine.** Also repairs motorcyles.

HOSPITAL: **Sitka Community Hospital**, Halibut Pt. Rd. 747-3241.

PETS: Vet is **Dr. Burgess Bauder**. Office is behind the city garage on Halibut Point Rd., open 3 p.m.–6 p.m., Monday–Friday. 747-3056. **Dr. Hunt**, 747-PETS, 8–5 daily, located on Jarvis St. behind Post Office. Pet boarding. Make reservations.

## Happenings

**Sitka Summer Music Festival** (chamber music) in Harrigan Centennial Hall, with performances Tuesdays and Fridays, through the month of June. The world's finest musicians perform here. June 4–25, 1999.

**Salmon Derby**, Memorial Day weekend and the following weekend.

**Alaska Day Festival**, Oct. 14–19, celebrating the Russian transfer of Alaska to the United States. Transfer is reenacted with period costumes, muskets and flags. Week-long celebration.

**Sitka Whale Fest**—annual festival celebrating Sitka's abundance of marine life, first weekend in November. Family event, entertainment,

Enjoy the forest and many totems along the wheelchair-accessible loop trail through Sitka National Historical Park, site of the last major battle between the Russians and Tlingit people. Parts of the trail are difficult for wheelchairs due to soft trail and wood chips, often wet.

whalewatching, marine mammal art show, etc. Visitors Bureau, 747-5940.

See the **Sitka Convention & Visitors Bureau** in 303 Lincoln St, Suite 4 for a complete list of activities, some not scheduled at presstime. 747-5940. Sitka has cultural and social activities throughout the year. E-mail: scvb@sitka.net. Website: www.sitka.org

Juneau

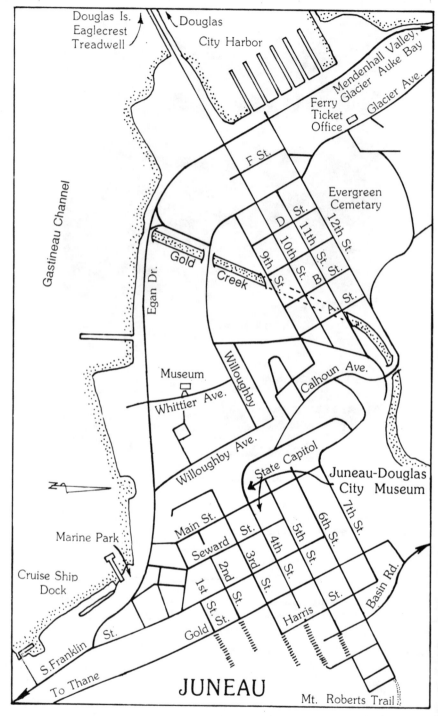

JUNEAU

Mt. Juneau looms over downtown Juneau and busy South Franklin Street. The state capital offers many historic sights and is the gateway to many wilderness areas including the Mendenhall Glacier which is just 13 miles from downtown.

## JUNEAU

(Area Code 907, Zip 99801, 2, 3, 11, 21, 24)

Juneau (city and borough pop. 30,000) is Alaska's state capital. It is nestled on the slopes between Gastineau Channel and Mounts Juneau and Roberts, which rise over 3,000 feet above the town. In 1880, prospectors Joe Juneau and Dick Harris were hired by geologist George Pilz to contact Auke Chief Kowee and confirm the presence of gold. They found gold in what is now Gold Creek, and a mining camp sprang up, named Juneau in 1881.

Besides placer gold from the creeks, gold was mined in three deep shaft systems: the Alaska Juneau Mine, the Alaska Gastineau Mine, and the Treadwell Mine on Douglas Island (extending under Gastineau Channel). Over $66 million in gold was removed before gold mining was declared a "nonessential wartime activity" during World War II, and the Alaska-Juneau Mine was closed. The Treadwell closed some years earlier when the shafts under the channel caved in and flooded with sea water.

Mining is again important to Juneau. Greens Creek on northern Admiralty Island produces silver and lead from a large deposit. A Canadian company plans to work the Alaska Juneau Mine and another near Berners Bay.

139

As Juneau grew past Sitka in size and activity, the district capital in 1906, the territorial capital in 1912, and later the state capital, were established here. Distances in Alaska are so great that most state departments have additional offices in other towns as well.

Juneau has so little flat ground in the downtown area that building has extended northwest into the Mendenhall Valley, where most residents now live. The airport and the Mendenhall Glacier also occupy the valley.

Since the glaciers dump sediment carried by the Mendenhall River and Lemon Creek into Gastineau Channel, ships cannot pass north of Juneau, and must go back down the channel and around Douglas Island. In order to avoid many miles of extra sailing, the ferries use a terminal at Auke Bay, 14 miles north of town. Distances are from the **downtown docks** unless otherwise noted.

There is bus service (**MGT**, 789-5460) and taxi service from Auke Bay terminal plus limited hotel courtesy van service to town and to the airport when the larger ferries dock. MGT stops at Juneau Airport on the way into town from the ferry terminal, providing service April through September, but questionable for winter. The hourly city bus runs between DeHart's store, 2 miles toward town from the dock, and town 6:50 a.m.– 11:36 p.m. Mon.–Sat. with fewer runs on Sundays. Airport area motels have courtesy vans to the ferry.

In daylight you have a fine view of the Mendenhall Glacier as you enter and leave Auke Bay. Unfortunately, many landings are scheduled at night, so if you want to see Juneau, you should stop over. For some summer arrivals there's a tour bus to the glacier or into town during longer daylight stops. Sharing a taxi for a trip to the glacier or town is another option, but do keep track of time if you're continuing on the ship. The drive from downtown to Auke Bay is at least a half hour one-way. Often the taxi must come from town to pick you up.

### To See and Do

Take a walking tour of downtown Juneau. Maps are available at the waterfront Marine Park information center (kiosk), most hotels, at the airport, the Auke Bay ferry terminal, and the Juneau Visitor Information Center in the log cabin at 3rd and Seward Streets. The tour passes historic sites and buildings of interest on Juneau's hills and waterfront.

Notice bald eagles on beaches, pilings, and trees around town and on the road north. Several nests are near the Auke Bay dock. Once I saw an eagle swim ashore to the parking lot with his fish. Another day a land otter used the culvert pipe as an underpass to cross under the road and popped out on the beach and down to the water beside the ship.

Visit the **Alaska State Museum**, on Whittier St. Open 9 a.m–6 p.m. Mon.–Fri., 10 a.m.-6 p.m. weekends in summer. Native culture, wildlife, historic exhibits, changing art exhibits. $4 charge. Closed Sunday and Monday in winter. Winter hours, 10–4, Tues.– Sat.

**Juneau Douglas City Museum**, at 4th and Main St. Exhibits and audio-visual programs, emphasizing local mining history, early social life, ships and planes of pioneer days. Summer hours: 9–5 weekdays, 10–5 weekends, mid-May to mid-Sept. Shorter hours in winter. Admission $2. 586-3572.

**Sealaska Heritage Foundation**, 2nd floor of the Sealaska building, One Sealaska Plaza, has books and videotapes on the history and culture of Tlingit, Haida, and Tsimshian people. Open weekdays, 8 a.m.–4:30 p.m.

See **St. Nicholas Orthodox Church**, 326 5th St., built in 1894. Frame building with a dome, icons, artifacts. Guided tours in summer. Donation requested, $1 per person.

Enjoy the view over Juneau and Gastineau Channel from Juneau's new library atop the parking garage next to the cruise ship dock.

Ride the **Mount Roberts Tram** from 490 S. Franklin Street about 2000 feet up the mountain to timber line. Enjoy the view, a native culture film, gift shops, and restaurants. 463-3412. May 1–September 25. Adult, $19.75, Child $10.50. You can ride the tram back down, or if you're comfortable hiking down a mile or so of switchbacked trail, you can have a close-up view of the rainforest. For safety, stay on the trail and don't take short-cuts. The top of the tram is at the edge of the alpine zone with trails on up the mountain, and alpine birds and wildflowers.

See the Mendenhall Glacier, 13 miles from downtown, 5 miles from Auke Bay ferry dock. Reach by car, bus tour, or municipal bus (daily, $1.25, you must walk the last 1.5 mile). You will find a U.S. Forest Service Visitor Center with programs, naturalists to answer your questions, nature walks, trails, and a good view of the glacier face. Rangers offer guided nature walks in summer. The **Visitor Center** is open weekends all year. From mid-May to late September, it's open 8:30 a.m.–5:30 p.m., seven days a week. Adult $3, family $6. Sockeye (red) salmon spawn in the stream in July and August, coho salmon from October to mid-winter, Arctic terns nest in the gravel, and in spring you may see mountain goats above by telescope.

Auke Lake, 12 miles from downtown. Also the location of Chapel By-The-Lake, and the University of Alaska campus. Get there on bus tour, or on municipal bus. The chapel has a famous view of the Mendenhall Glacier across Auke Lake.

**Auke Bay Marine Lab**, by car or municipal bus. Research lab has self-

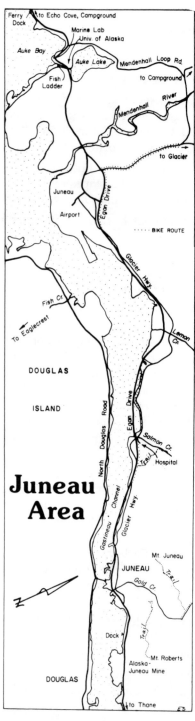

guided tour and exhibits, 9 a.m.–4 p.m., weekdays.

Auke Bay ferry terminal, 14 miles from downtown. In daylight, watch eagles, herons, a kingfisher who likes to dive off the dock, porpoises, seals, and an occasional whale. Eagles are often perched on the piling below the grocery store at Auke Bay small boat harbor.

Fish by boat or from shore, with an Alaska license even for saltwater. Get a tide table from any sporting goods, department, or hardware store. The tides are high here and currents strong. For rental and fishing charter information, ask at Visitor Information Center, 3rd and Seward.

For a "sure thing," with a fishing license, try the beach next to Gastineau Salmon Hatchery, 2697 Channel Drive, where locals fish to fill their freezers. In summer the hatchery puts out a floating dock for fishing, and an adjacent business sells snacks and rents fishing equipment and life jackets. It's a good place for children to fish, but they should never be on a dock without a lifejacket. You can buy fishing licenses here.

Enjoy beach fishing on Douglas Island, and north of Juneau, especially at the Shrine of St. Therese. For a recorded fishing report, call Alaska Fish and Game, 465-4116, April through November.

Fly over the Juneau Icefield. On a clear day this is an unforgettable experience. The icefield, which feeds the Mendenhall Glacier, covers 1500 square miles, supplying 39 glaciers. Many spectacular peaks. Local plane charters run about $110 per person. **Temsco Helicopters**, 789-9501, adjacent to the airport 9 miles from town, will fly you to Mendenhall Glacier and land. $160. Longer flights are available.

**ERA Helicopters** offers a 45-minute flight over the Icefield plus 15 minutes on the glacier for $175 per person. 586-2030.

State Office Building, 4th and Main. Free Concerts on old theater pipe organ, Friday noons, in spectacular 8th floor lobby with totem and view over channel.

Alaska Department of Fish and Game, 3/4 mile Egan Drive, behind KINY Radio, has a wildlife notebook series with information on all major land and water wildlife in Alaska.

State Capitol Building, 4th between Seward and Main. Free tours daily in summer.

Federal Building, Glacier Avenue and 9th, houses the offices of most federal agencies. The main post office and a Bureau of Indian Affairs exhibit of native artifacts are on the ground floor. Going higher requires a photo ID and security check. The cafeteria on the 2nd floor offers very good value lunch specials starting at 11:30, Mon.–Fri.

**Cooperative Extension Office**, in the Bill Ray Center of the University of Alaska, 10th & F Streets, near the Federal Building, has free or inexpensive leaflets on Alaskan lifestyle—everything from rhubarb and sourdough recipes, parka and mukluk patterns, to gardening in the north and making jerky.

**Gold Creek Salmon Bake**, 3 miles from downtown, near Salmon Creek. 1061 Salmon Creek Ln., Juneau, AK 99801. 789-0052, fax 789-1749. Courtesy bus picks visitors up for dinner at Baranof Hotel at 6 p.m. Operates for lunches and nightly dinners outdoors (under a roof, but often cool), 5:30– 9, mid-May to mid-September. All you can eat and your first beer, $25.50. Children 12 and under, $16.80. Music by local entertainers. Pan for gold in the creek and look at artifacts from gold mining.

**Thane Ore House Salmon Bake**, 4 miles south on Thane Road. Salmon, halibut, BBQ ribs. Mining operation, gold panning, mining exhibit. Indoor and outdoor seating. Handicapped accessible. Lunch and dinner daily, noon–9:30 p.m, May 1–September 30. 586-3442. Courtesy transportation from downtown for dinner—5:50 p.m. pick up from Baranof Hotel. Call to arrange later pick up times. All you can eat $18.50. With gold rush follies show, add $7.50.

Hike trails in Southeast Alaska's most extensive system. Guidebook *Juneau Trails*, $4, is available from the Forest Service, at bookstores. *90 Short Walks around Juneau* by Mary Lou King is a book featuring many delightful places to spend a few hours. The trail up Mt. Roberts (fine view of town) begins at the end of 6th Street. The trail up Mt. Juneau (have respect for weather and snow on trail) about one mile from beginning of Perseverance Trail at end of Basin Road. The trail to Pt. Bishop from end of Thane Road is 8 miles of flat hiking, through forest and along shore. Good camping and fishing at Dupont, 3 miles from start of trail. The trail from N. Douglas to Outer Point and Shaman Island is boarded through the forest and muskeg—even has turnouts for groups meeting so you don't have to step off into the mud! Watch the incoming tide so you aren't stranded on the island until the next low tide.

Free guided all-day hikes with Juneau Parks and Recreation, Wednesdays, Saturdays. Cross-country ski tours in winter. Distances and exertion vary. Weekend fun races May–October. Call 586-5226 Mon.–Fri.

Tour the **Gastineau Salmon Hatchery**, 2697 Channel Drive (frontage road adjacent to Egan Drive), 463-4810, to see salmon climbing a fish ladder, eggs taken for hatching, and *big* saltwater aquariums with many local fish and sea plants. Gift shop offers smoked and canned salmon and salmon leather crafts. Open 10–6 weekdays, 12–5 weekends, in summer. Adults $3 and children under 12 $1. Fishing pier and gravel beach for fish-

The great bronze bear presides over the state capitol in downtown Juneau.

ing next to hatchery. Foodstands nearby rent fishing poles and lifejackets for children.

Visit **Alaska Brewing & Bottling Co.**, 5429A Shaune Drive. 780-5866. Taste Alaskan Amber Beer and Pale Ale, Tues.–Sat., 11–4:30, in summer. Shorter hours in winter. Thursday is the best time to go as that's the day they bottle the brew! T-shirts, caps, etc. with label for sale. In the Lemon Creek area, from Glacier Highway turn north on Anka St., then right on Shaune Dr.

Drive your car or a rented one "out the road," a phrase Juneau-ites use to describe any place north of Auke Bay, for a picnic and beautiful view. Fire pits and picnic shelters (open with roofs for rain) at Auke Bay Recreation Area and Lena Cove. Fire pits and shelter at Eagle Beach. Pit toilets at all areas. Good picnicking and views from North Douglas Road. Some tourists drive these roads simply because they've never been where all the roads have ends!

Visit the lovely Shrine of St. Therese, 23 miles out Glacier Hwy. on a scenic rocky point. Excellent shore fishing from rocks below.

Ride the ferries on day or overnight excursions if you're using Juneau as a base. In summer the *Kennicott* and *Columbia* stay in Skagway for several hours at least once a week, or make an extra trip back to Juneau which could allow you a stopover in Skagway or Haines. You'd have time to explore either town on a one-day trip. The *Malaspina* will sail daily from Juneau to Haines and Skagway and return in daylight May 28–September 12, 1999. Check ferry schedule or our comments on the current season earlier in this book.

The *LeConte's* trips to Pelican, Hoonah, Tenakee, Angoon, and Sitka are popular. On her run leaving Juneau, Friday morning and returning early Sunday, you can go all the way to Sitka and sometimes have several hours Saturday in town or get off at any of the other ports and catch her on the return trip. At Tenakee for example, you would have about 21 hours. Remember that seniors 65 and over can ride the smaller ferries for 50% of the regular adult fare all year between Alaskan ports. In winter the promotional fare for drivers can be 75% off.

Join an adventure tour with **Alaska Travel Adventures**, 9085 Glacier Hwy., Juneau, AK 99801. 789-0052. Three-hour float trips on the Mendenhall River, May 1–Sept. 26. Gold panning and gold mining tour, 1 and 1/2 hours. Will pick you up at hotels. They also offer a nature tour to bird rookeries near Sitka and canoe trip in Ketchikan. **Grayline** desk at the Seadrome Visitor Center on the waterfront books these tours. They also have a "shuttle" to Mendenhall Glacier from downtown.

Kayak Juneau's sheltered waters or take off from here for longer trips. For kayak equipment, instruction, guiding, rentals, **Alaska Discovery**, 780-6226. Offers daily 6-hour guided small group kayak trips.**Adlersheim Lodge** at Mile 34 Glacier Highway, 780-4778, rents kayaks and offers tours.

Watch and photograph Juneau's scenery at sunrise or sunset with **Juneau Photo Tours**, 790-3937. Van tour with refreshments. For amateurs to experts. Raingear provided if needed.

Hike with **Alaska Rainforest Tours**, 463-3466, fax 463-4453. (800) 493-4453. At the airport, 1837 Shell Simmons Dr., Juneau, AK 99801. Day hikes, backpacking the Chilkoot Trail, and nature tours according to your interests. Has fishing, wildlife watching, whale watching, backpacking, camping adventures. Some require boat, plane, or helicopter transport. Rain gear provided.

Enjoy a Juneau Icefield flight and a salmon bake at fly-in **Taku Glacier Lodge**, 789-0790. Leaves seadrome in front of Merchants' Wharf for 3-hour trip, mid-May to late September. Icefield flight only, 45 minutes.

See Tracy Arm, a winding glaciated fiord about 60 miles south of Juneau. With granite walls several thousand feet high on both sides, waterfalls, and icebergs, it's like a flooded Yosemite without the people. The floating ice gets thicker as you reach the upper end where the North and

Mendenhall Glacier and Lake with Mt. Stroller White at left, named for a much-loved local journalist.

South Sawyer Glaciers reach the water, calving off icebergs while you watch. Seals with pups often lie on the icebergs. You may also see mountain goats, black bears, humpback and orca whales, and many bald eagles and sea birds on this trip. Companies offering tours to Tracy Arm are listed under Boats and Boat Tours later in this chapter. Some offer you a float-plane flight one-way and the boat ride the other. All serve meals on the boat. The tour takes 7–12 hours, less if you fly one-way. Suggestions: go as early in the summer as possible for longer daylight hours. Take a parka and cap for standing out on deck. It's an alternative to longer, more expensive trips to Glacier Bay.

Watch brown bears and cubs catching salmon at Pack Creek on Admiralty Island. For a one-day trip, charter a plane to take you over and pick you up later. With kayak or boat, you can get there and back in several days. The viewing area is at least 100 yards from most bears; also a viewing tower up a short trail. Call the U.S. Forest Service, 586-8751, and see them for a permit for the time you want to be there, as they now limit the number of people allowed, mid-July through August. All visitors must register with the Forest Service, year around. Some guide services have permits to lead groups there—the Forest Service can tell you which.

Tour "**House of Wickersham**," former home with memorabilia of Judge Wickersham and Alaska's early days. 213-7th Street, up steep hill from State Capitol. 586-9001. Call for info on hours, not announced at presstime.

Tours of Governor's Mansion can sometimes be arranged. 465-3500.

Enjoy the Mendenhall Golf Course, 2102 Industrial Blvd. 789-1221. 9 hole, par 3 course with driving range and club rentals in the Mendenhall Valley, west of the airport. Glacier view.

In winter ski downhill at **Eaglecrest Ski Area** on Douglas Island. Two chairlifts, x-c trails. X-c ski near Mendenhall Glacier and on hiking trails.

*1999 Tip:* On Friday and Saturday each week in summer only 1 or 2 small cruise ships are scheduled in town at presstime. For uncrowded shopping and downtown touring, these are your best bet. Tuesday, Wednesday and Thursday are the busiest days with several large ships in port.

INFORMATION AVAILABLE at **Visitor Information Center** in Davis Log Cabin, (corner of 3rd and Seward) 134 3rd St., Juneau, AK 99801. 586-2201, fax 586-6304. Toll Free, (888) 581-2201. E-mail: jcvb@ptialaska.net. Note: a very helpful brochure, *Free Things to see and do in Juneau Alaska* is available here. Web site: www.juneau.net for visitors' guide. The **Juneau Convention & Visitors Bureau** operates an information kiosk in Marine Park, adjacent to the cruise ship dock and desks in cruise ship terminal, and in the airport and ferry terminals, summers (both counters are self-service in winter).

For hiking, kayaking, and mountaineering trips and information, stop at the **Foggy Mountain Shop**, 134 N. Franklin. **U. S. Forest Service** information desk in Centennial Hall, 101 Egan Dr., 586-8751, has films, slide shows, maps, brochures, recreation cabin information and Pack Creek reservations. Open 8–5 daily Memorial Day to mid-September, 8–5 Mon.–Fri. rest of the year. Information on Glacier Bay National Park also available in summer.

## Transportation

FERRY: **Alaska Marine Highway**, daily in summer from Auke Bay terminal, 14 miles north. Ferry office for information, reservations, tickets, 1.5 miles, 1590 Glacier Ave. For actual time of arrival it's best to call the terminal, 789-7453. Terminal opens an hour or two prior to arrival, otherwise the message is recorded. Vehicle check-in time is at least 2 hours prior to departure. Reservations, 465-3941 or (800) 642-0066; daily recorded ferry arrivals 465-3940.

Passenger ferry to Gustavus, daily at 11 a.m., mid-May to mid-September. **Auk Nu Tours**, 586-6444. (800) 478-3610 US and Canada. (800) 820-2628 in Alaska. Carries kayaks, bicycles, pets in carriers, by reservation. More details in the Glacier Bay chapter.

Mendenhall Wetlands from Glacier Gardens overlook outside Juneau.

CITY BUS: Runs daily, less frequently on Sunday. Route goes from downtown cruise ship terminal through town to airport and DeHart's store at Auke Bay, 1.9 miles from Auke Bay ferry terminal. Some buses go to Douglas. Hourly, 6:50 a.m.–11:45 p.m., depending on route. Check schedule as no buses run during some hours at night. Ask for the express bus schedule (Mon–Fri only) as well—it's separate. The express bus stops at the airport. There is no city bus service to the Auke Bay ferry terminal.

BUS SERVICE: Bus and van service to airport and ferry: **MGT** (bright blue buses) meets ferries April 1–mid-September, and may extend dates. Will transport ferry passengers to downtown or to airport for $5. When ships are in port for several hours at a reasonable time of day, **MGT** offers a tour of the Mendenhall Glacier and town with return to the ferry terminal. **MGT** buses offer city/glacier 2 1/2 hour tours from the downtown cruise ship terminal and kiosk for $12.50. 789-5460.

Note that buses, and sometimes taxis, are parked in Juneau *behind* the ferry terminal building. You may not be able to see them from the parking lot until you walk around the building. All leave soon after ferry arrival, so you need to go up there as soon as the ship arrives or you will miss them. For pick up downtown to ride out to the ferry, ask at the Alaskan Hotel or call the bus company, 789-5460. make reservation the day

149

before if possible.

**Island Waterways** runs a bus between Juneau Airport and downtown, $8. 780-4977, year around.

TAXI: **Taku Taxi**, 102 Franklin St., Juneau, AK 99801. 586-2121. **Capital Cab**, 586-2772. Fare from downtown to Auke Bay terminal $22, $1 per add'l person.

TOURS: Starting in downtown Juneau, **Gray Line /Westours**, 586-3773, ticket desk in the Seadrome Bulding on the waterfront, mid-May to late September. Tours to Mendenhall Glacier ($34/person) and around Juneau. **Alaska Native Tours**, 3 hour tour of Juneau area sites emphasizing native culture and history. $15/person. 463-3231. **Island Waterways**, van tours, evening sunset tours, 780-4977. **MGT** from the cruise ship dock and ferry dock, 789-5460.

**Juneau Trolley Car**, motorized streetcar, tours town with narration and many stops, including the Mt. Roberts Tram, State Museum, and shopping district. Unlimited day use pass, Adult $11.50, Child $8.50. May–September, 8 a.m.–6 p.m. daily. 245 Marine Way. Also offers a Douglas Island tour. 586-RIDE.

CAR RENTAL: **Allstar/Practical Rent-A-Car**, across from Mendenhall Mall, (family-owned with airport pick up and drop off, excellent service). 790-2414, (800) 722-0741, fax 790-2412. **Avis**, Juneau Airport, 789-9450, (800) 331-0741. Call local number for one of few available compact cars. **Evergreen Ford**, 789-9386. **Hertz**, Juneau Airport, 789-9494, (800) 654-8200, fax 789-3519. **Mendenhall Auto Center**, 789-1386. **Payless Rent-a-Car**, 5245 Glacier Hwy., 780-6004, (800) 792-7219. **Rent-A-Wreck**, 789-4111, fax 789-7098. Has passenger vans, near airport. Some agencies let you drop off cars at the ferry terminal for a small charge (less than taxi ).

AIR: **Alaska Airlines**, 789-0600, (800) 426-0333, to Ketchikan, Sitka, Gustavus, Petersburg, Wrangell, Anchorage, Seattle, California, and Mexico.

**Air North**, 789-2007, fax 789-4228. Several days a week to Whitehorse, Old Crow, Fairbanks, and Dawson City. (403) 668-2228, fax (403) 668-6224, Whitehorse. Offers 21 day pass, allowing travel to all stops. DC-3 plane.

CHARTERS: Some operators have mail contracts requiring scheduled flights to outlying towns, on which you can ride at a flat rate (you don't have to charter the whole plane).

**Alaska Coastal Airlines**, 1873 Shell Simmons Dr., Juneau, AK 99801. 789-7818.

**Alaska Fly 'n' Fish Charters**, 790-2120. Floatplane trips to guided fishing, wildlife watching, Pack Creek.

**Haines Airways**, Box 470, Haines, AK 99827. 789-7990. Icefield and Gla-

Salmon climbing fish ladders at the Gastineau Salmon Hatchery in Juneau.

cier Bay tours. 2 hr. tour from Haines, $85/person.

**LAB Flying Service**, Terminal Building, Juneau Airport, Juneau, AK 99803. 789-9160. Scheduled flights to Haines, Skagway, Gustavus, Hoonah, Excursion Inlet.

**Alaska Seaplane Service**, 8995 Yandukin Dr., Juneau, AK 99801. 789-3331 and (800) 478-3360, fax 789-3221. Flightseeing Juneau Icefield and Glacier Bay.

**Reid Air**, 1873 Shell Simmons Dr., Juneau, AK 99801. 789-6968.

**Skagway Air Service**, Terminal Building, Juneau Airport, 789-2006. Two people minimum. Flies to Skagway, Haines, Hoonah, Gustavus.

**Ward Air**, Terminal Building, Juneau Airport, 789-9150. Charters only.

**Wings of Alaska**, Terminal Building, Juneau Airport, 789-0790. Mailing address: 1873 Shell Simmons Dr., Suite 119, Juneau, AK 99801. Scheduled service to Angoon, Gustavus, Hoonah, Pelican, Tenakee, Petersburg, Haines, Skagway, Kake, Elfin Cove. Tours of Juneau Icefield and to Taku Lodge salmon bake.

The following helicopter services offer flightseeing which can include landing on a glacier or the Juneau Icefield, letting you out to walk around and peer down crevasses. Bring your camera!

**Coastal Helicopters**, 1873 Shell Simmons Dr., Juneau, AK 99801. 789-5600.

**ERA Helicopters**, Box 1468, Juneau, AK 99802. 586-2030 or (800) 843-

1947 outside Alaska, fax 463-3959.

**NorthStar Trekking**, Box 32540, Juneau, AK 99803. 790-4530, fax 790-4419.

**Temsco Helicopters**, 1650 Maplesden Way, Juneau, AK 99801. 789-9501.

BIKE ROUTE: A cycle path follows the Mendenhall Loop Road from near the glacier to Egan Drive and along it to the Old Glacier Hwy. near Switzer Village to another segment along Old Glacier Hwy. beside Twin Lakes from Lemon Creek to Salmon Creek. From there a path goes north of Egan Drive to Glacier Highway in town. Thus you can cycle from DeHart's Store at Auke Bay to Juneau without getting on the freeway. A route map is available at Davis Log Cabin Visitor Center. You'll want time and daylight. Bicycle lanes parallel other main roads, including the Douglas Bridge and Douglas Hwy. to downtown Douglas, 4.5 miles from Juneau.

BICYCLE RENTALS: **Mountain Gears**, 586-4327, fax 586-2575. Rents bikes with helmet, lock, water bottle. Offers half-day and all-day tours.

BAGGAGE STORAGE at hotels for patrons, on day of departure. Juneau Airport terminal is open most hours daily. Auke Bay ferry terminal has lockers, but is locked when ships aren't in. **Alaskan Hotel** accepts bags of non-patrons, space available, usually at non-peak times, (small fee). The **Juneau Hostel**, 614 Harris St., has outdoor, unsecured storage. Check at Visitor Center or its manned kiosks for update.

## Hotels
(12% tax extra. High season rate shown; usually lower in off-season.)

**Adlersheim Lodge**—Mile 34, Glacier Hwy., 20 miles north of ferry terminal. Mail: Box 210447, Auke Bay, AK 99821. 723-4447, fax 780-4778. Only wilderness lodge near Juneau accessible by car. 9 rooms, 3 cabins (2 have 6 bunks and kitchens, 1 has 4 bunks (may add kitchen). Cabins use outhouses. Sea kayak, mountain bikes, hiking trails. Kayak rentals and kayak/lodging package rate. Heli-skiing in winter. Double in cabins, $55–75. Double in room, $65 per person incl. breakfast.

**Alaskan Hotel**—167 S. Franklin St., Juneau, AK 99801. 586-1000. For reservations (800) 327-9347, fax 463-3775. Sauna, hot tubs, cable TV, phone. Single w/o bath, $60. Single/Double with bath, $75. Studio 1–4 people $90. Children 12 & under free. Add'l $10  E-mail: akhotel@ptialaska.net Web: www.ptialask.net/~akhotel

**WestmarkBaranof Hotel**—127 N. Franklin St., Juneau, AK 99801. 586-2660, (800) 544-0970, fax 586-8315. Restaurant, lounge, hairstyling shop, travel agency, gift shop, coffee shop. Single/Double $149–159. Add'l, $15/person. No pets. Commercial and government rates.

**Bergmann Hotel**—434 Third St. Juneau, AK 99801. 586-1690, fax 463-

2678. Traditional hotel has restaurant, lounge, coin-op laundry, lawn with chairs, parking. Single $45, Double $65, weekly rates. All rooms with shared bath, maid service, have basin, phone,TV in room. No pets.

**Best Western Country Lane Inn**—9300 Glacier Hwy., Juneau 99801. 789-5005. Reservations (800) 528-1234, fax 789-2818. Near airport, 4 miles from Mendenhall Glacier. Courtesy transportation to airport, ferry, and downtown Juneau. 50 rooms. Complimentary continental breakfast. Free local phone calls, cable TV with HBO. Single $100, Double $108. Suites.

**Breakwater Inn**—1711 Glacier Avenue, Juneau, AK 99801. 586-6303. Fax 463-4820. 41 rooms have 2 double or 1 king-size bed. Kitchenettes in 26 rooms. 1 in-room jacuzzi. Dining room, lounge. Good view of waterfront, boat harbor. Single/Double $109 mountain view, $119 harbor view. Add'l, $10/person. Deluxe unit add'l. Children under 12 free. E-mail: breakwtr@ptialaska.net web: www.AlaskaOne.com/breakwater

**Cashen Quarters**—315 Gold Street, Juneau, AK 99801. 586-9863, fax 586-9861. Downtown. 5 units. Showers, kitchenettes, telephones, cable TV, microwave, laundry facilities. Renovated, lace curtains and Juneau atmosphere. Quiet back street near downtown. Pets allowed. Hearty continental breakfast. Single $80, Double $89. Two bedroom unit $156. e-mail: jsclc3@ptialaska.net. web: www.cahenquarters.com

**Driftwood Lodge**—435 Willoughby Avenue, Juneau, AK 99801. 586-2280, (800) 544-2239, fax 586-1034. 62 rooms, some kitchen units. Color TV, HBO, laundry facilities. Courtesy van to ferry and airport. Pets OK, $5/day. One block from Alaska State Museum. Near federal building, convention center, restaurant. Single $68, Double $78. Add'l, $7/person.

**Frontier Suites Airport Hotel**—9400 Glacier Hwy., Juneau, AK 99801. 790-6600, reservations (800) 544-2250, fax 790-6612. Four blocks from airport. 40 suites with queen beds, full kitchen, dishwasher, coffee-maker, safe, TVs, phone and modem connection. 2 handicapped-accessible. 2 in-room jacuzzis. Meeting rooms, lounge. Playground, basketball court, laundromat. Free shuttle airport. Single & Double from $119. Children under 12 free.

**Grandma's Feather Bed**—**A Country Inn**—2358 Mendenhall Loop Rd., Juneau, AK 99801. 789-5566, fax 789-2818. Near airport. 14 rooms, 12 with jacuzzis. Victorian farmhouse-style. Courtesy van. Single/Double $160 including full breakfast.

**Inn at the Waterfront**—455 S. Franklin St., Juneau, AK 99801. 586-2050. Restored hotel across from cruise ship dock in downtown historic district. Rooms with shared or private bath. Restaurant, lounge, steam bath. Shared bath, Single $60, Double $69. Private bath, Single $77, Double $86. Suites

$110–129.

**Juneau Airport Travelodge**—9200 Glacier Hwy., Juneau, AK 99801. 789-9700, (800) 255-3050. Half mile from airport, 5 miles from Auke Bay terminal. 86 rooms. Restaurant, lounge, indoor pool, jacuzzi. Free in room coffee. Cable TV with HBO. Courtesy transportation from airport or ferry terminal. Wheelchair accessible. Has executive room with desk, modem, computer hookups. No pets. Single $125, Double $135. Children 17 and under free with parents.

**Prospector Hotel**—375 Whittier St., Juneau, AK 99801. 586-3737. Reservations: in Alaska (800) 478-5866, elsewhere (800) 331-2711, fax 586-1204. Downtown, near convention center, waterfront. 60 rooms, restaurant, lounge, live entertainment. Single/Double from $95, varying with view. Suites. Continental breakfast included. Pets allowed with manager's okay.

**Silverbow Inn**—120 Second St., Juneau, AK 99801. 586-4146, (800) 586-4146. 6 room restored hotel in historic building downtown, private baths. Excellent restaurant. Single $115, Double $125, includes continental breakfast from bakery next door.

**Super 8 Motel**—Near airport, 2295 Trout St. (behind McDonald's). Juneau, AK 99801. 789-4858, (800) 800-8000. 75 rooms, cable TV, direct-dial phone, elevator, coin-op laundry, conference room, queen-size beds, wheelchair access. Courtesy transportation to airport and ferry. Pets with $25 deposit. Single $92.88. Double $102.88.

**Goldbelt Hotel Juneau**—51 West Egan Drive, Mail: Box 20929, Juneau 99802. 586-6900, (888) 478-6909, fax 463-3567. 105 rooms, cable TV, coffeemaker, hair dryers, irons & boards each room. Restaurant, lounge, free parking and airport transfers. Wheelchair accessible. Conference rooms. Single/Double $169. Add'l $15. Children under 12 free in room w/parent. Senior/government rates.

**Hostel**—Hill overlooking downtown, 614 Harris St., Juneau, AK 99801. 586-9559. Separate-sex dorm rooms, cooking facilities, showers, living room, dining area. Handicapped accessible. Groups welcome. One family room, reserved for travelers with children. Open all year. No pets. Register 5:00–11:00 p.m. in summer. Curfew 11 p.m. Closed 9:00 a.m.–5:00 p.m. 3-day limit. $10/person plus one short assigned chore. Affiliated with Hostelling International. Reservations recommended, by mail only.

**University of Alaska Southeast**—11120 Glacier Hwy., Juneau, AK 99801. 465-6389, fax 465-6832. For "university-affiliated people", accommodations are available in student housing from mid-May to mid-August, depending on the university's open dates. Single, $35–40 person/night. e-mail: jntch@acad1.alaska.edu web: www.jun.alaska.edu/uas/

Patsy Ann in bronze greets arrivals at Marine Park as the abandoned dog met ships for the rest of her life, looking for?

student_services/housing.html

### Bed & Breakfasts

**Alaska Bed & Breakfast Association,** Box 22800, Juneau, AK 99802. 586-2959, fax 463-4453. Reservation service, offering homes that specialize in hospitality. Serves all of Alaska and the Yukon. Rates average $65–95. Double. Reservations advised as many have 1–3 rooms, and the popular ones are often full. Free brochure and directory.

**Alaska Tours & Lodging**—Box 35403, Juneau, AK 99803. 780-5150, fax 780-4673. Reservations from day trips to B&B lodging, custom trip planning.

**Bed & Breakfast Assoc. of Alaska—INNside Passage Chapter,** Box 22800, Juneau, AK 99802. 789-8822, fax 586-9861. www. wetpage.com/bbaaip Reservation service for at least 140 rooms in all price ranges.

Samples from the Juneau 30+ B&Bs include **Mt. Juneau Inn,** 1801 Old Glacier Hwy., 463-5855, fax 463-5423. Channel view, north end of town on bus line, guest kitchen. **Crondahls' Bed & Breakfast,** 625 5th St., phone/fax 586-1464. Art-filled home on Starr Hill near Capitol. **The Lost Chord,** 2200 Fritz Cove Rd., 789-7296. Across Auke Bay from ferry terminal, overlooking the bay, great hospitality. **Windsock Inn,** 410 D St., Douglas, 364-2431. Pioneer Alaskans catering to retirees, teachers. Across channel from Juneau.

Call or write the **Visitors Bureau**, 134 Third St., Juneau, AK 99801. 586-2201. Their highly informative Travel Planner lists many independent B & Bs as well as other attractions.

## Campgrounds

**Mendenhall Lake**—5 miles from Auke Bay ferry dock, off Mendenhall Loop Road (turn right leaving ferry and follow signs for camping), 2 miles northwest of Visitor Center. USFS, from $8 per day, late May–mid-July in 1999. No reservations taken this year. Then will close to finish construction on upgraded facilities. Great views of glacier, hiking, some mosquitos. Firewood scarce and possibly green. Tables, fire grates, water, restrooms, central dump station. 60 spaces, some drive-through. Some walk-in tent spaces away from vehicle sounds.

**Auke Village Recreation Area**—2 miles northwest of Auke Bay ferry terminal. (turn left as you leave terminal) USFS, has 12 sites, $8 per day. Boating and beach adjacent, fewer bugs, flush toilets. Same facilities as above, except no dump station. No reservations.

Do not leave valuables in camp when you leave. I recommend marking equipment obviously and permanently with your name.

**City and Borough of Juneau** allows parking for self-contained RV's only, $8/night, limit 3 nights, at Savikko Park in Douglas. Permits available at Juneau Harbormaster's Office, across Egan Drive from high school. 586-5255, 586-5337. Mid-May to Sept. 30.

**Auke Bay RV Park**—11930 Glacier Hwy., 1.5 miles from ferry terminal toward downtown. Box 210215, Auke Bay, AK 99821. 789-9467. 25 spaces with full hookups. $18 per night. Reservations recommended, 2 night minimum.

**Spruce Meadow RV Park**—on Montana Creek Rd. en route to West Glacier Trail. 789-1990. Plan to open in summer 1999.

## Facilities

LAUNDROMATS: **Harbor Wash Board**, 586-1133, 1111 F. St., Juneau. Off Glacier Ave., behind Alaska Laundry, also has showers. **The Dungeon** is in basement of the Mendenhall Apartments, 326 4th Street, 586-2805. **Mendenhall Laundromat**, 789-2880, adjacent to supermarket off Mendenhall Loop Road in the Valley.

SWIMMING POOL: **Augustus Brown Pool** next to Juneau-Douglas High School on Glacier Avenue has open hours, weight equipment, a sauna, and showers. 586-2055, 586-5325.

DUMP STATIONS: **Mendenhall Campground. City Borough shop** in

The Mt. Roberts Tram hauls visitors 2000 ft. up Mt. Roberts to timberline overlooking Juneau and Gastineau Channel.

The Glacier Gardens of Juneau can take you back to the Ice Age.

Douglas at 3rd and Front St. **Valley Chevron**, Mendenhall Mall.

PROPANE: **Amerigas,** 10111 Glacier Hwy., 789-7897. **Gas 'N' Go,** 5165 Glacier Hwy., 780-4821. **MAPCO,** 6585 Glacier Hwy., 780-8697. **Petrolane Alaska Gas Service**, 3850 Mendenhall Loop Rd. (road to glacier). 789-7840. **Valley Chevron** in Mendenhall Shopping Center. 789-2880.

DIESEL: **Valley Chevron** in Mendenhall Shopping Center. **Gas 'N Go,** Grant's Plaza on Glacier Highway at Lemon Creek. **Airport Union**, Glacier Hwy. & Airport Rd. **Aurora Basin** fuel dock.

ICE: All supermarkets. **Breeze Inn,** convenience late-night grocery, Glacier Hwy. and Trout St., across from McDonald's.

EMERGENCY CARE: **Bartlett Regional Hospital**, 3.5 miles, Glacier Highway, 586-2611. **Juneau Urgent Care & Family Medical Clinic**, 8505 Old Dairy Rd. (1/4 mile south of Nugget Mall), 790-4111. Ambulance, fire department, dial 911.

PETS: Veterinarians: **Juneau Pet Clinic**, 8367 Old Dairy Rd., Juneau, AK 99801. 789-3444. **Southeast Alaska Veterinary Clinic**, 7691 Glacier Hwy., Juneau, AK 99801. 789-7551. Boarding: the vet clinics listed above plus **Gastineau Humane Society**, 7705 Glacier Hwy., Juneau, AK 99801. 789-0260. **Big Dog Bath House and B&B**, 790-2244/790-2BIG.

### Boats

CHARTERS: **Juneau Sportfishing**, P.O. Box 20438, Juneau, AK 99802. 586-1887. Boats 28–50 ft. available for fishing, wildlife viewing, overnights, Tracy Arm, mid-April through September. Courtesy shuttle to boat. Snacks provided. Wheelchairs accommodated. **Alaska Travel Adventures**, (800) 791-2673. Fax (425) 828-3519. Half-day, day, and multi-day trips for fishing, whalewatching, kayaking.

List of licensed charter operators available through **Visitor Information Center**. Boats can be hired for Tracy Arm (a spectacular fjord with glaciers), Berners Bay, Taku Inlet, or for **good** fishing. Rates from $110  for half day, $180 all day. 586-2201.

BOAT TOURS: **Alaska Sightseeing**, 586-6300, (800) 426-7702. Tours to Glacier Bay, 4 days–3 nights. **Anytime Cruises**, 789-0609, fax 789-1094. 3–10 day tours. **Auk Nu Tours**, 586-6444, (800) 820-2628 in Alaska. (800) 478-3610 outside Alaska. Tracy Arm cruises, May 15–September 12, 1999. $109 incl. lunch. **Dolphin Jet Boat Tours**, 463-3422. Whale and wildlife watching, several trips daily in summer. With these specialists, it's a real thrill to listen to the whales live via an underwater mike while watching them feed! **Glacier Bay Cruises**, 463-5510. Day trips to Glacier Bay, flying both ways, about $300 per person. Daily trips to Tracy Arm, $120–140, depending on whether you go round trip on the boat or fly one way in a floatplane, meeting the boat. **Alaska Rainforest Tours**, (800) 493-4453. 463-3466. Variety of land and sea tours.

**Princeton Hall**—15225 Point Louisa Rd., Juneau, AK 99801. 789-7558. Classic restored former missionary cruiser gives 3 and 5 day nature-watching tours around Admiralty Island, Tracy Arm, and other Southeastern spots. Fish, go ashore to beachcomb, etc. Charters for small groups.

**Adventure Sports**, 8757 Glacier Hwy., Juneau, AK 99801. 789-5696. Rents and sells kayaks and equipment. Offers 3-hour to 3-day tours.

**Alaska Discovery Expeditions**, Box 20669, Juneau, AK 99802. 780-6226, fax 780-4220. Kayaking trips with guide, 6 hours, also overnights and multi-day trips.

**Juneau Outdoor Center**, Rentals, arrangements. 586-8220

FUEL AND MOORAGE at Aurora Basin, Harris Harbor, Douglas, and Auke Bay. Dock space limited, especially in summer. **Harbormaster**, Channel 16 or 586-5255. **Juneau Yachting Services**, phone/fax 463-2628, offers shopping, business services, everything visiting boaters need.

## Happenings

**Concerts in The Park**, June to mid-August. Friday evening concerts in Marine Park, downtown, by local and visiting groups. Free.

**Juneau Jazz and Classics**, May 21–30, 1999. Ten day event with jazz and classical musicians from all over the country. 463-3378.

**Gold Rush Days** celebration, June 26–27, 1999. Miners' and loggers' skills events. Children's activities. 586-2497.

**4th of July**, July 3–4, 1999. Parade, fireworks over the channel, contests from sandcastle building to dog-frisbee!

**Golden North Salmon Derby**, August 20–22, 1999. Oldest salmon derby in Alaska, 53rd contest in 1999. Proceeds go to scholarships for students. Big prizes—recent winners won $15,000. 789-2399.

**Juneau Public Market**, November 26–28, 1999. Artists and craftmen from all over come to Centennial Hall for 3 days,

*Note*: Biennially, in June of even numbered years Alaska Native Americans meet in Juneau and offer public dance and theater performances. Artists may have special exhibits in addition to the works usually exhibited in galleries, stores, and the Alaska State Museum.

## Ferry Tale

A traveler looked at the Tongass National Forest map and concluded "We did get a good deal from the Russians. It looks like about a dollar an island".

The face of Margerie Glacier where you hear the cracking of moving ice and often see pieces "calve" off into Glacier Bay.

## GLACIER BAY NATIONAL PARK AND PRESERVE

This spectacular 65-mile-long bay is fed by a dozen glaciers at its upper end. It has bears, seals, whales, tufted puffins, and lots of icebergs. Many seabirds come ashore only to nest here. The park is some distance by boat or plane from Juneau. The nearest glaciers are 60 miles from park headquarters. Choices for getting there include:

A chartered flight over the bay from Juneau, Haines, Skagway, or Gustavus. Flights are cheapest from Haines, but the clouds must be high enough for the plane to get over the mountains, or at least between them.

Scheduled air taxi flights from Juneau, where you only have to pay per seat rather than charter the whole plane, fly at least once daily all year, several times daily in summer. Most lodges and inns are open from mid-May to September 30 with the excursion boat running trips to the glaciers and bird rookeries even though the airline has a shorter season.

The **Alaska Airlines** air-boat tour from Juneau. This can include a night at Glacier Bay Lodge, round trip boat service to the glaciers with a Park Service naturalist, and return flight to Juneau. Additional nights at the lodge can be added, as well as an overnight near a glacier on an excursion boat with staterooms. For package prices contact the airline or tour operators below. The season is mid-May–mid-September. Air fare from

The *Spirit of Adventure* waits in morning low tide at the Bartlett Cove dock before its daily tour up to the glaciers.

Juneau—regular coach $146 round trip. Sometimes special fares if flights aren't full—*ask*. Senior rates are 10% off any published fare. Airport transfers at Juneau and Gustavus ($10) are not included. (800) 426-0333.

**Air Excursions**, Box 16, Gustavus, AK 99826. 697-2375. (800) 354-2479 in Alaska. Air charter service based in Gustavus. Charter flights are available in park andto all Southeast Alaska airports.

**LAB Flying Service**, Terminal Building, Juneau Airport, Juneau, AK 99803. 789-9160. Scheduled daily air service all year between Juneau and Gustavus.

**Alaska's Glacier Bay Tours & Cruises,** 520 Pike St., Suite 1400, Seattle, WA 98101. (800) 451-5952. (206) 623-2417, fax (206) 623-7809. Web: www.glacierbaytours.com Offers multi-day tours throughout the summer, some starting from Juneau or Ketchikan. Vessels carry 36–86 passengers with staterooms.

Passenger ferry Juneau to Gustavus, daily at 11 a.m. Leaves Gustavus at 5:45 p.m. May 18–September 11, 1998. **Auk Nu Tours**, (800) 820-2628, 586-6444, US and Canada. Carries kayaks, bicycles, pets in carriers, by reservation. Adult $45 one way, $85 round trip. Children under 2 free, with reservation. No unaccompanied minors under 18. Kayak $40, bicycle $10.

From park headquarters at Bartlett Cove, you can take camping gear and a kayak "up bay" on the concessionaire's boat. For a drop-off fee, you can be left at camping spots. You'll be picked up some days later, or you may want to camp and paddle your way back down the bay to Bartlett Cove. You can thereby have a longer trip in this wild area for little more than the overnight trip.

There is a small extra charge for kayaks taken as luggage on the Alaska ferry to Juneau. **Taku Taxi** in Juneau will carry them on top. Tell the dispatcher you have kayaks when you call to be sure of getting a cab with rack. Airlines and chrters donKayaks are available for rent in Gustavus and park headquarters at Bartlett Cove, so you don't have to bring them.

The Park Service has a helpful information sheet for back country users and conducts camper orientation sessions daily at Bartlett Cove in summer. Kayaks to be dropped off the following day are loaded on the dayboat the night before. Arrangements must be made with the lodge.

Most cruise ships sailing the Inside Passage offer a day in Glacier Bay with a Park Service naturalist. Some air/boat packages as well as some charter boat trips include overnights.

Gustavus is an attractive, quiet settlement with enough outdoor activities to keep adults and families happily occupied for days—fishing for halibut and salmon, whalewatching, hiking along the rivers and beaches, bicycling, kayaking, and taking the excursion boat up to the glaciers one day. It's even a good honeymoon spot for those who don't need nightlife!

FOR INFORMATION about the park, write **Glacier Bay National Park**, Box 140, Gustavus, AK 99826. 697-2230. http:www.nps.gov/glba e-mail: GLBA_Administration@nps.gov Good people to call for bear information, and suggestions for trips at all times, especially off-season, when the lodge is closed and excursion boats and some flights aren't running. **Gustavus Visitor Association** has a brochure, info on inns and bed & breakfasts, as well as numerous charter boats for fishing or nature tours. Box 167. Gustavus, AK 99826. 697-2288.

## Hotels and Lodges

**Annie Mae Lodge**—Box 80, Gustavus, AK 99826. 697-2346, fax 697-2211. Family owned 11-room lodge near Good River. Good food, wildlife watching, hiking, biking. Glacier Bay tours and fishing optional. Courtesy van. Package includes meals, bicycle, and ground transportation to airport and Bartlett Cove, Single $130–145, Double $215–240, Child under 12, $92.50. Open all year. e-mail: anniemae@cheerful.com web: www.anniemae.com

**Fairweather Lodge**—Box 148, Gustavus, AK 99826. 697-2334. Three rooms with four beds each. Package tours include guided fishing for halibut and salmon, 5 days all inclusive except airfare, $2000. Room and all meals, adult $125. Room and breakfast $65. Open May 27–September 20.

**Glacier Bay Country Inn**—Box 5, Gustavus, AK, 99826. 697-2288, fax

Co-owner Joanne Lesh gathers fresh vegetables and flowers from the garden at Gustavus Inn. Inn's meals are famous, and Joanne has a cookbook with her recipes.

697-2289. E-mail: gbci@thor.he.net. Website: www.glacierbayalaska.com. Open April–September. Secluded retreat with 6 rooms, 5 cabins, private baths. Glacier Bay boat/plane tours and fishing charters arranged. Offers fishing, whalewatching, and sightseeing on 65' yacht (Grand Pacific Charters). Single $183, Double $322, cabins $352, double, add'l. $85, includes meals, snacks, airport transfers, use of bicycles. Child, aged 3–12, $50/day.

**Glacier Bay Lodge**—Open May 15–September 10. For info and reservations all year: Glacier Bay Park Concessions, Inc., 520 Pike St., Ste. 1400, Seattle, WA 98101. (206) 623-2417 in Seattle. Toll-free from U.S. and Canada (800) 451-5952, fax (206) 623-7809. Lodge (907) 697-2226. E-mail: gbinfo@cruisetours.com Web: www.glacierbaytours.com 56 rooms, dining room, lounge, gift shop, day and overnight tour boats, kayaking, whale-watching. Package tours available from Juneau: 2 day/1 night tour $481, 3 day/2 night $563.50/person. A one-day fly/cruise trip from Juneau to Bartlett Cove, up to the glaciers and back is $346.50. Tours from Haines and Skagway higher. Single $142, Double room $165. Dormitory, $28.

**Glacier Bay's Bear Track Inn**—P.O. Box 255, Gustavus, AK 99826. (888) 697-2284, locally 697-3017, fax 697-2284. e-mail: Beartrac@aol.com Web: www.beartrackinn.com Open May 8–September 15. New, expansive log lodge with 14 rooms, 2 handicapped accessible, large, with 2 queen beds each, private baths. Second floor rooms have great views. Conference room. Glacier tours, charters, fishing, whale watching, kayak trips available. Package rates include air transportation from/to Juneau, ground transportation, lodging, and meals. Per person, double ocupancy, one night/two days $393, two nights/three days $633. Add'l day packages.

**Gustavus Inn**—Box 60, Gustavus 99826. All year, (800) 649-5220. Summmer phone, 697-2254, fax 697-2255. Open May 15-Sept. 15. Winter address: 7920 Outlook, Prairie Village, KS 66208. Fax (913) 649-5220. Family, farm style, fireplace, private baths, 14 rooms (one handicapped accessible). Meals famous, feature home-grown produce, local seafood. Glacier Bay fishing/ sightseeing packages available. All inclusive tour, one night/two days, $310/adult, $155/child, all meals, lodging, transfers, all day cruise to Glacier Bay's West Arm. Can arrange flights to/from Juneau, overnight Glacier Bay cruises, whalewatching and fishing charters on lodge's four boats. Daily rate, including all meals, bicycles, fishing poles, transfers to/ from airport and Bartlett Cove, $135 per adult, $67.50 per child 4–12, ocean-view rooms with shared bath $10 less.

**A Puffin's Bed & Breakfast**—Box 3, Gustavu, AK 99826. 697-2260, fax 697-2258. In Alaska (800) 478-2258. E-mail: puffin@compuserve.com Web: http://www.compuserve.com/homepages/puffin Open May 10–Sept. 10. Five cabins among trees, with attached private baths. Wheelchair accessible cabin. Bicycles and full breakfast included. Central lodge, coin-op laundry, covered picnic area with microwave and refrig. Single/Double $85. $20/add'l. adult. Senior and child rates. House for up to 6 people with kitchen and laundry, $125 double. Package rates with boat tours, air fares to Juneau, Haines, Skagway. Offers fishing and sightseeing charters, kayak rentals.

**Salmon River Cabin Rentals**—Box 13, Gustavus, AK 99826. 697-2245. Housekeeping cabins with pvt. bath, oil heat, well separated in mossy woods. Bicycles. Transportation available for Glacier Bay tours. Free airport and dock pickup. Cabins $70/day double. $350/week. Cabins can serve families with children. Mid-May– mid-September.

**Whalesong Lodge**—Box 389, Gustavus, AK 99826. Same phone and ownership as Glacier Bay Country Inn above, an alternative for families and groups. Four attractive rooms with private baths and one 3 bedroom apartment with kitchen. Rooms $140/person including breakfast. Add'l meals available. Apartment $299 without meals, up to 6 people.

### Bed & Breakfasts

**Aimee's Guest House,** 697-2306. **The Bear's Nest,** 697-2440. **Fairweather Lodge,** 697-2334. **Faraway Nearby Studio Cottage,** 697-2429. **Growley**

**Bear,** 697-2730. **Good River Bed & Breakfast,** 697-2241. **Noah's Ark,** 697-2307. **Spruce Tip Lodge,** 697-2215. **TRI Bed & Breakfast,** 697-2425. Accommodations vary from rooms in house to nearby cabins, some with kitchens. All can arrange tours to the glaciers, take you to the day boat that goes from Bartlett Cove to the glaciers, and offer guided fishing or arrange it.

*Note*: When comparing cost of Gustavus inns, ask if rate includes transfers to/from airport and/or Bartlett Cove. Several loan bicycles for exploring around Gustavus. Some loan fishing gear for fishing in rivers or from dock and beach.

## Campgrounds

**Bartlett Cove**, in park. Walking distance from lodge, on shore. Pit toilets, bearproof food caches. Seals and whales often just offshore. Can sometimes buy fresh seafood from commercial fishing boats at dock. Pets allowed in Bartlett Cove area on leash, but not allowed in back country.

## Boats

EXCURSION boat cruise from Bartlett Cove on *M/V Spirit of Adventure*, $156.50 round-trip to glaciers, includes lunch. Child under 12 $78.25. Infant under 2 free. Boat cruise with drop off and pick up service for hikers or kayakers at any of several specified points, $168.10 per person.

Whalewatching, 1/2 day, $89. Overnight cruises on Wilderness *Explorer* to glaciers. **Glacier Bay Tours and Cruises,** (800) 451-5952.

CHARTERS for fishing, whalewatching, and exploring Glacier Bay are offered by many Gustavus operators and can be arranged by your lodge, or call the Visitors Association for a list. 697-2288.

MOORAGE, but no dock space, fuel at Bartlett Cove. Private boats need permit from National Park Service to enter park during June, July, and August.

KAYAK rentals from **Glacier Bay Sea Kayaks** in Gustavus. 697-2257. May 15-Sept. 15. **Spirit Walker Expeditions,** 697-2266, (800) 478-9255 in Alaska, offers guided kayak trips, 1-7 days. **Alaska Discovery** offers guided kayak 1-9 day trips. (800) 586-1911.

## Facilities

Gustavus has gift shops, an art gallery, restaurants, and a hair salon.

GROCERIES: **Beartrack Mercantile,** 1/4 Mile, Dock Rd., 697-2358. Groceries, camping supplies, batteries, film. Open Mon.–Sat. For boat orders delivered, call VHF "WRS 957".

CAFES: **Strawberry Point Cafe,** 1/4 mile, Dock Rd., 697-2227. Lunch and dinner Mon.–Sat. **The Bear's Nest,** Wilson Rd., 697-2440. Breakfast, lunch, dinner. Healthy fare (including emu!) , seafood.

SMOKED FISH: **The Salmon River Smokehouse**, 697-2330. On main road, west side of Salmon River. Sell smoked fish or will process your salmon, halibut, trout. Open 9–9.

FISHING SUPPLIES, LICENSES: **Gusto**, 1/4 Mile Dock Rd. 697-2297.

TAXI: **TLC Taxi**, 697-2239.

GOLF: **Mt. Fairweather Golf Course**, 9 holes plus driving range. Golf clubs and push carts available.

CAR RENTAL: **BW Auto Rental**, 697-2403. Has cars, pickups. $50 a day. For family or group rental may be cheaper than transfers or taxi to park, airport, etc.

FUEL: **Gustavus Dray**, 697-2299, on and across from airport. Plane, boat, car, and stove fuels, lubricants.

AIRFIELD: Runways at Gustavus Airport 7,500' and 5,000' paved. Avgas 100LL and Jet A fuel, **Gustavus Dray**, 697-2299. Radio repeater 122.5 to Juneau on field.

The Rainbow Glacier near Haines and its attendant waterfall.

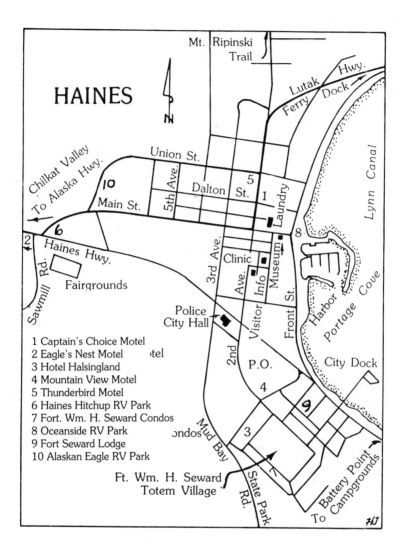

# HAINES

1 Captain's Choice Motel
2 Eagle's Nest Motel        tel
3 Hotel Halsingland
4 Mountain View Motel
5 Thunderbird Motel
6 Haines Hitchup RV Park
7 Fort. Wm. H. Seward Condos
8 Oceanside RV Park
9 Fort Seward Lodge
10 Alaskan Eagle RV Park

# HAINES
## (Area Code 907, Zip Code 99827)

CHILKAT INDIANS lived in this area and traded with inland natives long before John Muir and S. Hall Young arrived in 1879 and selected it as a mission site. The mission was established in 1881, followed by salmon canneries, mining, and an army post in 1903. During the Klondike Rush this was the southern end of the Dalton Trail, a toll road over which stock could be driven to supply meat to the northern settlements. The Haines Highway, connecting the Inside Passage with the Alaska Highway, generally follows the Dalton Trail. Today Haines (pop. 2,500) has a large fishing fleet, and the hotels and other tourist facilities that mark the end of the Marine Highway and the beginning of the land road to interior Alaska. Near the ferry docks, a tank farm marks the end of a six-inch oil pipeline to Fairbanks, built in 1953 and now in dead storage.

Haines has attracted many artists in a variety of media. You will find their work in local galleries and stores. An enthusiastic small theater group performs its own productions.

Bald eagles are a big attraction, in fall and winter, at the Chilkat Bald Eagle Preserve along the Chilkat River flats between Mile 8 and Mile 31 out of Haines. The river has warm springs running into it, so it seldom freezes and supports a late fall salmon run, providing the eagles with a dependable food supply. The largest known congregation of bald eagles meets here to fish and spend hours perched in snowy trees along the highway. Over 3,000 have been counted here in a single day! November is the peak month, but you'll see many from October through January.

As 250–400 eagles nest in the Haines area, you will see them fishing and perched in trees all year. Several nests are near the ferry dock.

### To See and Do

Tour Fort William H. Seward, 5 miles from ferry, just south of town. Walking-tour brochures are available at the Visitor Center.

Visit the **Alaska Indian Arts** workshop and totem village (on walking tour). Watch totem carving, and purchase crafts made here.

See the Chilkat Indian dancers in authentic costumes. **Chilkat Center for the Arts**. Adult $10, Student under 18, $5. Children under 5, free. Five miles from ferry at Ft. William H. Seward. Phone/fax 766-2160 or ask at the Visitor Information Center for times of performances.

Enjoy a salmon bake over alderwood fire, served at the **Chilkat Raven** tribal house, Port Chilkoot. All you can eat. Beer and wine served. Daily except Thursday, June through August, 5 p.m.–8.p.m. Adult $21.75, Child $12.75. Information at Hotel Halsingland, 766-2000.

The Sheldon Museum and the town center of Haines.

Visit **Sheldon Museum**, 5 miles from ferry, Main St. Historic native artifacts, changing exhibits, video and slide shows. Open daily in summer. 766-2366. Hours as posted, or ask at Visitor Center. Adults over 18, $3.

Visit the **American Bald Eagle Foundation's** natural history museum at Haines Highway and 2nd Ave. Wildlife exhibits with over 100 examples of local birds, fish, and animals, video of eagles' fall gathering, gift shop. Non-profit, supports education, habitat preservation, research. Open daily 10 a.m.–6 p.m. $2.

Walk down to the boat harbor where 65 fishing boats are based all year, in addition to several hundred during fishing season. Watch fishermen mending nets and get close-up look at the different types of boats and gear used in Alaska.

Watch salmon pass fish weir in the Chilkoot River, below Chilkoot Lake, about 5+ miles north (to the right) of the ferry terminal, June–October.

See Rainbow Glacier, a hanging glacier which doesn't reach the bottom of the mountain, from Mud Bay Rd. across inlet from Chilkat State Park.

Fish in Lynn Canal and Chilkat River for salmon, in Lynn Canal for halibut, and in Chilkoot Lake for trophy cutthroat trout, Dolly Varden and salmon. Fishing charters available. Haines Visitor Center has a current list.

Watch bald eagles at the 48,000-acre Chilkat Bald Eagle Preserve on the Chilkat River flats along the Haines Highway. Although many eagles nest in the preserve, the greatest number are there October through December, especially between Miles 18 and 21 from Haines.

*Note:* Truck traffic along the narrow road is fast, so you should use the newly-developed pullouts which are good eagle-watching view-points with interpretive displays, restrooms, and a paved walkway. The eagles will be disturbed and fly away when approached closely, but you can watch easily from the pullouts and get good photos. They often perch for hours on the same branch, making photography easy. Dress warmly and bring a hot thermos. Rental cars and tours are available in Haines if you don't bring your own vehicle. The Haines Visitor Center has a brochure on the Eagle Preserve.

Hike the trails up Mt. Ripinsky, Mt. Riley, or 7-Mile Saddle for grand views down Lynn Canal and over surrounding mountains.

Visit Chilkat State Park on Mud Bay Road. Visitor Center, camping, picnicking, boat launch, dock, trails. Some programs in summer. Dates open according to snow. Great scenery.

See old salmon cannery at Letnikof Cove on Mud Bay Road.

Hike trails on Chilkat Peninsula. Get "Haines is for Hikers" brochure, with maps, descriptions, and distances for hikes along the shore of the peninsula, on the Chilkat River Flats, and up nearby mountains. In winter, cross-country skiing and snowmobiling are popular on some trails and back roads.

Fly over Glacier Bay and the Juneau Icefield. Air charters are available at Haines Airport. The Visitor Center has infomation. **Mountain Flying Service**, 766-3007, offers tours of Glacier Bay and a beach landing on the outer coast of the Gulf of Alaska for beachcombing.

Tour Haines by bus on longer ferry stops. Most southbound ferries stop in Haines about two hours. Though the dock is five miles from town, there is bus service and perhaps time for shopping or a tour if you have boarded at Skagway. Bus meets ferries, in summer only.

Drive the Golden Circle in whole or part, from Haines to Haines Junction, Whitehorse, and Skagway, returning to Haines by ship. With daily ferry service between Haines and Skagway in summer 1998, this is a convenient, *very* scenic trip! Vehicles can be rented or stored in Haines.

Take a walking tour of town including the waterfront park. Get a self-guiding brochure at the Visitor Center.

Enjoy the library with a good Alaska section, newspapers, restrooms. Browsers welcome.

Go on a guided nature tour with **Alaska Nature Tours**, 766-2876. Tours

A special sighting in southeast Alaska. A moose emerges from a swim in Haines.

feature forest and Chilkat River flats. Hikes, nature walks, photography with naturalists. You'll see some eagles any time of year though the greatest concentration is in fall. Daily tours mid-May to mid-September. Winter tours by appointment in the preserve. 3-hour tour, Saturday special , . and 6-hour tour.

Tour Chilkoot Lake in launch with **Chilkoot Lake Tours,** 766-2891, for fishing, wildlife watching, photography.

Rent a bicycle to explore Haines, Port Chilkoot, Chilkat State Park, and ride up to Chilkat Lake on your own. They also rent kayaks. **Sockeye Cycles** in Fort Seward, 766-2869.

Rent single or double kayaks with complete gear, or go on a guided trip with **Deishu Expeditions & Alaska Kayak Supply,** Portage Street just above cruise ship dock. 766-2427.

Golfers try the **Weeping Trout Sports Resort** 9-hole course near Chilkoot Lake where you can also catch trophy cutthroat trout. 766-2827.

Winter visitors enjoy cross-country skiing and snowmobiling on logging and mine roads near Haines. Haines has generally drier snow than Juneau. Call the **Visitor Center** for dates of winter holidays, snowmobile races.

INFORMATION AVAILABLE at 2nd and Willard St., downtown, **Haines Visitor Center,** P.O. Box 530, Haines, AK 99827. 766-2234, (800) 458-3579 in U.S. and Canada. Fax 766-3155. 8 a.m.–8 p.m., daily in summer, 8 a,m,–

10 p.m. Monday through Thursday. Shorter winter hours. They have hiking information and bird lists. U.S. Forest Service and Alaska State Parks have a summer office in town.

## Transportation

FERRIES: **Alaska Marine Highway**. Ships run daily in summer. Dock is 4 miles north of town on Lutak Inlet. 766-2113 or 766-2111.

Take a side trip to Skagway with **Haines-Skagway Water Taxi**, 766-3395 and (800) 766-3395. Two round trips daily between Haines and Skagway for walk-on passengers only, $32 round trip, from Haines small boat harbor. **Chilkat Cruises,** 766-2100 or (888) 766-2103, offers 2–3 round trips daily from Port Chilkoot. Both companies offer package tours including a White Pass train ride from Skagway. Boat tickets available at docks or most hotels in either town.

BUS: Runs to and from ferry dock and airport. Stops at all hotels. **Haines Tours & Taxi**, 766-3138, also has tours of Haines and Fort Wm. H. Seward during ferry stops. May–September.

**Alaskon Express** to Tok, Glennallen, Anchorage, Whitehorse. Ferry dock (meets Bellingham ferry), and 277 Main St. downtown. Division of Grayline. Toll-free in cont. U.S. (800) 544-2206. Runs Tuesday, Thursday, and Sunday, so it's best to call for info.

BUS TOURS (local): **Haines Tour & Taxi**, 766-3138. **Yeshua Guided Tours**, 766-2334. Local fishing and photography, also bus tours to Yukon.

TAXI: **Haines Tour & Taxi**, 766-3138. Offers all year transport between town and ferry dock. **New Other Guys Taxi**, 766-3257.

CAR RENTALS: **Eagle's Nest Car Rental**, Eagle's Nest Motel, 766-2891. **Avis,** Halsingland Hotel, 766-2733. **Captain's Choice Motel Car Rental**, 766-3111.

DRIVE-OFF FERRY SERVICE (for cars whose drivers don't accompany them): **Ward's Transport**, 766-2221. If you put your car on the ferry with reservation to Haines, but want to stop off en route without it, these people can drive it off and store it by prior arrangement.

AIR: **LAB Flying Service**, Box 272, Haines, AK 99827, 766-2222. Juneau office: **Wings of Alaska**. Haines office: 766-2030. Juneau office: 789-0790. **Haines Airways**, Box 61, Haines, AK 99827. 766-2646. **Mountain Flying Service,** 766-2665 and (800)766-4007. Most have scheduled service to Juneau and Skagway, plus charters.

BAGGAGE STORAGE at hotels for patrons, on day of departure. Also at ferry terminal.

## Hotels

Sales tax 5.5% additional. In Haines the line between hotels and bed & breakfasts is blurred. Former officers' quarters in Fort Seward have been converted into hotels, condos and B &Bs with more rooms than usual in B & Bs. A third of the rooms are open all year. Check with Visitor Center for additional facilities added recently. Bus stops at all hotels en route to ferry in summer.

**Captain's Choice Motel**—5 miles, downtown Haines, corner 2nd and Dalton. Box 392, Haines, AK 99827. 766-3111, fax 766-3332. (800) 478-2345 in Alaska and Canada. (800) 247-7153 in Lower 48. 40 rooms. TV, Showtime, phone, refrigerators, room service, courtesy coffee, view of Lynn Canal. Rental cars, tour booking. Courtesy transfers. Single $91, Double $98. Pets allowed, some rooms, $10.

**Chilkat Eagle B & B**—5.5 miles from ferry in Fort Seward, adjacent to Chilkat Center for the Arts. Box 387, Haines, AK 99827. 766-2763, fax 766-3651. 4 rooms, 2 share each bath. Full breakfast, diets OK. Non-smoking. Multi-lingual. Art gallery. Single $65, Double $75. Winter & multi-day ratesr. Ferry shuttle $3/person. Open all year. e-mail: eaglebb@kcd.com web: www.kcd.com/eaglebb

**Dalton Street Cottages**—5 miles from ferry, 116 6th & Dalton St. Box 1528, Haines, AK 99827. 766-3123. Cottages for 2–4, private bath, kitchenette, deck, phone, microwave. Smoking outside only. Hot tub available. Single/Double $75, $10 ea. add'l. Open May–Sept. and late fall.

**Eagle's Nest Motel**—5 miles from ferry, 3.5 miles from airport. Haines Highway at Sawmill Rd. Box 250, Haines, AK 99827. 766-2891, fax 766-2848. (800) 354-6009. 13 rooms, some kitchenettes, 7 doubles, all with queen-sized beds. Color TV, Showtime, courtesy coffee. Single $75, Double $85, Twin $95. Car rentals. Walking distance to downtown. e-mail: eagles_nest@wytbear.com web: eaglesnest.wytbear.com

**Fort Seward Bed & Breakfast**—5.5 miles from ferry, in Fort Seward. House # 1 Seward Drive. Mail: Box 5, Haines, AK 99827. 766-2856, (800) 615-NORM. Website:www.haines.ak.us/norm// Former officers quarters. Full breakfast. Handicap access, non-smoking. Courtesy transfer from airport or ferry. Single $74, Double $84–110. Suite $110–198. Add'l. $28. Children welcome. Open April 15–October 15. e-mail: fortseward@yahoo.com

**Fort Seward Condos**—5.5 miles from ferry in Fort Seward. Gregg Enterprises, Box 75, Haines, AK 99827. 766-2425 phone & fax. Converted apartments in officers' quarters at historic Ft. Wm. H. Seward. 1 and 2 bedrooms, some with fireplaces, overlooking bay and mountains, fully e-quipped with kitchens. $90 per day, 2 day minimum, $540 weekly, $900 monthly. www.hp11/haines.ak.us/condos

**Fort Seward Lodge**—5.5 miles from ferry. Box 307-B, Haines, AK 99827. 766-2009. (800) 478-7772. Ten rooms in former Post Exchange. Courtesy van, deck with Lynn Canal view. Restaurant featuring seafood. Rooms with private bath, Single $60, Double $70. Shared bath, Single $45, Double $55. Ocean view rooms with kitchenettes Single $75, Double $85. Open all year. web: www.fortsewardlodge.com

**Hotel Halsingland**—5.5 miles from ferry, 4 miles from airport, in Fort Seward. Mail: Box 1589, Haines, AK 99827. 766-2000, fax 766-2445. (800) 542-6363 in U.S. (800) 478-2525 in Yukon and B.C. 60 rooms. Restaurant, cocktail lounge, salmon bake, gift shop, car rental. Courtesy transfer from ferry. Building was the commanding officer's house in Fort Seward. Single $89. Double $93. Twin $97. Economy rooms with shared bath from $49-59. Fall rates after Sept. 30. Open Mar. 1–Nov. 30.

**Mountain View Motel**—5.5 miles from ferry, 151 Mud Bay Rd., Port Chilkoot. Mail: Box 62, Haines, AK 99827. 766-2900. Fax: 766-2901. (800) 478-2902 in Alaska, B.C., and Yukon. Seven housekeeping units. TV, Showtime. Single $69.30. Double $74.55. Triple $79.80. Open all year. Pets OK.

**Officers Inn**—5.5 miles from ferry, in Fort Seward. Box 1589, Haines, AK 99827. 766-2000, fax 766-2445. (800) 542-6363 in U.S. In Yukon and B.C., call (800) 478-2525. 14 rooms in former officer's house, Fort Seward. Views, phones, TV, fireplaces. Private & shared baths. Courtesy transfers. Senior rates. Reserve with Hotel Halsingland. Breakfast included. Well behaved pets allowed. Private bath, Single $84, Double $89. Twin $94. Shared bath, Single $50, Double $55. Open May 15–Sept. 15.

**Officer's Suites**—5.5 miles from ferry, in Fort Seward. Box 1589, Haines, AK 99827. 766-2000 or (800) 542-6363, fax 766-2445. Victorian house on Officer's Row has 1 and 2 bedroom suites with full kitchens, TV, courtesy transfers, 2 verandas, barbecue. $95-125. Open March 1-Dec. 1.

**Pyramid Island B&B**—6.5 miles from ferry, 1.5 miles from Port Chilkoot on Mud Bay Rd., facing water and Pyramid Island. Box 604, Haines, AK 99827. 766-2771. Apartment and 2 rooms, 2 bathrooms, kitchen, living room, TV and deck. Good for family or group.Single $85, Double $95–125. Weekly and winter rates. Open all year. e-mail: pyramid@wytbear.com web: www.wytbear.com/pyramid

**A Sheltered Harbor B & B**—5.5 miles from ferry, 57 Beach Rd. on waterfront, upstairs with balcony facing channel. Box 806, Haines, AK 99827. 766-2741. 5 rooms with pvt. bath, TV, phone. Gazebo in yard, barbecue. Breakfast included. Single $75, Double $85. Suite $115. Open all year.

**The Summer Inn Bed & Breakfast**—5 miles from ferry in town at 117 Second Ave. Mail: Box 1198, Haines, AK 99827. 766-2970. Fax: 766-2970.

Chilkoot Lake is a favorite and beautiful spot for fishing, boating, picnicking and camping.

Five rooms, shared bath, views, breakfast. Single $75, Double $85, Triple, $100. Open all year.

**Thunderbird Motel**—5 miles from ferry, downtown, Dalton and 2nd. Mail: Box 589, Haines, AK 99827. 766-2131, fax 766-2045. (800) 327-2556. 20 units (6 have kitchenettes), restaurant and bar around corner on 2nd. Phone, TV. Small pets allowed. Senior & military discounts. Single $70, Double $80. Triple $90. Kitchenette $115. Open all year.

Additional B&Bs not inspected: **River House B&B**, Box 1173, Haines, AK 99827. 766-3215, (888) 766-3215. web: www.rhbb.com **Inn-Between B&B** 766-2057. web: www.kcd.com/innbetween

**Youth Hostel**—6 miles from ferry, 1.5 miles from post office on Small Tract Rd. **Bear Creek Camp & Hostel**, Box 908, Haines, AK 99827. Phone/ fax 766-2259. Cooking facilities, laundry. Cabins surround lawn with hot tub. Bunks in dorms, $14. Family cabins $38/2 people, add'l. $4. Tent space $8/1 person, $4/add'l. Bike rentals $10/day. Cabins open April through December. Dorms open May 1–September 30. Ferry shuttle $3 person each way—call from terminal. Meets ferries in summer. e-mail: hostel@kco.com

### Wilderness Cabins

**Chilkat Wilderness Lodge**—at headwaters of Chilkat River. Box 881, Haines, AK 99827. 766-2665, 766-2349. Fishing, hiking, photography. Open year around.

**Alaska Cross Country Guiding & Rafting**—31 miles from ferry, Mile 26 on Haines Hwy. Box 124, Haines, AK 99827. 767-5522. Housekeeping cabins open year-round near Klehini River in the bald eagle preserve. Also outlying wilderness cabins. Rafting, hunting, photography, winter x-c skiing and snowshoeing.

## Campgrounds

STATE (Camping $10 per vehicle, or $100 for annual pass. Day parking $2 per vehicle, or $25 for annual pass):

**Chilkat State Park**—7 miles, Mud Bay Road. 32 vehicle spaces and 12 hike-in-camper spaces. Boat launch, dock. Tent pads, picnic tables, fireplaces, restrooms, water. Open dates according to snow. Note that the land just *outside* the entrance is private and camping is not allowed on it.

**Chilkoot Lake State Recreation Site**—5 miles to right of ferry dock on Lutak Road; 10 miles from town. 32 spaces, some with lake view. Picnic tables, restrooms, water pump, fishing, boat launch.

**Portage Cove**—1 mile from town, 7 miles from ferry, on Beach Road. Limited spaces. Tent campers and picnickers. Picnic tables, water, toilets. Scenic. No vehicles.

**Mosquito Lake Campground**—32 miles from ferry, Mile 27 Haines Highway. Turn off at Mosquito Lake Rd. 7 spaces. Fishing, boat launch.

PRIVATE (plus 5% tax): **Port Chilkoot Camper Park**—5.5 miles from ferry, Port Chilkoot. Box 473, Haines AK 99827. 766-2755. All facilities, showers, laundromat. Sixty spaces, most with electricity and wate—no pull-throughs, but spaces are large. Dump station. Full hookups $15, electrical only $12.50, without hookups $10. Tent space $6.75. Walking distance to town. Wooded.

**Alaskan Eagle RV Park**—5 miles from ferry, downtown at end of 6th Street. Box 28, Haines, AK 99827. 766-2335. 52 spaces, 30 with full hookups including cable TV, $18/day. 22 with electricity only, $15/day. Tent camping, $12 for 2 people. Showers, dump station. Laundry for guests. Good Sam park. Senior discounts.

**Haines Hitch Up RV Park**—5 miles from ferry, 1/2 mile west of downtown, 851 Main St. Mail: Box 383, Haines, AK 99827. 766-2882. 92 spaces, (20 are pull-throughs). Full hookups, $21–25. Laundromat, restrooms, and gift shop. Cable TV sites available. Open May 1–September 30. e-mail: hitchuprv@aol.com

**Oceanside RV Park**—5 miles from ferry, Front and Main near museum. Box 149, Haines, AK 99827. 766-2437, fax 766-2832. 20 spaces with full hookups including cable TV. $18. Open May 1–September 30.

**Salmon Run Adventures RV Campground**—1.8 miles to right from ferry dock, 7 Mile Lutak Rd. Box 1122, Haines, AK 99827. 723-4229. 30 sites, restrooms, showers, tables, firepits, 1/2 mile waterfront. $12.50 for 1 tent.

2 cabins sleeping 4 each, elec. & heat, use shared bath in lodge, no kitchens, $45. Has charter fishing boat.

**Swan's Rest RV Park**—Mile 27 Haines Hwy., plus 3 miles gravel road, near Mosquito Lake.Box 2860, Haines, AK 99827. Phone/fax 767-5662. RV sites $15, tent $5. Cabin $80. Overlooking lake.

PARKING is allowed off pavement toward town from dock along first 1/4 mile of road, though not recommended due to chance of vandalism. Overnight parking is done here "all the time."

## Facilities

ICE: **A & P, Alaskan Liquor Store, Howser's Supermarket, Pioneer Bar and Liquor Store, Haines Quick Shop.** Freezer space rental: Bear Den Mall, Main St. across from the museum.

PROPANE: **Eagle Chevron**, Mile 0 Haines Hwy., **B & L Service**, 1 Mile Haines Hwy. at Totem Oil, **33 Mile Roadhouse**, 33 Mile Haines Hwy.

DIESEL FUEL: **Valley Fuel Service** (50 gal. minimum), **Charlie's Repair, 2nd Ave.**

CAR WASH: Union and Main St. *Note*: Southbound vehicle owners who wash their cars before loading on the ferry's crowded car deck will save their own clothes and others' from rubbing on dust-covered cars.

DUMP STATIONS **Eagle Chevron**, 0 Mile Haines Hwy. **Eagle Camper Park**, 751 Union St. **Charlie's Repair**, Second Ave. on way to ferry. **B & L Service** at Totem Oil, Main St. and Haines Hwy. at Y in the road.

CLINIC: **Lynn Canal Medical Center**, 766-2521, South 2nd St., doctors, nurses. Dentist on Main St.

HORSE STALLS & EXERCISE AREA: Three transient box stalls available, more by arrangement, except during Southeast Alaska State Fair in August $5/night, negotiable if left clean. Riding area. 766-2476, or 2478. Southeast Alaska Fairgrounds at southwest edge of town. For trailers or vans of horses going between South Central Alaska and the Lower 48, this is probably the best place en route to give them a break.

LAUNDROMATS: **Port Chilkoot Camper Park**—Port Chilkoot, 10 a.m. to 10 p.m. **Haines Quick Laundry**, also has showers, restrooms. Open 7 a.m.–midnight, daily. Between Fort Seward and the post office. **Susie Q's**—Main St., across from museum. Has showers.

## Boats

Launching facilities at small boat harbor. Fuel available. For charters see Visitor Center or harbor bulletin board. Several fishing charter boats and guides operate in summer and fall. Hunting guides are also available in Haines for deer, goat, and bear hunting.

RIVER RAFT TOURS: There are several operators working out of Haines in summer. The following outfitters run trips on the Chilkat, Alsek, Tatshenshini, and other rivers: **Chilkat River Guides**, Box 170, Haines, AK 99827. 776-2409. **Alaska Cross Country Guiding & Rafting**, Box 124, Haines, AK 99827. 776-5522. Open year around. **Alaska River Expeditions** specializes in raft trips on the Arctic North Slope, and runs 10-day trips on the Tatshenshini River, with trips starting from Haines. 419 K Street, Salt Lake City, UT 84103. (801) 322-0233.

## Happenings

**King Salmon Derby,** May 22–24, 29–31, Memorial Day weekend. Great prizes. 766-2490.

**5th Annual Alaska Mardi Gras,** June 6. Alaska style, costumes, contests. 766-2000.

**Summer Solstice Celebration,** June 19. 766-2476. Also **Kluane to Chilkat Bicycle Relay,** 160 miles. 766-2869.

**Independence Day,** July 4. Parade, contest, fireworks.

**Southeast Alaska State Fair** at the fairgrounds on the southwest edge of town, August 11–15, 1999 regional fair with crafts, logging contests, carnival, parade, and horse show. 766-2476.

**Bald Eagle Music Festival** with day and evening performances, August 11–15, 1999. 766-2476.

**Sam Donajkowski Memorial Triathlon.** Run, bike, & swim, August 9, 1998. Team and individual competition. 766-2700. Chip Lende has info.

**4th Annual Alaska Bald Eagle Festival**, November 11–14, 1999. Speakers, seminars (including bird handling, slideshows, photography workshops, tours of preserve, entertainment. (800) 246-6268.

**Alcan 200 Snowmachine Race**, January 2000, dates TBA. 200 mile race from the Canadian border on the Haines Highway to Dezadeash Lake and back. Oval track races on the frozen river. Auction. 766-2503.

Ask at the Visitor Center about performances and exhibits by local and touring artists. Winter and spring are busy times in this cultural town. In spring and summer, there are bicycle and running races, often up surrounding mountains.

Haines was a busy place during the Klondike Gold Rush. The Dalton Trail, which the Haines Highway follows, was an important route north, the only one on which stock could be driven. Cattle were driven to provide food for the stampeders. The local Indians had long used it as a trading route, and made money druing the gold rush carrying loads for miners and traders.

CUSTOMS: U.S. and Canadian customs stations are about 40 miles out of Haines on the Haines Hwy. They are closed from midnight to 8 a.m. and there are no facilities in the area or for some miles north. Requirements for Canadian customs are described at the end of the Prince Rupert section.

## UP THE HIGHWAY (THE LAND ONE!)

From Haines it's 775 miles to Anchorage and 653 miles to Fairbanks. The Klondike Highway from Skagway to Whitehorse is partly gravel. Even in summer, you will enjoy the trip more as well as be safer if you don't try to hurry, but drive at reasonable speed, allowing for wildlife around the next bend. At night those animals are hard to see. Drive a reasonable number of hours per day and pull off to enjoy views or rest. Gas stations and mechanical service are far apart. Carry a few spares and basic tools as well as the service manual for your car. Screen protection for your headlights and radiator from flying rocks is recommended. So are a tow chain, flares, and extra water and fuel cans (which are best filled after you get off the ferry as they can't be stored on your car on the ship).

In winter all the above precautions apply, plus others. Think of Wyoming in January for driving conditions. Avoid driving in storms which can lead to white-out conditions and at night when unlit moose find the road an easy trail. With short daylight, you will probably drive some hours in the dark, but be careful. The RCMP, Alaska State Troopers, and the ferry terminals have latest road condition reports. If the weather ahead is awful when you get to Haines, your best bet is to wait a day or more.

If you've driven in Montana in winter, you already know that fuel systems require thought at -25°F and below. Gasoline engines require additives to remove water even above freezing. If you fill a diesel car or truck in Washington with the #2 fuel usually sold there, it will not run at winter temperatures in the Alaskan and Canadian interior. Stations in Haines, Skagway, and Canada do sell #1 diesel for winter use. Using your engine block heater before you start will help. You should carry a heavy duty extension cord to reach the nearest electrical outlet for it.

Be **sure** your car is in good condition for cold weather driving, with good studded snow tires or chains, plenty of antifreeze, winter oil, and engine block heater. Carry a flashlight and spare batteries and shovel and something for traction such as sand, kitty litter, burlap sacks, or pieces of expanded metal screen to put under spinning tires. Have plenty of warm clothes and sleeping bags for everyone in the car. Be prepared to spend the night in the car without running the engine for heat and carbon monoxide, and to be able to walk a few miles for help (if it's more than a very few or there are any vehicles coming by, don't walk). Keep your gas tank

Chilkat River rafters seen from the Haines Highway.

full as bad conditions can force you to drive miles in low gear. Allow enough time for the drive and take more, if needed, to avoid driving while tired or to wait out storms.

Driving to or from Prince Rupert in winter requires the same planning. In rare winters the road may be intermittently closed or cars led through in convoys due to avalanches on the highway between Smithers and Prince Rupert. Keep your speed down on this scenic 2-lane paved road and be prepared for several well-marked sharp turns the road makes across the railroad tracks. It's easy to forget while negotiating those turns to look for the occasional train as well! If you pull off at scenic points, you'll enjoy one of the most beautiful drives in the world.

The Alaska Highway is still an experience to drive even though most of it is paved and many bends have been straightened. In 1942 its construction in less than a year when it was so desperately needed was an incredible achievement. Near Fort Nelson there are more than 70 tractors under the road bed where they sank in the muskeg and the road was built over them. The road served as a supply route for truck traffic and as a major navigational facility and forced-landing strip for planes being ferried to Alaska. It still performs both functions today. The 50th anniversary of the Alaska Highway was commemorated in 1992. On my first flight to Alaska in the 70s I didn't land on it, but took off from it twice when the strips I had landed on were too rough or soft for takeoff.

The Haines Highway, completed in 1943, changed the village from a fishing town and former gold rush trailhead to a modern port and gateway to Alaska and the Yukon.

Broadway in Skagway features the Native Brotherhood Hall and Museum.

# SKAGWAY

(Area Code 907, Zip Code 99840)

SKAGWAY (pop. 800) was founded in 1888 when Captain William Moore and his son settled here. They were overrun by the stampede to the Klondike in 1897. Skagway is at the head of the Taiya Inlet, the northern end of the Inside Passage, and the south end of the White Pass Route. Skagway served the White Pass Trail, and the ghost town of Dyea served the Chilkoot Trail. Both mushroomed into tent and clapboard cities during the winter of 1897–98. Later, when the White Pass and Yukon Railroad was built, Dyea died and Skagway became the main gateway to the Klondike, over 500 miles to the north. In Skagway, Soapy Smith, the notorious con artist, and his gang were expert at separating prospectors from their money and goods. Today the town lives on its historic past, with a good museum and many original buildings. In 1976 Klondike Gold Rush National Park was authorized, including the Chilkoot and White Pass trails, and most of Broadway (the main street of Skagway).

The Klondike Highway is open all year over White Pass to Carcross and on to Whitehorse. For 14 miles it climbs to an altitude of 3,290 feet along the route of the Klondike gold seekers. The scenery is fabulous and the road is paved from Skagway to Whitehorse, 108 miles. You can connect with the Alaska Highway near Whitehorse. There is fishing at lakes along the way if you have the appropriate British Columbia or Yukon fishing

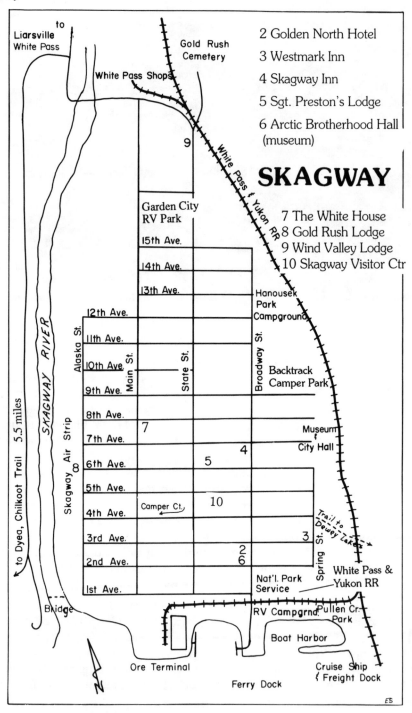

2 Golden North Hotel
3 Westmark Inn
4 Skagway Inn
5 Sgt. Preston's Lodge
6 Arctic Brotherhood Hall (museum)

# SKAGWAY

7 The White House
8 Gold Rush Lodge
9 Wind Valley Lodge
10 Skagway Visitor Ctr

license. At stops to enjoy the view, you can also enjoy the tiny alpine tundra flowers at your feet.

There are several good spots to camp or picnic between the summit and Carcross. There are no facilities other than the customs station between Skagway and Carcross. Carcross has a visitor center in the former White Pass and Yukon train depot, restaurants and gasoline. It is about 31 miles from Carcross on to Whitehorse.

## To See and Do

Explore historic streets and buildings from the Gold Rush days.

Stop at the restored railroad depot on 2nd Avenue and Broadway for exhibits and programs by the National Park Service. Films and talks are given several times daily in summer, as are walking tours of historic features in Skagway. Open daily from mid-May to mid-September. You can get the latest Chilkoot Trail information at the trail center across the street.

Visit the museum on Broadway, inside AB Hall. 9–5 daily from May to September. 983-2420. Very entertaining collection of costumes, tools, photos, and other artifacts from the Klonkdike Gold Rush. Donation, $2 adults, $1 for children.

See the **"Days of '98 Show"** in Eagle's Hall, Broadway and 6th. Adults $14, children $6. Daily mid-May to mid-September, fun gambling starts at 7:30 p.m., the show at 8:30 p.m. Matinee performances and sometimes morning shows on cruise ship days. One-man Soapy Smith show for matinees; full show with gambling, evenings only. Jim Richards as Soapy Smith should *not* be missed! For times see the board in front of the hall. 983-2545.

See **"Buckwheat"** performing "The Cremation of Sam McGee", and other ballads of Robert Service at the National Park Visitor Center, 2nd & Broadway, in June, July, and August.

**Gold Pan Theatre**, 7th & Broadway, 983-3177. Deli, sarsparilla bar, Victorian parlor. June through September.

Most ferries stop long enough in Skagway for a walk around town. Some stops are long enough for a drive to Dyea and the Chilkoot trailhead. Wait and see what time the ship actually arrives before counting on that if you are riding back on the same ship. The longer stops make this a good one-day excursion from Juneau.

Ride the **White Pass & Yukon Railroad** on a 3-hour excursion to the summit of White Pass and back. The historic narrow gauge train runs daily, mid-May through mid-September, leaving at 8:45 a.m. and 1:15 p.m. Trains may run earlier some days—check with **White Pass & Yukon**, (800) 343-7373. Extra trains may run when several cruise ships are in port. Fare adults $78, children 12 and under, $39. Besides enjoying the train experience, you can see more of the historic route from the train than from the highway.

There is scheduled service to Whitehorse in summer. Ride the train from Skagway to the summit, leaving at 12:40 p.m., use a motorcoach between Fraser, B.C. and Whitehorse, and arrive at 5:30 p.m. Southbound, the bus leaves Whitehorse at 8 a.m., arriving in Skagway at noon. One-way fares, adults $95, Children $47.50.

Also offered in 1999, **Yukon Territory Adventure**, Sundays in June, July, and August. Train leaves at 8 a.m., goes to summit, stops at Bennett and Carcross in the Yukon. You ride the bus back to Skagway. Trip including lunch, Adult $128, Child $64. For the same price, **Lake Bennett Adventure** goes to Bennett Monday, Thursday, Friday, Saturday in June, July, August giving you an all-train round trip back to Skagway. Lunch and a 2 hour stopover at Bennett are included. The same trips return Chilkoot hikers to Fraser $25, Skagway $65.

**Special Steam Excursions** to Bennett with an historic steam engine pulling the train all the way will run on Saturdays, June 12 and 26, July 10 and 24, and August 7 and 21. Adult $156, Child 12 and under $78, includes lunch. It's an 8 hour trip, leaving at 8 a.m.

For reservations or info, **White Pass & Yukon Route**, Box 435, Skagway, AK 99840. (800) 343-7373, fax (907) 983-2658. Call from NW Canada (800) 478-7373. All fares are in U.S. dollars. Times are local, Alaska or Yukon (in Whitehorse).

See both bald and golden eagles in the area. Swans sometimes stop near Dyea during migration.

Fish Taiya Inlet, Skagway and Dyea rivers, and Dewey Lakes. Salt water fishing is generally better than lake fishing here. Dolly Varden in May and June, and salmon and halibut have all been caught from shore, dock, or skiff very near the ferry dock. Ask the locals and remember to get a license even for salt water fishing.

Visit Dyea, the takeoff point for the Chilkoot Pass. See the remains of buildings, boats, and the slide cemetery for victims of the avalanche on the Chilkoot Trail in 1898. Any taxi will take you on the 9 miles of gravel road each way.

See the Gold Rush cemetery at the north end of Skagway, with the graves of Soapy Smith and Frank Reid.

Hike up to Dewey Lakes , 1/4 mile, Reid Falls 1/2 mile, and Icy Lake 2 miles. Beautiful views and forest.

The White Pass Railroad snowplow kept the lines open. Now it has retired to the entrance of Skagway.

Walk over the footbridge across the Skagway River and follow the trail to Yakutania Point for short, level hike to a good picnic spot on a rocky point looking down Taiya Inlet. Picnic tables and fire pits. Parcours excercise stations line this trail. Ambitious hikers can hike the trail from that point up the ridge overlooking Skagway 5.5 miles each way to A.B. Mountain at 5100 ft. Several view points along the way offer good photography and shorter hiking goals.

Backpack the historic and strenuous 33-mile Chilkoot Trail. Information on trail conditions is available from the National Park Service. Additional comments and suggestions on hiking the Chilkoot Trail are in the next chapter.

Go flightseeing by helicopter over Skagway, the Chilkoot and White Passes, and the Juneau Icefield, including a landing on the ice. **Temsco Helicopters**, 1st & Broadway, near ferry. Box 434, Skagway, AK 99840. 983-2900. From May through September you can fly over Chilkoot and White Pass Trails and nearby glaciers with tours from 30 minutes to 1 hour, the latter touring both passes.

Go flightseeing by plane over Juneau Icefield, Klondike Trails, Glacier Bay. Take a lunch tour to see the Chilkat Dancers in Haines. **Skagway Air Service**, Box 357, Skagway, AK 99840. 983-2218.

Take a day bus tour over White Pass to Carcross and back or over-night to Whitehorse. The scenery and history combine to make this a great trip. Enjoy flowers in summer and fall colors in September.

In winter and spring, ski cross-country near White Pass. Dry snow and gentle, rolling country for miles! March and April are best for dry snow, good weather, and long daylight hours. Buckwheat Classicr aces in March.

INFORMATION AVAILABLE at the **National Park Service Visitor Center** all year in the restored railroad depot at 2nd and Broadway. Box 517, Skagway, AK 99840. 983-2921. Web: www.nps.gov/klgo E-mail: klgo_ranger_activities@nps.gov The Park Service has good maps. Exhibits, lectures, guided walks around town. Open 8 a.m.–7p.m. in summer.

For Chilkoot Trail info and permits, see the trail center across the street which is manned by both U.S. and Canadian park personnel. **Skagway Convention and Visitors Bureau**, Box 415, Skagway, AK 99840. 983-2854. Fax: 983-3854. Open 8:00 a.m–5 p.m., daily in summer, May 15–Sept. 30. Same hours in winter, Mon.–Fri. Maps of town and of hiking trails, and a walking tour brochure are available. 333 5th Ave., just off Broadway. Web: www.infoskag@ptialaska.net E-mail: infoskag@ptialaska.net

**U.S. Customs and Immigration**, (907) 983-2325. **Canada Customs** at Fraser, B.C., (403) 821-4111.

## Transportation

FERRY: **Alaska Marine Highway**, 983-2941. daily in summer, 4 times per week in winter. Terminal is at south end of Broadway.

**Haines-Skagway Water Taxi**,Skagway 983-2083. (888) 766-3395. Two round trips daily between Haines and Skagway for walk-on passengers only, $32 round trip, $20 one-way. Will take a few bicycles. Cruises close to shore for scenery, wildlife viewing. **Chilkat Cruises,** 766-2100 or (888) 766-2103, offers 2–3 round trips daily in summer. Both companies leave from Skagway small boat harbor. Boat tickets available at docks or most hotels.

BUS: None local. **Alaska Direct**, (403) 668-4833. (800) 780-6652. Has daily service between Skagway and Whitehorse, also scheduled service throughout the Yukon and Alaska. In summer **Gray Line Alaskon Express**, 983-2241, (800) 544-2206, has bus service from Skagway to Whitehorse.

TRAIN (& bus): **White Pass & Yukon Route**. Scheduled service to Whitehorse, by train from Skagway to the summit, leaving at 12:40 p.m. and by bus from Fraser, B.C. to Whitehorse, arriving at 5:30 p.m. Southbound, the bus leaves Whitehorse at 8 a.m. Mid-May to mid-September. One-way, Adults $95, Children $47.50.

TAXI: Most hotels have courtesy transportation to/from the ferry if you ask when you reserve. **Frontier Tours & Taxi** 983-2512. **Southeast Tours**

Skagway Hack picks up passengers in front of Keller's Curios to tour Skagway and perhaps go to the historic cemetery.

983-2990. **Klondike Taxi** 983-2075.

TOURS: **Skagway Tours** 983-2294, **Frontier Tours** 983-2512, **Gray Line of Alaska** 983-2241, **Klondike Tours** 983-2075, **Princess Tours** 983-2895, **Skagway Streetcar Company** 983-2908, **Southeast Tours** (800) 478-2990. Also offers horseback tours with **Chilkoot Horseback Adventures**. Horse-drawn **Skagway Hack** buggies await you in front of Keller's on Broadway, for tours of town and to cemetery. All these operators run tours around Skagway. Some also go to Dyea and to Carcross and Whitehorse.

BICYCLE RENTAL: **JD & Paul Bike Rental & Repairs**. Corner of 4th & State. **Sockeye Cycle**, 983-2851. Tours and rentals. **Sourdough Shuttle**, 983-2523.

CAR RENTAL: **Avis**, 983-2247. **Sourdough Shuttle,** 983-2523. Car & van rentals. **ABC Motorhome Rentals**, 983-3222, (800) 421-7456. Also cars and vans. All year.

AIR: **Skagway Air Service**, Box 357, Skagway, AK 99840. 983-2218, fax 983-2948. **LAB Flying Service**, 983-2471, fax 983-2122. **Wings of Alaska**, 983-2442.

ROAD: The Klondike Highway to Carcross, the Alaska Highway (99 miles), and on to Whitehorse (108 miles) is open all year, paved. Just north of Skagway there's an 11.5 mile grade up to White Pass, 3290'. The rest of the way is rolling upland with beautiful, unpopulated scenery. Both U.S.

and Canadian Customs are open 24 hours a day all year at Fraser near White Pass.

BAGGAGE STORAGE at hotels, for patrons, on day of departure.

## Hotels
(rates plus 8% tax)

**Gold Rush Lodge**—.5 mile from ferry, 6th and Alaska. Box 514, Skagway, AK 99840. 983-2831, fax 983-2742, e-mail grl@ptialaska.net Courtesy van. Queen or double and twin beds, with private bath. Street level, modern. Cable TV. 12 rooms, all non-smoking. Senior rate, 5%. Standard room Single/Double $79–89. Deluxe room $99 Single/Double, $99 Triple.

. **Golden North**—.35 mile from ferry, on Broadway and 3rd, Box 343, Skagway, AK 99840. 983-2451 and 983-2294, fax 983-2755. 31 rooms with Gold Rush era furnishings, maps, photos, renovated. With private bath, from $90.. Shared bath, from $65. Restaurant, lounge, gift shop, microbrewery, tours. Open mid-April–early October. Shoulder season rates.   e-mail: corrington@msn.com  web: www.alaskan.com/goldenorth

**Miner's Inn**—.5 from ferry, 6th & Broadway. Inn established 1899. Box 589, Skagway, AK 99840. 983-3303, fax 983-3304. Eight rooms, shared bath. Ferry pickup. Single $45, Double $60.

**Portland House**—.5 mile from ferry. 5th and State. Box 393, Skagway, AK 99840. 983-2493. Built in 1897. Eleven basic clean rooms with shared baths. Greek-American restaurant downstairs. Single $35, Double $45. Open May–September 30.

**Sgt. Preston's Lodge**—.6 mile from ferry, on 6th between Broadway and State. Box 538, Skagway, AK 99840. 983-2521. 30 rooms, private baths, telephone and cable TV. Single $75, Double $80, Triple $85. Also has economy and deluxe rooms. Open all year. Winter rates. Courtesy van from ferry and train. E-mail: sgt-prestons@usa.net

**Skagway Home Hostel**—.5 from ferry, 3rd between State and Main. Box 231, Skagway, AK 99840. 983-2131, fax 983-2131. 10 beds in male and female dormitories. Private double rooms available. Hot water, cooking facilities. Sleeping bags recommended. No pets, drinking, or smoking. Curfew 11 p.m. Check in 5–10 p.m. $15. Open all year. Reservations advised always, required Sept. 1–May 1. Reservations require 1 night's fee deposit.

**Skagway Inn Bed & Breakfast**—.5 mile from ferry, Broadway and 7th. Box 500, Skagway, AK 99840. 983-2289, fax 983-2713. Inside Alaska, (800) 478-2290.e-mail: sgyinn@ptialaska.net. Web: www.puffin.ptialaska.net/ ~sgyinn Living room, shared baths, some rooms on ground floor. Built in 1897, it has friendly Gold Rush atmosphere with 12 rooms named, instead of numbered, with the names of the "girls" who worked here. Full

The White Pass Railroad train crosses a trestle between Skagway and White Pass.

breakfast included. Courtesy pick up, ferry, airport. Single/Double $85. Winter rates: Single $60, Double $70. Add'l $15. Open all year.

**Westmark Inn**—.4 mile from ferry, 3rd Ave. between Broadway and Spring. Box 515, Skagway, AK 99840. 983-6000, fax 983-6100. (800) 544-0970. Restaurants, cocktail lounge, entertainment. Laundromat, travel agency. Courtesy van from ferry, airport. Avis car rental. In room phone, TV. Single/Double $99, including breakfast. Children 18 and under free. Annex, Gold Rush, and Backpacker rates, $69–89, space avail. Open mid-April–late September.

**The White House**—1/2 mile from ferry, 8th Ave. at Main. Box 41, Skagway, AK 99840. 983-9000, fax 983-9010. Restored family-owned hotel. Ten rooms with private baths. One is wheelchair accessible. Beds 1 queen or 2 twins. Full breakfast included. Open all year. Single/Double from $99. e-mail: whitehse@ptialaska.net web: www.skagway.com/whitehouse

**Wind Valley Lodge**—.8 mile from ferry, 22nd and State Street. Box 354, Skagway 99840. 983-2236, fax 983-2957. 30 rooms, modern, AAA rated, cable TV. Non-smoker and handicap rooms. Restaurant, laundry. Standard rooms, 2 double beds. Single $69, Double $79. Add'l. $10/person. Children under 12, cribs free. Deluxe rooms larger, have 2 queen-sized beds and sitting area. Open Mar. 15–Nov. 1. Courtesy transportation. e-mail: wvl@ptialaska.net web: www.alaskan.com/windvalleylodge/

Not inspected, but attractive: **Mile 0 B&B**—Box 165, Skagway, AK 99840.

983-3045, fax 983-3046. New, non-smoking, handicapped acessible.

## Trailer Parks/Campgrounds

**Backtrack Camper Park**—.7 mile from ferry, 12th & Broadway. 983-3333. RVs and tents. Has water, electricity, restrooms, showers, dump station, laundromat, TV, ice. With water and electrical hookups $16, $8 without.

**Hanousek Park**—.8 mile from ferry, Broadway at 14th. 983-2297. 12 spaces without hookups and tent sites $8. Firepits, tables, water, restrooms, hot showers, dump station. Open May 1–Sept. 30.

**Garden City RV Park**—1 mile from ferry, State between 15th and 17th. Box 228, Skagway, AK 99840. 983-2378, fax 983-3378. RV camping with and without hookups, pullthrough spaces. Dump station, restrooms, showers, laundromat. With hookups $16, without $8.

**Pullen Creek Park & RV Campground**—.2 mile from ferry, to right of Broadway. Box 324, Skagway, AK 99840. Summer 983-2768. Oct.–April (800) 936-3731, fax (208) 233-7003. City-owned campground. All spaces with hookups. Park has a creek, pond, picnic shelter. $10 tents. $15 dry. $20 with water, electricity, dump. Bathhouse with showers. Central dump station, $5 if not registered at park. Open May 1–Sept. 30.

Call ahead to reserve campground space, especially on Sunday and Monday nights with the *Columbia* from Bellingham arriving Monday.

## Facilities

LAUNDROMAT: **Service Unlimited**, 2nd and State.

DUMP STATION: **Pullen Creek Park.**

PROPANE: **Corner Gas Station,** 4th Ave., between State and Main.

DIESEL: **Service Unlimited**, International Chevron. 2nd and State Streets. Also car wash. (If you use it southbound, you'll save your clothes & paint when you slide between your car and the next on the car deck.)

ICE: **Fairway Supermarket** and all liquor stores.

CLINIC: **Skagway Medical Clinic** 11th Ave., between State and Main, 9–5 weekdays, 983-2255. After hours, 983-2418.

## Boats

Charters for fishing and tours available. Information at **Skagway Convention & Visitors Bureau**. Moorage and fuel at harbor.

**Westours** at the Westmark Inn, 983-2241, has a 2-hour scenic and historic boat tour.

## Happenings

Skagway *is* a celebration of the Klondike Gold Rush, but the late 90s are special, the centennial of the stampede. Watch for special displays, films, and activities in town and along the route to Dawson.

The picturesque church at Lake Bennett built by stampeders.

**Skagway Windfest**, March 28, 1999. Games, races, contests with Klondike theme—Ore Truck Pull, Chainsaw Toss, Chili cookoff, etc. Winter festival. 983-2854.

**Buckwheat Ski Classic**, March 22, 1999. Cross country ski races on groomed course near White Pass and lakes. Call 983-2544 or 983-2234.

**Mini Folk Festival**, late April. 983-2276. Music.

**Solstice Picnic**, June. Annual picnic sponsored by the Elks Club.

**July 4 Parade and Celebration**. Tradition started when Soapy Smith led the parade as grand marshall on a white horse in 1898, four days before he was shot. Full day and evening of games in frontier tradition—Children's Foot Races, Ladies' Rolling Pin Toss, Arm Wrestling, Pie Eating Contest, Egg Toss, Volunteer Fire Department Water Fight, etc. 983-2297.

**Flower Show and Gold Rush Garden Club Awards**, August. Features Skagway's gardens at their peak in the long summer days as well as floral displays by local businesses. Tea and cookies. 983-2365.

**Klondike Trail of '98 Road Relay**, Skagway to Whitehorse. Sept.10–11, 1999. Ten-person teams from all over the western U.S. and Canada start Friday at midnight from the Skagway waterfront and race 110 miles up the highway and over White Pass to Whitehorse, finishing Saturday afternoon in time for dinner and dance that night. The race has grown until

Jim Richards, completely believable as Soapy Smith, veteran of thousands of performances of "The Soapy Smith Show," takes a break between acts.

it's now limited to 70 teams. Teams come from all over North America to join the locals. For info, call (403) 668-3331 in Whitehorse.

**Victorian Yuletide Celebration**, early December. Tree lighting ceremony with Santa and Mrs. Claus, business open house, caroling, and a Yuletide Ball at the Arctic Brotherhood Hall. 983-2289.

**Eagles Christmas Party**, December 24, 1999. Town Christmas program has been held by the Fraternal Order of Eagles since 1937, with band and choir. Presents for town children. 983-2234.

# THE CHILKOOT PASS

Gold was discovered in creeks running into the Yukon's Klondike River in August 1896. As word spread through the north country, prospectors for many hundreds of miles around converged on the camp that became Dawson City. They staked claims, struggled and starved with bottles of gold nuggets on the shelf (there was gold but not enough food for so many people in the Yukon that winter). Finally in July 1897 the *Portland* arrived in Seattle with a load of gold, and the rush was on, world-wide.

Despite its difficulties, the Chilkoot Pass proved to be the quickest and one of the easiest routes to the Klondike. During the winter of 1897–98 thousands struggled over the pass, not once but many times, as they shuttled back and forth moving the ton of supplies the Mounties now required for entry to the Yukon (to avoid a repetition of the starving times). By spring, when the ice went out on the river, over 20,000 miners waited on the shores of Lakes Lindeman and Bennett with hand-built boats to float the last 500 miles. They arrived to find all likely land and much unlikely area already staked. Few got any gold, but for all the trip was the most memorable time of their lives.

Today the trail is included inthe Klondike Gold Rush International Park on both sides of the border and maintained by U.S. and Canadian personnel. Many artifacts remain, and must be left as they lie. Along the trail are remains of wagons, boots, harnesses, stoves, and sleds once pulled by miners. There are metal pictures of views as they were then from the places you are standing now. The Chilkoot Trail is much more than a rugged 33-mile backpack trip. Even in summer it's a walk for several days through the world's most scenic historical museum.

To enjoy this trip requires some planning. The trail goes from sea level at Dyea to 3739 ft. (Parks Canada says 3502!) at the summit, mostly from mile 13.5 to mile 16.5 (which is very hard on legs if you start from the north end and go in reverse), and back to 2153 ft. at Lake Bennett. July is the most popular month, as much of the winter's snow is gone and the wildflowers are lovely. The trip takes three to five days for most people.

You still can expect wind and rain any time. In the pass this can be miserable and force you to concentrate on the trail markers so you don't lose the trail. The trail is often muddy, crosses streams, has several miles of snow at any season and several miles of loose rock near the U.S. side of the pass.

On the Canadian side avalanches sometimes run across the trail even in mid-summer. Canadian wardens you'll meet near the pass have good advice on snow and weather conditions. For the latest information on trail conditions you should see the **National Park Service** in Skagway, which can give you a useful trail profile. Topographic maps are available at the **Skagway Sports Emporium** on Fourth Avenue.

Adequate clothing and boots, well broken-in, are critical. The shelters are widely separated and nowhere near the pass. Good rain gear that's windproof is essential—rain pants and parka or cagoule. Ponchos don't work in wind, and the new breathable synthetics haven't proven waterproof in this climate for anyone I know. Pants must be wool or polyester fleece. (Synthetic *inner* layers and insulation do work well in this climate and dry quickly in camp.) Damp cotton pants lose heat, even under rain pants, faster than if you were undressed. Wearing them here leaves your whole safety margin to the luck of the weather and says things about your judgment you wouldn't want to advertise. A wool cap and water repellent gloves that dry quickly are essential. Breathable gaiters are *very* good for keeping mud and snow out of boots, and keeping pants dry.

Camping is only approved in designated spots, and campfires are prohibited. You are advised to bring a stove and fuel for cooking. Shelters are only for drying out—not for camping in. You should also bring 50 feet of light rope for hauling your pack up out of bears' reach on the horizontal poles provided at most campsites. Water, especially from lakes with campsites, should be boiled or treated with water tablets.

Deep Lake is the prettiest campsite on the trail, but is located so it doesn't fit many people's schedules. The flowers here are lovely in July, and you can easily spend an afternoon discovering artifacts hidden by the brush. Happy Camp is *not* in the first trees you come to on the Canadian side, and the "four miles" the map says it is from the summit are a sadistic underestimate. But this is a great trip and one I want to do again!

The **White Pass & Yukon** will have a Chilkoot Hikers Service from Bennett back to Fraser $25 and Skagway $65, on Monday, Thursday, Friday, and Saturday during June, July, and August, 1999. (800) 343-7373 or 983-2217.

You can choose to leave the trail at a fork just beyond Bare Loon Lake at about Mile 30 for a 5 mile walk out along the train tracks to a place on the road called Log Cabin where there's no longer a cabin, to meet the bus (get schedule in Skagway).

From Log Cabin on the Klondike Highway you can catch the bus going either north or south, to Whitehorse or back to Skagway.

*Suggestion:* If you don't want to climb the pass, but want an interesting trip, you could leave the highway at Log Cabin and hike to Bennett or Lake Lindeman for a few days in the beautiful, rolling upland with flowers and history. I highly recommend this trip as the weather is drier on this side of the mountains, the terrain is gentle, you start from over 2000

Triumphant hikers at the end of Chilkoot Trail at Lake Bennett.

ft. above sea level, and you can do as much or as little as you like. Beginning backpackers and less-conditioned people could enjoy this variation no matter how the weather turned out. You will need a trail permit from Parks Canada.

Seeing the award-winning film "City of Gold" narrated by Pierre Berton and reading his book *Klondike Fever* (U.S. edition) or, as it's titled in Canada, *Klondike*, will make the trip mean more, I think. The film is shown sometimes on the ferries and often in Skagway. Berton's father went over the pass, and Pierre grew up in Dawson. With that preparation, a friend and I panted up the pass on a sunny July day trying to imagine spending weeks on it in mid-winter and marvelled "they did all this for *gold*?"

For additional information, write or call Area Superintendent, Yukon National Historic Sites, Box 5540, Whitehorse, Yukon Territory YIA 5H4 Canada. Phone (403) 668-2116 or (800) 661-0486. In Skagway you can write or call Superintendent, Klondike Gold Rush N. H. P., Box 517, Skagway, AK 99840. (907) 983-2921.

*Very important note:* In Skagway, visit the Chilkoot Trail center across the street from the restored railway depot at 2nd and Broadway for current information on trail conditions and to get the required backcountry per-

Yukoners celebrated the centennial with a commerative tent bakery at Lake Bennett where for the summer of '98 they served free pancake breakfasts to Chilkoot hikers.

mit. This office is manned by the U.S. National Park Service and Parks Canada. Here you can get info, the trail permit, and customs clearance with one stop!

Canadian park authorities limit the number of hikers on the Chilkoot Trail into Canada to 50 per day, mainly due to crowding at Happy Camp. Groups are limited to 12 hikers. The majority of the permits are available for reservations with a limited number held open for hikers arriving without reservations. These are available starting at noon on the day before the day you plan to start hiking. Your permit is good for a specified number of days but doesn't require you to go over the pass on a particular day—allowing you some flexibility to wait out bad weather.

Permits cost C$35 plus a reservation fee of C$10 per person. Youths age 15 and under pay C$17.50 plus the C$10 fee. If you want to go to Bennett from the highway or train, the day hiking fee is C$5 per day per person. Add C$10 per tent/night if you camp at Bennett. If you hike all the way to Lindeman, you pay the whole trail permit fee and are limited by its numbers.

The main impact of the limit is on the peak period of the last two weeks of July and the first two weeks of August. There is presently no limit or fee on the U.S. side.

You should get a copy of "A Hiker's Guide to the Chilkoot Trail" from the Klondike Gold Rush International Park for $3. It has lots of useful information, including a recommended equipment list.

# SMALLER PORTS

(Served by the *Aurora*, and *LeConte*, but not by the larger ferries)

## METLAKATLA

(Area Code 907, Zip Code 99926)

METLAKATLA (pop. 1600) was established in 1887 when Father Duncan and 823 Tsimshian Indians from Canada to Annette Island. The island remains a reserve. A neat, well-planned community, Metlakatla has seasonal fishing, timber operations, and tourism. A cannery and a saw-mill are in town. The eastern half of the island is mountainous with lakes and waterfalls, while the western half, where the town, roads, and 7500 ft. airport are, is flat.

### To See and Do

See Alaska's only Native American reserve and the only legal ocean fish traps in the United States.

See the Duncan Cottage Museum, open 10–2, Mon.–Fri. Weekends by request. Call 866-4441, ext. 232 for special group or individual visits. $2 admission.

Tour Annette Islands Packing Company to see processing of 4 species of salmon and other fish and shellfish. Their gift shop sells salmon gift boxes and native art. Shipping available.

Complete the history of Missionary Duncan by visiting his gravesite and the Duncan Memorial Church, replica of the original burned in 1948.

Visit the tribal longhouse, used for ceremonies. See the Tsimshian Dancers in traditional dance regalia of leather, wool, beadwork, buttons, and clan crest as they dance tribal legends. Tsimshian crafts displayed and for sale. Performances given when cruise ships are in, and occasionally for groups of 10 or more.

Beachcomb and picnic at Pioneer Park or Point Davidson, 10 miles by gravel road (good birdwatching). The walk out the road west, past cemetery is popular. Purple Lake Trail, 3 miles, is steep and rugged, but beautiful. The Yellow Hill trail is boarded and starts on the right side of Airport Rd.

Bring bicycle on ferry for tour of island roads, trip to Pt. Davidson. May be able to rent one from local people.

Visit the Tamgas Fish Hatchery to see how fish are farmed and harvested.

Founder's Day, August 7, celebrates arrival of Father Duncan and his followers in 1887. Tribal dances, community lunch, special events.

The Harvest Celebration, first Friday in October, celebrates another year of gathering provisions for winter with native feast and dancing.

Walk trails like Yellow Hill Viewpoint Trail, 2 miles south of town, and Skaters Lake Trail (1/2 mile long), 1/4 mile from town toward airport.

## Facilities

ACCOMMODATIONS: **Metlakatla Hotel and Suites,** Box 670, Metlakatla, AK 99926. 886-3456. 7 rooms with private bath, phone, VCR, cable TV, 2 with kitchenettes. Free video films. Single/Double $78. Winter rates. Open all year. E-mail  methots@metlakatla.net

**Ethel's B&B,** 886-5275. **Bernita's B&B,** 886-7563

RESTAURANTS: **Chester Bay Cafe,** 886-5667, pizza, bay view. **Leask Mini Mart,** 886-3000, fast grill foods. **Uncle Fred's Cafe,** 886-5007, daily specials, ocean view. **PaPa's Place,** 886-3144, coffee.

AIR SERVICE: **Taquan Air Service**, charter and regular service to Ketchikan. 886-8800. **Pro Mech Air,** 886-3845. Both use float planes.

Tour: offered by **Taquan Air Service**, round trip from Ketchikan, with self-guided walking tour, brochure, $49.

CAR RENTAL: **Rent-A-Dent** in Metlakatla. Toll-free reservation from U.S. outside Washington, (800) 426-5243. Metlakatla, 886-4622.

GAS, REPAIR: Annette Islands Gas Services, 886-7851. Leask Garage, 886-3499.

BUS SERVICE: None public.TAXI: **White Cab & Van Tours,** 886-1212. **Major Taxi,** 886-5241.

GROCERY/SNACKS: **Leas**k market, **Leask** mini-mart, **Starlight Video**.

ART & CARVING: **House of The Wolf,** Tsimshian artist Jack Hudson sells his art work. 886-4923, fax 886-1936.

SWIMMING POOL, with sauna and fitness room, open to public at Lepquinum Recreation Center.

BOATS: Visiting boats and vehicles can get fuel at Guthries' on dock, tie up. Must check in with Harbormaster on arrival, 886-4646, VHF Ch 16. A new breakwater and small boat harbor are completed. **Jim Beal Charter**, for fishing, exploring, 886-1122.

FERRY: Ferry service is almost daily, 1.5 hours from Ketchikan on *Aurora*. The ferry dock is 1 mile from downtown. Vehicles arriving on the ferry must check in with Metlakatla Police Dept. to report your length of stay on the reserve. **In summer 1999, Saturday** is only day the ferry makes 2 trips. You can have the whole day in Metlakatla if  you leave Ketchikan at 6:15 a.m. and return at 10 p.m., $14 each way, or $7 senior fare if you're over 65. Since **Taquan** has several scheduled flights daily from Ketchikan in summer, special and senior rates, you could ride one way on the ferry and the other by plane, quite inexpensively.

In 1999 a road is being built around the north end of the island which will allow Metlakatla to be served by a shuttle ferry across the channel from Mountain Point south of Ketchikan. during construction, some roads are closed to the public.

INFORMATION AVAILABLE: Metlakatla Tourism Dept., Box 8, Metlakatla, AK 99926. 886-8687, toll free (877) 886-8687.

Note: Metlakatla is legally dry. There is no place to buy alcohol, and it cannot legally be brought to the island.

# HYDER

(Area code 250 for Hyder and Stewart, Zip code 99923)

Hyder is a village of 100 people at the head of Portland Canal, a long scenic inlet George Vancouver followed, hoping it was the Northwest Passage. Adjacent is Stewart, B.C. with about 700 people. The Alaska ferry, *Aurora*, makes a weekly trip in summer from Ketchikan, actually docking in Stewart. You can drive from the Cassiar Road to the ferry and board with a vehicle up to 25' long. Or you can ride one way on the ferry from Ketchikan and fly the other way on the mail plane. The ferry terminal in Ketchikan can tell you which air taxi has the run.

Hyder and Stewart have both seen bigger days in their scenic fiord, surrounded by cliffs leading up to icefields and glaciers above. Both were busy mining towns—Hyder had over 10,000 people. More recently Stewart was the base for the Grand Duc copper mine until the fall of copper prices closed it. The Premier and Big Missouri gold mines near Hyder have rebuilt bunkhouses and other buildings and have reopened. Anything you can't find in Hyder you probably can in Stewart. Stewart has 2 motels and 3 restaurants and an air strip. Most Hyder children go to school in Stewart.

Note that Hyder's phone area code is British Columbia's 250, but the zip code is a U.S. code.

## To See and Do

See the museum collection of local history in the hall of Hyder's new community building.

Walk around the quiet unpaved streets, the banks of the Salmon River or the Portland Canal and enjoy the scenery.

Photograph scenery and wildlife: salmon spawning, July–September; bears at Fish Creek, four miles from Hyder, July–September; Salmon Glacier, 20 miles up Grand Duc Mine Road above Hyder, July–October; Bear Glacier, all year; Alpine flowers, May–September; birds, all year.

Fish in Salmon River or Portland Canal. If you have a boat, set a crab or shrimp pot in Portland Canal.

Watch bears fishing at Fish Creek, four miles north of Hyder. Near the bridge, park and walk about a block to a viewing platform built over the creek. In summer Forest Service interpreters are there to answer questions. Be quiet and don't bring food.

As this is a mineralized area, rockhounds can enjoy flashy mineral specimens from roadside or abandoned slag heaps at mines.

Pick berries and enjoy summer flowers everywhere.

At your own risk in summer, with a good car or pickup and plenty of gas, you can drive *very* carefully up the Salmon River Valley Road from Hyder toward the Grand Duc Mine for great scenery and glacial views.

Help the residents celebrate International Days, July 1 through the 4th. The Canadians start on the 1st with Canada Day and the holiday runs through the U.S. Independence Day, including games, fireworks, and a bed race from Hyder to Stewart.

Enjoy the Stewart/Hyder International Rodeo, second weekend in June.

Get Hyderized. Anyone can tell you how. Hint: with 3 bars, open until 5 a.m. seven days a week, it's easy.

## Facilities

BUS (also tours): **Seaport Limousine** in Stewart, 636-2622. **Grandview Express**, 636-9174.

AIR: Not serviced but fuel available on call at **Granmac Service Station**.

DIESEL, GAS: **Yankee Trader,** Hyder, 636-9143. **Shell**, Stewart, 636-2344. Note **RV Wash** next to the old jail on the road to the Hyder dock.

PROPANE/ICE: **Granmac**, Stewart, 636-2402.

GROCERIES: **Ghost Town Groceries**, in Hyder, 636-2422. Laundromat in Stewart.

RESTAURANTS: **Border Cafe**, 636-2379; **Sealaska Inn**, 636-9001. **Wildflower Sweets,** subs and soups, 636-2878.

HOSPITAL: **Stewart General Hospital**, 11th Ave., 636-2221.

BOAT MOORAGE and launching: Hyder 636-9148.

BOAT CHARTERS: several, both in Hyder and Stewart. Some of the best fishing in Alaska (a good place for a crab or shrimp pot, too).

ACCOMMODATIONS: **Sealaska Inn**, 1/2 mile from ferry dock, in middle of Hyder. Box 33, Hyder, AK 99923. 636-2486. 14 rooms, queen-size beds. Double $36. Restaurant, bar, gift shop. Open April–Nov. e-mail: sealaskainn@hotmail.com

**Grand View Inn,** 1 mile from ferry. P.O. Box 49, Hyder, AK 99923. 636-9174. Hyder's newest hotel has 10 rooms, TV, kitchenettes. Single $50, Double $55. Open all year. e-mail: grandview@myhome.net

CAMPGROUNDS: **Camp Run-A-Muck South,** Tent sites, showers, laundromat. Downtown Hyder. **Camp Run-A-Muck North,** RV hookups, laundry, showers. Half mile north of town center. Register for either at Sealaska Inn. 636-2486. Open May– Oct.

Stewart has several additional motels, camping, and an airstrip with fuel.

LIBRARY: Reading and additional information on Hyder.

INFORMATION: **Hyder Community Association,** Box 149, Hyder, AK 99923. 636-9148. Fax: 636-2673. E-mail: hcainc@hotmail.com In summer there's a **Visitor Information Center** with a small museum on the right entering town on the main road. 636-2879. **U.S. Forest Service,** 636-2367.

# PRINCE OF WALES ISLAND, CRAIG, KLAWOCK
(Area Code 907, Zip Codes Craig 99921, Klawock 99925, Hydaburg 99922)

PRINCE OF WALES, 45 miles west of Ketchikan, is the largest island in Southeast Alaska with over 1000 miles of shoreline. It's served by ferry to Hollis, daily in summer, several times weekly in winter. From there a paved road reaches Craig, 35 miles, pop. 2043, and Klawock, pop. 729, seven miles from Craig and 28 miles from Hollis. A paved road goes to the native fishing village of Hydaburg. Gravel roads reach the big logging camp of Thorne Bay and the north island logging camps of Whale Pass, Coffman Cove and Naukati. The native village of Kassan, north of Hollis has a road. Pt. Baker is reachable only by air and boat.

Excellent fishing is found in both fresh and saltwater. The west coast has many islands with sheltered coastline—a good place for boat touring, kayaking, and camping. Fishing and logging are the main activities on the island. There is abundant wildlife, including black bears and eagles, even wolves.

## To See and Do
Visit totem park at Klawock, 21 totems.

See the fish hatchery in Klawock.

Watching birds and wildlife is rewarding here—and there's lots to photograph. Eagles are everywhere. A wolf crossed the road in front of us.

Fish both fresh and salt water and hunt, many places, in season.

Enjoy July 4th celebrations in Craig and Klawock— games, fireworks.

Watch logging contests in Thorne Bay during July.

Big king salmon here. Fishing derby.

Kayak between islands in many protected bays. Bird and whale watching are great, especially on west coast.

Camp dry in Forest Service cabins, most reached by boat or floatplane.

Walk the scenic bike path in Craig and One Duck Trail (sign on the Hydaburg Rd. 2 miles south of its start on the Craig–Hollis Rd.) to timberline and shelter.

Bring a mountain bike and explore the road system, camping at lakes and bays. Be careful with logging truck traffic and with black bears that might come into camp.

Watch gravel beaches and road shoulders for interesting rocks. Prince of Wales Island has a great variety, including the marble used for the pillars in front of the state capitol.

Explore the north part of the island, including its caves. Cavern Lake Cave, 2.5 miles from Whale Pass is open with viewing platform and creek pouring out of it. Do not enter the cave on your own as their are hazards. El Capitan Cave is closed and protected, 11 miles west of Whale Pass, 94 miles from Hollis, via Klawock. You can explore the first 200 ft. on your own. Beyond a closed gate, it's open on guided Forest Service tours from late May to early September. Call the Forest Service, 828-3304, in Thorne Bay for information and reservations.

### Facilities

FERRY: **Alaska Marine Hwy**. from Ketchikan to Hollis where the road ends. A small terminal building is open for ferry arrivals. Note that traffic has increased greatly in the past few years between Ketchikan and Prince of Wales Island. If you're taking a vehicle any time of year, you should have reservations. Hollis terminal, 530-7115. Craig, 826-3432.

ROADS: Most extensive road system,over 1200 miles, in Southeast Alaska, mostly gravel, though some in central part of island are now paved. Vehicles going to northern area should carry extra fuel and two spare tires. Watch for logging trucks. Hollis, a former logging camp, has no facilities. The first person with a mobile coffee/sandwich van here can probably retire early.

AIRPORT: State-maintained airport at Klawock is 5000' paved, lighted. Free tiedowns. Unicom 122.8. Attended irregularly. No phone, fuel, or facilities. Paved road from Klawock to airport. Instrument approach added in 1997. Fuel on call.

ACCOMMODATIONS: **Haida Way Lodge**, downtown Craig, 31 miles from Hollis, on Front St. Box 690, Craig, AK 99921. 826-3268, fax 826-3267. 25 units. TV, coffee, phones. Open all year, Single $90, Double $100. Jacuzzi suites, $120. Corporate, government, senior, weekly rates.

A bald eagle perches in a Sitka spruce tree.

**Fireweed Lodge-Riptide Outfitters**, 28 miles from Hollis. On Craig-Hollis Hwy., Box 116, Klawock, AK 99925. 755-2930, fax 755-2937. Open all year. Boats, summer ocean fishing charters, island touring, hunting outfitters. 18 rooms with private bath, family style dining. Budget rental cars available. $95 per person with meals. e-mail: fireweedlo@aol.com

**Ruth Ann's Hotel**, 31 miles from Hollis. Box 145, Craig, AK 99921. 826-3292, fax 826-3293. Restaurant and lounge, fishing charters. 15 rooms. Standard rooms with fridge and coffeemaker, Single/Double $90. With kitchenette Single/Double $125.

**Shelter Cove Lodge**, 31 miles from Hollis. Box 798, Craig, AK 99921. 826-2939, (888) 826-FISH, fax 826-2941. 10 non-smoking rooms, queen and single beds, phones, cable TV, restaurant. Charter boat fishing. Fishing packages include room and fishing. Room $90–100, land and ocean view. Winter rates. Open all year.

**Log Cabin Campground & Resort**, 28 miles from ferry. Box 54, Klawock, AK 99925. 755-2205. (800) 544-2205. Rents showers, freezers, boats and trailers, canoes, separately or as package. Fishing, adventure, and eco-tour packages (including trip to El Capitan Caves, hike on off-shore island). Halibut and salmon charters, dive charters. Fishing packages include transportation from Ketchikan, boat and gear, beach cabin with shared kitchen. Free moorage for guests' boats to 26'. Cabin is $50 for 2 people. Log house or apartment, $120 for 2, plus $10/person add'l. Weekly rates.

The cabins and campground are among big trees facing gravel beach and boat dock. There are so many eagles fishing nearby and perched in the trees overhead that you may wish our national bird wasn't such a chatterbox at 4 a.m. Photography with still cameras and camcorders is easy here, though 200 and 400 mm lenses are helpful. Campground has some spaces with hookups, $23 per vehicle and two people. Tent space, $7/person. Kitchen and showers in adjacent building. Weekly rates.

**Eagle's Nest Campground**, near Thorne Bay, about 1.5 hours from the Hollis ferry terminal (U.S. Forest Service), has RV and tent sites. Pit toilet, water, kayak launch site.

TAXI: **Jackson Cab**, 755-2557, **Screaming Eagle Taxi**, 755-2256, Klawock. In Craig, **Craig–Klawock Taxi**, 826-3448. **MyCab**, 826-3151.

BUS SERVICE: There is no bus service at presstime, but others are discussing reopening the service.

CAR RENTAL: **Allstar Rent-a-Car**, Klawock. 755-2524. **Prince of Wales Lodge** and **Fireweed Lodge** have rental cars and pickups.

GROCERY STORES: three in Craig, one open 9–6, one 8–8, in summer, supermarket, beauty shop, clothing stores. Klawock has a convenience store and a grocery store. **Thorne Bay Market** is a full service store with groceries, bait and ice, open 7 days/week. Coffman Cove, Whale Pass and Hydaburg have small grocery stores. Supermarket in Klawock, 7 a.m.–8 p.m. Mon.–Sat., 9 a.m.– 6 p.m. Sun.

RESTAURANTS: 3 in Craig—**Dante's Restaurant, Ruth Ann's, Pan Handle Bar & Grill, Burger King, Submarina, Papa's Pizza. Dave's Diner, Papa's Pizza, Supervalue Deli**, and **Fireweed Lodge** in Klawock.

LAUNDROMATS: In Craig, **T.L.C. Laundry & Rooms**, 826-2966, has laundromat and bunkhouse rooms above with shared bath. $30–45. Weekly rates. One in Klawock near road from Hollis.

GAS STATIONS in Craig, Klawock, Thorne Bay, Whale Pass. Note that there is no gas anywhere else on the island, and miles of gravel road can use a lot of it. Fill up any time you pass a station. Auto parts store in Craig.

PROPANE and DIESEL: **Black Bear** in Klawock. For propane only, **Klawock Fuels** in Klawock, **Island Propane** in Craig.

ICE: all grocery stores, liquor stores in Craig and Thorne Bay.

HEALTH CLINIC: Craig, with doctor and physician's assistant. Open 10–4, Mon.–Fri. Radio contact with hospital in Ketchikan. 826-3257, after hours 826-3330. For emergency in Craig, dial 911.

BOAT FUEL: Craig, Klawock, and Thorne Bay (only as a convenience here). Boat rentals at Thorne Bay. Launch ramp, Craig, at City Center

A quiet morning in Hydaburg's boat harbor, a fine place to launch a skiff or kayak for miles of calm boating.

(North Cove).

TOURS: **Adventure Outdoors** offers small-group van tours using ferries including four days on the island for fishing and sightseeing. Box 4461, Rolling Bay, WA 98061. (206) 842-3189.

Kayak rental, tours, fishing charters: **S. E. A. Coastal Adventures**, Box 268, Craig, AK 99921. 826-3425.

**Craig's Dive Center**, Box 796, Craig, AK 99921. 826-3481. In kAlaska, (800) 380-DIVE. Diving and nature charters, air fills, instruction. Bike and canoe rentals.

Fishing charters, sightseeing: **Craig Charters,** Box 495, Craig, AK 99921. 826-2939. **Catch-A-King Charters**, Craig. 826-2938. Call **Prince of Wales Chamber of Commerce**, 826-3870, for latest listings on the island.

CHARTER AIR SERVICE from Ketchikan by any of the operators there. **Taquan Air,** 826-8800, has scheduled service, allowing you to pay by the seat instead of for the whole plane.

INFORMATION AVAILABLE at City Hall, **City of Craig**, Box 725, Craig, AK 99921. 826-3275, fax 826-3278. **U.S. Forest Service**, Box 500, Craig, AK 99921. 826-3271. You can get the "Prince of Wales Road Guide" for $4 from the Forest Service office here or in Ketchikan. **City of Klawock**, Box 113, Klawock, AK 99925. 755-2261. Has lots of info including suggested kayak loop trips, trails, and more. **Prince of Wales Chamber of**

**Commerce**, 826-3870. Box 497, Craig, AK 99921. Has latest list of B&Bs, including some at northern end of island.

# HYDABURG

Hydaburg is a village of 464 people, mostly native American Haidas, on the south shore of Prince of Wales Island. Until the gravel road (now paved) was cut through from the Craig-Hollis Highway in 1983, it could only be reached by boat and plane. The village has excellent fishing and kayaking as well as a totem park with 15 totems carved during the 1930's. The road to Hydaburg is scenic with good berry picking in season (blueberries and red huckleberries) and fishing in several streams.

Villagers fish for salmon and halibut. Some work in logging, and most fish and hunt for part of their food. They appreciate your sensitivity to their culture.

Kayakers and campers with skiffs will find more miles of sheltered water and bay shoreline reachable (without being exposed to open water) from here than from any other town in Southeastern Alaska. It's a great starting point for many trips—exploring the shores and deep bays of Prince of Wales, Long, and Dall Islands. Part of this land is included in the 91,000 acre South Prince of Wales Wilderness Area.

## Facilities

BUS: from Hollis ferry terminal to Hydaburg 36 miles, about an hour.

AIR: **Taquan Air,** 285-8800, from Ketchikan.

PROPANE: **Island Fuel**, 285-3425 and **Haida Oil**, 285-3283, also has diesel and boat fuel.

GROCERIES: **Do Drop In**, a general store.

CLINIC: on Main Street with limited first aid. 285-3462.

BOAT MOORAGE: **City Harbor**, 285-3761.

ACCOMMODATIONS: There are no hotels but some people will take boarders. **Molly Edenshaw,** 285-3254.

INFORMATION AVAILABLE: **City of Hydaburg**, Box 49, Hydaburg, AK 99922. 285-3761, 235-3793, and 235-3954. Has list of homes lodging visitors.

# KAKE

(Area Code 907, Zip Code 99830)

KAKE (pop. 861) is a Tlingit Indian fishing village on Kupreanof Island, west of Petersburg. It is scenic, has paved roads in town and gravel logging roads. It has excellent fishing, and is home of the world's tallest one-piece totem pole, 132 feet tall, centerpiece of the Alaska pavilion at the 1970 World's Fair in Japan. Ferry dock 1.5 miles from center of town.

## To See and Do

Fish anywhere, even at the ferry dock, for halibut, salmon, sole. Rainbow trout in streams.

Hike, camp, beachcomb. Logging roads provide some trails and ski touring in winter. Road south leads short distance to Boot Lake picnic area, then on to Hamilton Bay, 20 miles.

See the totem pole above town.

Canoe or kayak in bay between Kupreanof and Kuiu Islands. Many inlets and small islands. Several Forest Service cabins.

## Facilities

ACCOMMODATIONS (plus 5% tax): **Waterfront Lodge**, Box 222, Kake, AK 99830. 785-3472, fax 785-3885. 1 mile from dock, in town. Has 8 rooms, meals family style for hotel guests. Cable TV, phone. Coin laundry. Single $70, Double $90.

**Keex'Kwaan Lodge**, Box 207, Kake, AK 99830. 785-3434. 12 rooms with phone, cable TV, view. Full service restaurant. Single $78, Double $98. Fishing charters.

**Nuggett Inn**, 785-3132, 785-6469. 3 rooms—2 singles $45, 1 double. $65. Often rented for summer to workers.

RESTAURANTS: **Nuggett Inn**, known for its good food. **Ozzie's Arcade**, fast food. **Jule's Pizza**, pizza only. **Keex'Kwaan Lodge Restaurant**, full service, breakfast, lunch and dinner.

GROCERY STORES, 2, **SOS Value-Mart**, 785-6444, general store with Alaska souvenirs and postcards. **Ace's Variety**, 785-4444, variety items, snack food, video rentals.

BOAT FUEL available at Kake Cold Storage dock, launch ramp. Boat charters, 785-3434.

PICNIC AREA at Portage Area, 1.5 miles, to right of dock, no facilities.

TAXI: CB Channel 4.

FERRY SERVICE from Petersburg, Sitka, Juneau 2X/week, *M/V LeConte* .

AIR SERVICE: **LAB**, 785-6435, to Juneau, Petersburg, Hoonah, and Angoon daily. **Taquan Air,** 785-6411 Sitka and Juneau daily. Airstrip: Paved, 4000'. No facilities. 100 octane fuel is available at seaplane base on waterfront.

CLINIC: **City of Kake Health Clinic,** 785-3333. Physician assistant and four health aides available. No on-site physician.

INFORMATION: There is no Chamber of Commerce and Kake does not have brochures available. **Petersburg Chamber of Commerce** or **U.S. Forest Service** in Petersburg may have information. **Kake City Hall,** 785-3804. Box 500, Kake, AK 99830. Or call Diane Wilson, 785-4815.

# ANGOON
(Area Code 907, Zip Code 99820)

ANGOON (pop. 639), is the only settlement on Admiralty Island. It is a Tlingit fishing village at the mouth of Mitchell Bay, a narrow-mouthed saltwater "chuck" featuring incredible currents at the tide change. This is also the end of the Cross-Admiralty canoe/kayak route, a system of cabins, trails, lakes and creeks, connecting the east and west sides of Admiralty Island. There is fishing in season for salmon, trout, herring, and halibut.

Most of Admiralty Island has been declared a national monument and wilderness. For information, check with U.S. Forest Service Information Center in Centennial Hall in Juneau, 586-8751. Wildlife watching is good— but note that this island has brown bears, an estimated average of one per square mile, considered the densest brown bear population in the world. Occasionally one is even seen from the ferry docked at Angoon. Note— bears may regard a piece of stream or lakeshore as *theirs*.

## To See and Do
Fish, hike, beachcomb, kayak, canoe. Be careful of tides and rough water that can develop quickly in Chatham Strait. Weather changes rapidly.

See **Historical Center** with new totems, artifacts, historical photos.

## Facilities
FERRY SERVICE: Several times weekly from Juneau and Sitka.

CHARTER PLANE SERVICE from Juneau and Sitka. **Bellair Service,** 788-3641 from Sitka, six days a week. **Wings of Alaska,** 788-3530.

ACCOMMODATIONS: **Kootznahoo Inlet Lodge,** Box 134, Angoon, AK 99820. 788-3501. At plane float, 2 miles from ferry dock. 11 units, 6 with kitchen. Restaurant. TV , coffee service in rooms. Single $125, Double $150, including 3 meal. Suite $150. Kitchenettes $15 extra. Fishing packages include room, meals, flights to/from Juneau or Sitka, guide, boat: 3 day $1600, 5 day $2200, 7 day $2800. Laundry facilities. Kayak and skiff rentals. Bring own fishing gear. Chartered fishing. Sightseeing rates negotiable.

The Point Retreat light house from the ferry route.

web: slblackhurst@hotmail.com

**Favorite Bay Inn Bed and Breakfast,** Box 101, Angoon, AK 99820. 788-3123, (800) 423-3123. Overlooks Favorite Bay, walking distance from village. 4 guest rooms, 3 baths, family room, library, deck. Courtesy transportation from ferry dock or seaplane terminal. Boat, canoe, and kayak rentals. Salmon, halibut, and trout fishing available. Whale watching, natural history and wildlife tours. Single $89, Double $129, including breakfast. Other meals available. E-mail: favoritebayinn@juno.com

**Whaler's Cove Lodge,** on Kilisnoo Harbor, 3 miles south of Angoon, on island across from ferry dock. Box 101, Angoon, AK 99820. 788-3123, (800) 423-3123. Sportfishing for all saltwater fish, trout, steelhead. Fishing packages all-inclusive: round trip air fare from Juneau, meals, boat, tackle, fish processing. Guided or self-guided packages starting from $1995. Open late May through September. Web: www.whalerscovelodge.com  E-mail: whalerscovelodge@juno.com

GROCERY STORES: Two. **Seaside** and **Angoon Trading Company.**

BOAT FUEL: at **Angoon Standard Oil.**

BOAT RENTALS: **Alaska Discovery** through Dick Powers, 788-3123.

CRAFTS: The villagers make and sell blankets, moccasins, and other beaded items at their homes.

Angoon is a dry community, so alcohol cannot be legally bought locally.

LAUNDRY FACILITIES at hotels, coin operated. Public laundry at Angoon Community Association.

TAXI: **Eagle Taxi**, 788-3343.

ICE: at the grocery stores.

INFORMATION AVAILABLE at the **Angoon City Office**, 788-3653 and 788-3663. Box 189, Angoon, AK 99820.

# TENAKEE SPRINGS
(Area Code 907, Zip Code 99841)

TENAKEE SPRINGS (pop. 141) is a settlement near Tenakee Hot Springs on Chichagof Island. It is scenic, quiet, and marks one end of a good canoe route from Hoonah. Main street is a path. The only "cars" in town are the oil truck and fire truck. Hot springs feed the bath house adjacent to the dock and Main Street. The ferry dock is in the center of town. There are 16 miles of excellent footpath along the shoreline, extending 8 miles east and west of town.

Tenakee is an idyllic place to get "unhurried" for a few days. Watching the seals out at the reef, fishing boats coming and going, the eagle on the piling in front of your lodge, salmon spawning in Indian River, and soaking yourself in the hot spring while visiting with the local people is a fine break even in the middle of a tourist trip through the rest of Alaska.

If you're staying over, particularly on weekdays when the cafes keep shorter hours, you may have to plan eating times. Dinner after 4 p.m. means cooking it yourself if you have housekeeping facilities or are camping—or making reservations earlier with the Blue Moon Cafe for the time you want to eat. On weekends everyone keeps longer hours.

Accommodations are limited. Get reservations, ask if there's anything new, stay with a friend there, or plan to camp.

The people of Tenakee are a tough and resourceful lot. They've rebuilt after storm wave damage and fires.

### To See and Do
Walk the path that's Tenakee's main street. Enjoy the relaxed atmosphere, variety of cabins and gardens, friendly people, and beautiful views. Draw, paint, photograph, or simply relax.

Birdwatch, pick berries outside of town, kayak, and canoe.

Whalewatch for humpbacks and orcas.

Fish for salmon, halibut, and trout. Set a pot for crab or shrimp.

Enjoy hot mineral springs in Tenakee Bathhouse, next to ferry dock.

Floatplane from Juneau lands at Tenakee Springs after a 30 minute flight.

Men's and women's hours posted. Donations accepted at Snyder's Mercantile to help maintain building.

### Facilities

ACCOMMODATIONS: **Snyder Mercantile Co.**, Box 505, Tenakee Springs, AK 99841. 736-2205. Cottages for rent, with cooking facilities. Supplies available at Snyder's General Store. Near ferry dock and plane float. Cottages from $40/day. Cabins sleep 2 to 6. Ask for one of the modern ones with deck just east of the store. Reservations a must. Full info on services and ferry and plane schedules provided when booking reservations.

**Tenakee Hot Springs Lodge**, Box 3, Tenakee Springs, AK 99841. Phone/ Fax 736-2400. Full package luxury fishing lodge with guided fishing for salmon, halibut, trout. 5 days/5 nights, $2590/person plus tax, includes round trip air, Juneau–Tenakee. Open mid-May to mid-September. e-mail: tenakeehsl@juno.com

CAMPGROUND at Indian River, 2 miles east of town. No facilities. Brown bears sometimes, especially when salmon spawn in the river during late summer. I wouldn't camp here then. Be careful with food and garbage and don't argue with bears—anything they've taken, including space, is now theirs.

RESTAURANTS: **Blue Moon Cafe** next to dock. **The Bakery in the Shamrock**, baked goods, continental breakfast, sandwiches, light lunch. Open 7 a.m.– 2 p.m.

GROCERY STORE adjacent to dock, open 9 a.m.– 5 p.m. Mon.– Sat.

LAUNDROMAT: open daily.

PUBLIC COIN PHONE in booth near store and bath house. Available 24 hours/day. Also a public coin phone at the boat harbor.

BOAT FUEL and tie space available. A Juneau friend cautions boaters to tie near cafe carefully. He moored a skiff to the dock and failed to allow for its tidal swing. When he used the open-bottom restroom at the back of the cafe, he thought a skiff underneath looked familiar. It was!

BOAT CHARTERS: **Jason's Custom Charters**, Box 4, Tenakee Springs, AK 99841. 736-2311. Sightseeing, photography, fishing.

FERRY SERVICE: *LeConte* northbound from Sitka twice a week, southbound three times a week. The trip southbound from Juneau, Friday afternoon, returning Sunday morning makes a nice excursion with about 22 hours in Tenakee (arrival and departure are in middle of the night both ways). Note schedule variations the weeks the ferry goes to Pelican. People in Tenakee are sensitive to gawkers with cameras tramping through their yards, etc. Please be considerate.

SCHEDULED AIR SERVICE: operators in Juneau and Sitka. **Wings of Alaska**, 736-2247, has daily flights from Juneau. **Taquan Air**, 747-8636, has scheduled flights from Sitka.

INFORMATION AVAILABLE, **Snyder Mercantile Co.**, Box 505, Tenakee Springs, AK 99841. 736-2205.

# HOONAH
(Area Code 907, Zip Code 99829)

HOONAH (pop. 932) is the site of a very old Tlingit settlement on Port Frederick, a good natural harbor that remained ice-free during the last glacial advance that filled Glacier Bay only 200 years ago. Most houses in the village are similar as the U.S. government sent prefab housing after the village burned in 1944. Commercial fishing, subsistence hunting and fishing, and logging by the local native corporation are the main activities. Due to the logging, miles of gravel roads run almost to Tenakee. Hoonah has frequent ferry service from Juneau and Sitka. On the north shore of Chichagof Island, it's at one end of the canoe route to Tenakee Springs, about 40 miles including a portage from Port Frederick to Tenakee Inlet.

## To See and Do

Walk around the scenic village with its beautiful views across Port Frederick.

Visit the **Hoonah Cultural Center** on Roosevelt street overlooking town. Historical and cultural exhibits. Open 8 a.m.–4:30 p.m., Monday–Friday. Admission free, but donations appreciated. Hoonah Indian Association, 945-3545.

Hoonah's old cannery cold storage facility on the point.

Hike Spasski Trail, 3 miles, east of airport. Minimal marking and maintenance.

Walk the road to the left of the ferry dock, northwest, past the old Indian cemetery to the picturesque cannery at its end—about 15 minutes each way. Fishing is good for Dolly Varden from the point.

The nearby dump attracts brown bears and is a good place to see them if you're in a vehicle, preferably with a villager who knows how far you must stay away.

The beach north of cannery has a fascinating variety of banded pebbles and rocks, including jasper. Wave-worn now, they were carried miles by the glaciers that shaped Glacier Bay.

Fish for salmon, trout, halibut.

### Facilities
(Rates plus 5% tax. Most have winter rates.)
ACCOMMODATIONS: **Hoonah Lodge**, Box 320, Hoonah, AK 99829. 945-3636, fax 945-3610. 24 rooms with TV and phone. Restaurant featuring seafood, American, Italian, and Mexican dishes. Lounge, gift shop, fax, e-mail, and computer printouts. Fishing and hunting charters can be arranged. Single/Double $63.

**Dancing Bear**, Box 312, Hoonah, AK 99829. 945-3500, fax 945-3497. 1.5 miles from ferry, Garteeni Hwy. 4 non-smoking upstairs rooms share 2 baths, kitchen, living room with TV. Full breakfast. Single/Double $85.

**Whalewatch Lodge**, Box 245, Hoonah, AK 99829. On 2nd St., up hill from town center. Phone/fax 945-3327. Operates as fishing lodge May–August with guided fishing packages. September–April it's a B&B. 3 rooms (1 has private bath) share kitchen, laundry, satellite TV. Continental breakfast. Single $65. Double $75. e-mail: fishes@hoonah.net web: www.ptialaska.net/~kevinw

**Wind 'n Sea Inn**, Box 490, Hoonah, AK 99829. 945-3438 and (888) 945-3438. At 527 Garteeni, 1 mile from airport and ferry dock. 8 rooms, shared bath and kitchen, living room with TV. Coin-op washer & dryer. Rooms small and bright, double bed, screened window. Continental breakfast. Single/Double $65.

Bed & Breakfasts: **Bucking Salmon B&B**, 945-3326. **Hubbard's B&B**, 945-3414. **Tina's Room Rentals**, 945-3442, 2–9 p.m.

RESTAURANTS: **Mary's Inn**, 945-3228. **Hoonah Lodge**, 945-3636.

CAMP: Check with harbormaster, Paul Dybdahl for acceptable place. 945-3670.

HARBOR FACILITIES: Transient floats inner harbor, under 40 ft. $2/night, over 40 ft. $4/night. Free first 24 hours on outer harbor float. Telephone, showers, and coin-op laundry. Paul Dybdahl, harbormaster, 945-3670.

GROCERY STORES: There are 2.

LAUNDROMAT: Located at Harbormaster's office.

BUS: none. TAXI: **Papa's Cab**, 945-3685. **Huna Taxi**, 723-4862.

TOURS: **Janaggen Touring & Guiding**, 945-3511, fax 945-3706. Van tours with Jan Skaflestadt on Chichagof roads for scenery, wildlife watching and photography.

FERRY SERVICE: dock about 1 mile west of center of town, 945-3292.

AIRPORT: 3600 ft. runway, lighted, paved. Scheduled air service from Juneau, **LAB Flying Service**, 945-3661. **Wings of Alaska**, 945-3275. **Haines Airways**, 945-3701.

BOAT FUEL: **Hoonah Trading Company**, 945-3211. Tie-up space.

REGISTERED HUNTING GUIDE SERVICE (for deer and bear): **Ken Schoonover**, Box 13, Hoonah, AK 99829. 945-3223. **Wendell Skaflestad**, Box 214, Hoonah, AK 99829. 945-3229. **John Ericson**, Box 251, Hoonah, AK 99829. 945-3274.

BOAT CHARTERS: **Floyd Peterson**, F.I.S.H.E.S., 945-3327. Brochures available. **Fish Slammer Charters**, (800) 6HOONAH. **Galatea Charters**, 945-3525. **Hoonah Charters**, 945-3334.

CLINIC: **Hoonah Health Clinic**, behind the Senior Apartments, 9 a.m.–4 p.m., Monday–Friday. 945-3235 or 945-3386. Emergency 911.

INFORMATION AVAILABLE, City Hall, Mon–Fri., 945-3663, 945-3664, fax 945-3445. City Clerk, **City of Hoonah**, Box 360, Hoonah, AK 99829. **U.S. Forest Service Hoonah Ranger District Office**, Box 135, Hoonah, AK 99829. 945-3631. Has "Hoonah Area Road Guide" for $4 showing topography, shoreline of north Chichagof Island including Tenakee Inlet, and logging roads.

## Happenings

**Kid's Trout Derby**—June.

**4th of July**—Parade and booths with games and food.

**Fall Carnival**—October

# PELICAN
(Area Code 907, Zip Code 99832)

PELICAN, pop. 200, is a tiny fishing village with a cold storage plant on Lisianski Inlet, a scenic fiord on the northwest corner of Chichagof Island. Ferry service is twice a month in summer, and monthly in winter. The ferry stays about two hours, but that is time to get off (and plan to fly back to Juneau) or walk up the one-lane boardwalk main street to the far end of town. Sometimes fish and crab can be bought from the cold storage plant. It is a bustling place during fishing season or on 4th of July, the big annual date in town. The round trip on the ferry makes a good day excursion from Juneau, with great scenery and, frequently, whales and sea otters.

## To See and Do

Walk around town, including fishing harbor with lots of boats and gear, surrounded by spectacular scenery in the fiord. Few places in America have this lifestyle in the 20th century.

Fish anywhere. Peak seasons: King salmon in April, May, June. Coho salmon in July, August. All summer, trout and halibut.

Kayak scenic West Chichagof Island (West Chichagof-Yakobi Wilderness) if you've solved the problem of how to return to Juneau or can stay until the ferry's next trip. Some experienced paddlers go from Pelican to Sitka, a multi-day trip for experienced sea kayakers.

## Facilities

ACCOMMODATIONS: **Rosie's Bar & Grill**, 100 yards from ferry dock, has 4 rooms for rent. Box 42, Pelican, AK 99832. 735-2265. Adjacent to Rosie's. Gift shop and museum. Open all year. Single $65, Double $95.

**Lisianski Inlet Lodge**, Box 776, Pelican 99832. 735-2266. (800) 962-8441. Web: www.alaskaone.com/starbuck/index.htm  E-mail: kuhook@aol.com

Cabin and charter boat just outside Pelican. Beach cabin for 5 and lodge rooms for 8, bed and breakfast. Can furnish all meals. Complimentary packing of your fish. Per person: $150/day room /board, $370/day for room, meals, guide and boat. Guided hikes, $50/day. Whale watching.

**Otter Cove Bed & Breakfast**, Box 618, Pelican, AK 99832. 735-2259. Toll free (888) 687-2683. Website: www.AlaskaOne.com/ottercove. On beach, short walk from downtown. 1 room, 1 cabin. Private baths. Open year round. $65-$200. Guided hikes and boat trips for wildlife viewing and photography, $105-$275.

**Beyond the Boardwalk Bed & Breakfast,** Box 12, Pelican, AK 99832. 735-2463, Open Mid-June through August. Three rooms, $75–95. Winter phone (360 297-3550.

CAMPING: Ask the locals. Very little level ground in area. The flats across the creek south of town flood at high tide. No camping within city limits. Must have boat or hike out of town.

GROCERY STORE: 1 general store.

RESTAURANT: 1 restaurant and 2 bar/ grills.

BOAT FUEL at Chevron in center of town. 735-2206.

LAUNDROMAT: downtown.

FISHING CHARTERS: **Starbuck Charters**, P.O. Box 765, Pelican AK 99832. 735-2266, (800) 962-8441. **Otter Cove B&B Nature Tours**, 735-2259, **Pelican Charters**. 735-2460. **Chikobi Charters**, 735-2233. **Howard Charters**, 735-2207. **FV Demijohn**, 735-2266.

KAYAKING: **Pelican Paddling**, 735-2495.

KAYAK RENTALS: **Lisianski Inlet Lodge, Loken Aviation**

SCHEDULED AIR SERVICE: From Juneau 7 days/week, **Loken Aviation**, 735-2244. (800) 478-3360. From Sitka, 3 times/week, **Taquan Air Service**, 747-8636.

INFORMATION AVAILABLE: **Pelican Visitors Association**, Box 737, Pelican, AK 99832. 735-2282 and 735-2259. Fax 735-2258.

## Elfin Cove

Nearby, but accessible only by floatplane or boat from Pelican or Juneau, is the tiny village of Elfin Cove, in a rocky cove near the entrance to Lisianski Inlet, adjacent to great salmon and halibut fishing. The ferry does not stop here, though it gives you a glimpse from one of its alternate routes to Pelican.

**The Cove Lodge** offers fishing packages for up to 8 people. Rooms for 2 with private bath. Open mid-May to mid-September. Summer: Box 17,

Elfin Cove, AK 99825. Phone/fax 239-2221. Winter: 10013 NE Hazel Dell Ave., Ste. 146, Vancouver, WA 98685. Phone/fax (800) 382-3847.

**Elfin Cove Charters** offers fishing packages, using their **Cross Sound Lodge** and boats from Elfin Cove, for salmon and halibut. Freshwater river fishing available. Fully guided five day trips. Can accommodate up to 16 guests. (800) 323-5346. Summer: Box 85, Elfin Cove, AK 99825. Winter (October through April): 15917 NE Union Rd., Suite 115, Ridgefield WA 98642.

**Tanaku Lodge**, fishing for halibut and salmon. Box 72, Elfin Cove, AK 99825. 239-2205, (800) 482-6258. Web: www.tanaku.com E-mail: tanaku@msn.com Fishing packages, 4 days/3 nights $2195 and 6 days/5 nights $2595.

Chichagof Island salmon stream and bear watching spot (above). A lone whale breeches, and falls back with a mighty splash (below).

# Notes For Inside Passage Travelers

Accommodations and activities for tourists have multiplied recently, especially bed & breakfasts, tours, and charter boats. These change often and would fill many pages (which you would have to carry) for larger towns. I have listed associations, but suggest you get current lists from visitors' bureaus in towns where you'll stay. If you want complete lists rather than just the bureaus' members, ask for their convention/meeting kit or other complete list— you may have to be insistent.

Bed & breakfasts aren't inexpensive, but offer more hospitality and individuality than hotels and a chance to meet local people and sample Alaskan living. Many have just 2 or 3 rooms, so you need reserations. If having a private instead of shared bath is important, ask what's available.

Most facilities, especially lodgings, have low season rates as much as 20–30% lower than their summer rates. From mid-September to mid-May, you should definitely ask. While there is no state sales tax, note that a 5–6% hotel tax is often added to a town's 4–6% sales tax for a hefty 12% addition to your bill.

As tourism has grown, now almost every town (certainly every mainline port) has someone renting kayaks and/or bicycles, and offering kayak trips and guided walks. Fishing charters boats and wildlife-viewing boat trips are available everywhere. The visitors' bureaus have current lists. Some operators in main ports have contracted with cruise ship lines and may be unavailable to individual travelers, or operating such assembly-line operations with large boats that you'd rather ride with someone else.

Alaska is celebrating its Gold Rush Centennial (1894–1904) with events and exhibits in many towns. For info, note the Klondike Gold Rush web site, http://Gold-Rush.org and the Alaska Division of Tourism e-mail address for a Gold Rush Trails Map: GoNorth@commerce.state.ak.us or call (907) 465-2010.

Alaskan distances are so great, you'll enjoy your trip more if you concentrate on one area unless you have several months. On a recent 17-day trip in August, my husband and I flew to Juneau, spent several days there, rode a ferry to Sitka and spent three nights (rode a boat out to the bird rookeries on St. Lazaria Island), flew to Ketchikan as there wasn't a ferry that day, and spent two nights there. We rode a ferry to Wrangell for three nights there and a jet boat trip to watch bears at Anan Creek. Then we rode a ferry back to Juneau (a daylight run through the narrows) for two more nights before flying home. We rented a car in each town, stayed in a hotel, several b&bs, and with friends, hiked and photographed, and missed the August crowds almost completely. You have lots of choices in Southeast Alaska and can make the trip your way!

# HAVING FUN, WITHOUT ACCIDENT, OFF THE BEATEN TRACK

Southeastern Alaska is a big area with few people and lots of cool, wet weather, poor visibility, and miles of **very cold** water. One quickly develops respect for prehistoric Indians who roamed these forests and paddled open canoes as far as Portland, Oregon. They must have been very good at staying dry, or very stoic about being cold and wet.

Judgment and planning are everything, whether you're hiking, boating, or flying. Any time you move into a new climate and an unfamiliar area, you have a new set of nature's rules to learn, and in Alaska, nature can be very quick and violent.

**Weather, tides, and currents** change rapidly here. When 20 vertical feet of water go somewhere every 6 hours, the currents in narrow channels and the constricted mouths of wider bays can easily exceed 8 knots. Winds and downdrafts in mountain passes can do the same thing. Visibility may drop rapidly, far from harbor, airport, or campsite.

**Clothing** should include the rain gear and warm woolens you'll need if it gets cold and wet. If it's warm now, you can wear light clothing, but have the other with you. Passengers who fly with me wear a lifejacket or floatcoat flying over water, and wear or bring boots, parka, etc. for flying over the icefield. If a boat sinks or capsizes, what will you have with you on the beach? Down is useless when wet—wool and fiberfill retain some warmth. Wet blue jeans are deadly. Surplus stores and the Salvation Army have inexpensive wool pants.

**Shelter.** Some light emergency shelter should be in your boat, plane, or pack, adequate for overnight in rain on wet ground. A tube tent fastened to your floatcoat or lifejacket, so it and you reach shore together, is a good idea.

**Fire starter** or stove can be useful, though it's best not to count on being able to burn wet wood. Large clear plastic playing dice make an excellent fire starter that doesn't crumble in a pocket. Bring an ample supply of starter and dry matches. Practice starting fires in wet conditions if you haven't done it before. Spruce sap or gum pulled off tree trunks was used by Indians as fire starter.

**Insect repellent** is a must. Besides the standard ones in every drugstore, you may want to try diluted Avon "Skin-So-Soft" bath oil which is effective and easier on your skin. It works for black flies as well as mosquitoes, though you'll need to replace it more often for the latter. In a pinch you can use the native solution—rubbing your skin with the inner bark from alder trees.

**Distress signals** and extra food are musts. People are hard to see in this big country, so make it easier for those looking for you. Pocket flares or a strobe are good and don't weigh much. Carry a copy of the air-to-ground emergency signals. Waving OK to a plane or helicopter could send the pilot off when you need him.

**Let someone know** where you're going, and don't go alone. The smaller the area anyone has to search for you, the sooner you'll be in where it's dry and warm. Do let people know when you've returned. Stay together.

**Bears** need respect if we're to coexist. Brown bears, especially, can claim a territory or fishing stream as theirs. Keep food and food smells away from camp and out of your pockets. Burn all garbage. Make some noise anywhere you go. Bears are apparently attracted to human menstrual odors. Ask local people about recent bear sightings. Anything a bear takes is now *his*.

**Turn back** if weather or sea get bad. Check weather before going, and then watch it. Listen for reports if you have radio. Weather can change very rapidly here.

**Don't have to get there,** or back today. Hole up and wait it out. Bring the supplies you'll need to do that.

**Learn the area as soon as possible**, carry charts and ask the locals a lot of questions. Many aviation radio repeaters have been installed in Southeast Alaska. With current charts, you can talk to Flight Service Stations in Ketchikan, Sitka, or Juneau from most areas even if you're below hilltops.

**For pilots and boaters:** In air or water, know the rules of the road and obey. Know your equipment and your ability. Always have an alternative goal—not easy when bays or airports are far apart. Don't overload—always have a margin. Carry adequate personal flotation gear, and wear it when the sea is rough. Watch for partly submerged logs and ice.

**Work up** to bigger things; don't just jump in. A hiker on his first backpack trip ever, on the Chilkoot Pass, complained to the ranger about the steep trail. "But didn't the pictures in town show you it would be steep?" "Oh, I thought with all the people going over, it would have worn down some."

*Note:* :You can reserve campgrounds and cabins by calling (800)444-6777. From outside US and Canada, call (518)885-3639. Internet users can reserve at www.reserveusa.com

Author's husband, Hank Jori, casts into Kowee Creek north of Juneau for pink salmon.

A favorite walk is the trail on the dike around Juneau's floatplane pond at the airport, overlooking the Mendenhall wetlands. Birding is always good, and you may even see swans during migration. Late afternoon light on the wetlands and a view of the glacier are memorable.

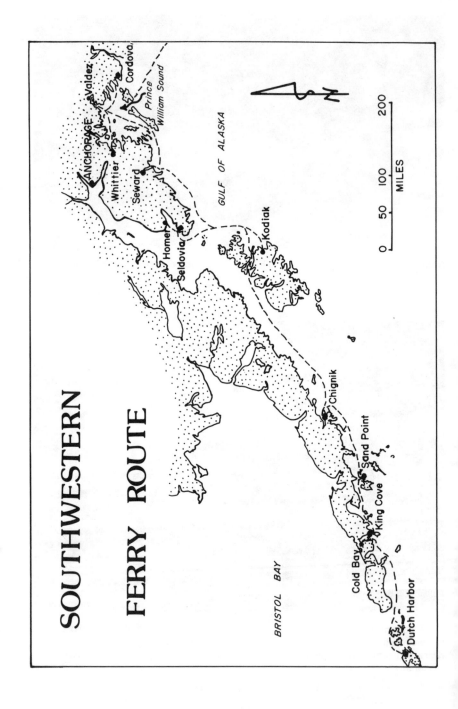

SOUTHWESTERN FERRY ROUTE

222

Outbound from Kodiak Harbor, a tug passes under the bridge and heads up the channel.

## THE SOUTHWESTERN FERRY SYSTEM

The two ferries, *Bartlett* and *Tustumena*, make up the Southwest System, also part of the Alaska Marine Highway. In summer the *Kennicott* now makes a monthly run from Juneau to Valdez and Seward, connecting the two systems on a regular basis for the first time. In winter the *Kennicott* replaces the *Tustumena* on its route for several months. The *Bartlett* serves Prince William Sound with stops at Whittier, Valdez, and Cordova. The *Tustumena* serves Seward, Seldovia, Homer, Kodiak, Port Lions, Valdez, and Cordova, and has monthly trips in summer out the Aleutian Chain with stops both ways at Kodiak, Chignik, Sand Point, King Cove, Cold Bay, and Unalaska. Reservations are needed, even for walk-on passengers on all these runs.

The *Bartlett's* trips in Prince William Sound are beautifully scenic and make a fine excursion from Anchorage, using the Alaska Railroad to reach the ferry at Whittier, which doesn't have road access. You can also drive to or from Valdez, which has bus service as well. Cordova doesn't have road connections with the rest of Alaska, though it has daily service from Anchorage and Juneau with **Alaska Airlines**. The nearby Copper River Delta is one of the world's important rest areas for migratory waterfowl and has nesting swans in summer.

The *Bartlett* 's round trip from Valdez to Whittier and return makes a fine all-day excursion. The ship tours Prince William Sound, passing bird rookeries, whale feeding areas, sea otters and other marine mammals, and perhaps Bligh Reef. On weekends there is a Forest Service naturalist on board helping you spot wildlife. Whether you ride the ferry or one of the tour boats between Valdez and Whittier, this is a fine trip.

The *Tustumena* sails between Seward and Valdez on Thursdays, returning on Fridays, offering an unhurried and uncrowded trip on which you may be able to get a stateroom if you want it for the day.

Tour boats go from both Valdez and Whittier to the Columbia Glacier which calves into a fiord near Valdez.

We can all hope that in future summers Alaska's state government will again allow the ferries to turn up the inlet to give passengers a view of the Columbia Glacier. Tour boat operators lobbied to prevent this in 1999.

The *Tustumena's* runs to Kodiak Island are an experience. These are not protected "inside" waters, and the 10-hour trip is locally known as the "Dramamine Run." In summer it is often calm with many puffins flying by, sea otters, whales, and bird rookeries on the Barren Islands. If you want the experience or want to get your car to Kodiak, you can enjoy a real ocean trip. For the runs out the Chain you definitely need reservations. The *Tustumena* has some staterooms, but the *Bartlett* , sailing in Prince William Sound between Whittier, Valdez, and Cordova, has none.

If you're going out the Chain, most direct access is from Homer. If you get on the ferry at Seward, the ship goes to Kodiak and back to Homer and returns to Kodiak before going west. You can stay on for several crossings of the Gulf, paying for the additional distance, or you can stop over in Kodiak. For trips west or to Kodiak, you could go one way on the ferry and fly to or from Anchorage the other way.

Kodiak has famous scenery, sportfishing for halibut and salmon, and hunting for bear and deer. It is the site of the first permanent Russian settlement in Alaska and has a fine museum in the Russian-built Erskine House a block from the ferry dock. The harbor is home to one of Alaska's largest fishing fleets and to charter boats for fishing, hunting, and trips to bird rookeries. The bird, otter, and whale watching alone would be worth the trip, whether you go by sea or air. Seniors have noted that the senior travel privilege on the *Tustumena* (space available) makes this an inexpensive trip from Seward or Homer.

If you're traveling on the senior or disabled pass reduced rate, note that such travel is **not** allowed between April 1 and September 30 on the *Bartlett* or *Tustumena* between Valdez and Whittier or Seward or at any sea-

At Halibut Cove, across Kachemak Bay from Homer, guests and life-size wooden figures mingle on the deck of a small lodge. Can you spot the wooden ones?

son on roundtrip sailings between Homer and Unalaska, Seldovia and Unalaska or Kodiak and Unalaska on the same Aleutian Chain trip.

The towns on the Alaska Peninsula and the Aleutian Chain are famous for birdwatching during migration, as is the Copper River Delta near Cordova. Whole species of waterfowl pass through here, stopping off to rest and feed at the world's largest eelgrass beds in Izembek Lagoon near Cold Bay. The Copper River Delta is a nesting area for waterfowl, including swans.

Homer and Seward are popular destinations for travelers, especially RV campers. Both towns have hotels, bed & breakfasts (several on small farms east of Homer), campgrounds, fishing charter boats, and bicycle and kayak rentals. Nearby are state parks, wilderness areas, U.S. Forest Service cabins, glaciers and hiking trails.

In recent winters the *Tustumena* has made several trips between Seward and Juneau, offering an alternative to winter driving up the highway. A smooth ride isn't guaranteed across the Gulf of Alaska in winter! The *Kennicott's* winter schedule was not announced at presstime.

Both Southwest ferries have solariums and dining room service, but the *Bartlett* has no elevator or baggage cart. The *Bartlett* doesn't have rental blankets or pillows as most of its runs are in daylight.

For another dimension to Alaska and unbeatable scenery, why not try the marine buses of the Southwest? You can make reservations and buy tickets at any ferry terminal in Southwest Alaska, in Anchorage, or by calling the **Juneau** main office, (800) 642-0066 or 465-3941. Other terminal numbers are: **Anchorage**, 272-4482; **Cordova**, 424-7333; **Homer**, 235-8449; **Kodiak**, 486-3800; **Seldovia**, 234-7868; **Seward**, 224-5485; and **Valdez**, 835-4436.

INFORMATION AVAILABLE: **Cordova Chamber of Commerce**, 424-7260; **Homer Visitor Center**, 235-7740; **Kodiak Island Visitor Center**, 486-4782; Kodiak **National Wildlife Refuge**, 487-2600; **Seward Chamber of Commerce**, 224-3094; **Valdez Visitor Center**, 835-2984; **Chugach National Forest**, 271-2500 (for trail and Forest Service cabin info).

Note: Railway connections required between Portage and Whittier for all Whittier arrivals and departures. No reservations, but holders of ferry reservations get priority in loading train. Alaska Railroad, (800) 544-0552 or 265-2494 .

### Railroad Shuttle Fares, One-Way

| | |
|---|---|
| Adult Vehicle Occupants other than driver | $12 |
| Child 2–11 (under 2 free) | 6 |
| Motorcycles & Kayaks | 30 |
| Vehicles to 23 feet | 60 |
| Vehicles to 40 feet | 90 |

*M/V E. L. Bartlett*

May 1–August 29, 1999. Maximum size vehicle, 60 feet long, gross weight 35 tons.

**PORTAGE TO WHITTIER***

| | | |
|---|---|---|
| LV | PORTAGE | 10:15 AM |
| AR | WHITTIER | 10:55 AM |
| LV | PORTAGE | 1:20 PM |
| AR | WHITTIER | 2:00 PM |

**WHITTIER TO PORTAGE**

| | | |
|---|---|---|
| LV | WHITTIER | 3:30 PM |
| AR | PORTAGE | 4:10 PM |
| LV | WHITTIER | 6:15 PM |
| AR | PORTAGE | 6:55 PM |

*Check-in time in Portage is one hour earlier than departure.

## M/V E. L. Bartlett

EFFECTIVE  MAY 27, 1999 — AUGUST 29, 1999

| **MON** | LV | VALDEZ | 7:15 AM | | **THU** | LV | VALDEZ | 7:15 AM |
|---|---|---|---|---|---|---|---|---|
| | AR | WHITTIER | 2:00 PM | | | AR | WHITTIER | 2:00 PM |
| | LV | WHITTIER | 2:45 PM | | | LV | WHITTIER | 2:45 PM |
| | AR | CORDOVA | 9:45 PM | | | AR | VALDEZ | 9:30 PM |
| | | | | | | | | |
| **MON** | LV | CORDOVA | 10:45 PM ** | | **FRI** | LV | VALDEZ | 5:00 AM ** |
| **TUE** | AR | VALDEZ | 6:15 AM | | | AR | CORDOVA | 12:45 PM |
| | LV | VALDEZ | 7:15 AM | | | LV | CORDOVA | 6:30 PM |
| | AR | WHITTIER | 2:00 PM | | **SAT** | AR | VALDEZ | 12:15 AM |
| | | | | | | | | |
| **TUE** | LV | WHITTIER | 2:45 PM | | **SAT** | LV | VALDEZ | 7:15 AM |
| | AR | VALDEZ | 9:30 PM | | | AR | WHITTIER | 2:00 PM |
| | LV | VALDEZ | 11:45 PM | | | LV | WHITTIER | 2:45 PM |
| **WED** | AR | CORDOVA | 5:30 AM | | | AR | VALDEZ | 9:30 PM |
| | | | | | | | | |
| **WED** | LV | CORDOVA | 7:00 AM | | **SUN** | LV | VALDEZ | 7:15 AM |
| | AR | WHITTIER | 2:00 PM | | | AR | WHITTIER | 2:00 PM |
| | LV | WHITTIER | 2:45 PM | | | LV | WHITTIER | 2:45 PM |
| | AR | VALDEZ | 9:30 PM | | | AR | VALDEZ | 9:30 PM |

**     Tatitlek Whistle Stops available by notifying Valdez or Cordova Terminal.

Train arrives at Portage with cars that rode from Valdez to Whittier on the *Bartlett*. A highway under construction is scheduled to open in 2000.

## *M/V Tustumena*

### JUNE EASTBOUND

| Leave SELDOVIA | | Leave HOMER | | PORT LIONS | | Arrive KODIAK | | Leave SEWARD | | Arrive VALDEZ | |
|---|---|---|---|---|---|---|---|---|---|---|---|
| T1 | 5:00P | T1 | 7:55P | W2 | 6:30A | Lv. W2 | 4:00P | TH3 | 9:45A | TH3 | 11:00P |
| SU6 | 6:00A | SU6 | 9:30A | | | SU6 | 7:00P | | | | |
| | | M7 | 9:30A | | | M7 | 7:00P | | | | |
| T8 | 4:00P | T8 | 11:30P | | | W9 | 9:00A | | | | |
| ***FROM ALEUTIAN CHAIN TRIP*** | | | | | | M14 | 8:15P | | | | |
| T15 | 4:00P | T15 | 7:55P | W16 | 6:30A | Lv. W16 | 4:00P | TH17 | 9:45A | TH17 | 11:00P |
| SU20 | 6:00A | SU20 | 9:30A | | | SU20 | 7:00P | | | | |
| | | M21 | 9:30A | | | M21 | 7:00P | | | | |
| T22 | 4:00P | T22 | 7:55P | W23 | 6:30A | Lv. W23 | 4:00P | TH24 | 9:45A | TH24 | 11:00P |
| SU27 | 6:00A | SU27 | 9:30A | | | SU27 | 7:00P | | | | |
| | | M28 | 9:30A | | | M28 | 7:00P | | | | |
| T29 | 4:00P | T29 | 7:55P | W30 | 6:30A | Lv. W30 | 4:00P | TH1 | 9:45A | TH1 | 11:00P |

### JUNE WESTBOUND

| Leave VALDEZ | | Leave SEWARD | | Leave KODIAK | | PORT LIONS | | Leave HOMER | | Arrive SELDOVIA | |
|---|---|---|---|---|---|---|---|---|---|---|---|
| F4 | 6:30A | F4 | 9:30P | S5 | 12:45P | S5 | 3:45P | SU6 | 3:30P | SU6 | 4:55A |
| | | | | SU6 | 10:30P | | | Ar. M7 | 8:00A | | |
| | | | | M7 | 10:30P | | | T8 | 12:30P | T8 | 2:00P |
| | | | | W9 | 4:55P | ***TO ALEUTIAN CHAIN TRIP*** | | | | | |
| | | | | M14 | 10:30P | | | T15 | 12:30P | T15 | 2:00P |
| F18 | 6:30A | F18 | 9:30P | S19 | 12:45P | S19 | 3:45P | SU20 | 3:30P | SU20 | 4:55A |
| | | | | SU20 | 10:30P | | | Ar. M21 | 8:00A | | |
| | | | | M21 | 10:30P | | | T22 | 12:30P | T22 | 2:00P |
| F25 | 6:30A | F25 | 9:30P | S26 | 12:45P | S26 | 3:45P | SU27 | 3:30P | SU27 | 4:55A |
| | | | | SU27 | 10:30P | | | Ar. M28 | 8:00A | | |
| | | | | M28 | 10:30P | | | T29 | 12:30P | T29 | 2:00P |

### JULY EASTBOUND

| Leave SELDOVIA | | Leave HOMER | | PORT LIONS | | Arrive KODIAK | | Leave SEWARD | | Arrive VALDEZ | |
|---|---|---|---|---|---|---|---|---|---|---|---|
| SU4 | 6:00A | SU4 | 9:30A | | | SU4 | 7:00P | | | | |
| | | M5 | 9:30A | | | M5 | 7:00P | | | | |
| T6 | 4:00P | T6 | 7:55P | W7 | 6:30A | Lv. W7 | 4:00P | TH8 | 9:45A | TH8 | 11:00P |
| SU11 | 6:00A | SU11 | 9:30A | | | SU11 | 7:00P | | | | |
| | | M12 | 9:30A | | | M12 | 7:00P | | | | |
| T13 | 4:00P | T13 | 11:30P | | | W14 | 9:00A | | | | |
| ***FROM ALEUTIAN CHAIN TRIP*** | | | | | | M19 | 8:15P | | | | |
| T20 | 4:00P | T20 | 7:55P | W21 | 6:30A | Lv. W21 | 4:00P | TH22 | 9:45A | TH22 | 11:00P |
| SU25 | 6:00A | SU25 | 9:30A | | | SU25 | 7:00P | | | | |
| | | M26 | 9:30A | | | M26 | 7:00P | | | | |
| T27 | 4:00P | T27 | 7:55P | W28 | 6:30A | Lv. W28 | 4:00P | TH29 | 9:45A | TH29 | 11:00P |

### JULY WESTBOUND

| Leave VALDEZ | | Leave SEWARD | | Leave KODIAK | | PORT LIONS | | Leave HOMER | | Arrive SELDOVIA | |
|---|---|---|---|---|---|---|---|---|---|---|---|
| F2 | 6:30A | F2 | 9:30P | S3 | 12:45P | S3 | 3:45P | SU4 | 3:30P | SU4 | 4:55A |
| | | | | SU4 | 10:30P | | | Ar. M5 | 8:00A | | |
| | | | | M5 | 10:30P | | | T6 | 12:30P | T6 | 2:00P |
| F9 | 6:30A | F9 | 9:30P | S10 | 12:45P | S10 | 3:45P | SU11 | 3:30P | SU11 | 4:55A |
| | | | | SU11 | 10:30P | | | Ar. M12 | 8:00A | | |
| | | | | M12 | 10:30P | | | T13 | 12:30P | T13 | 2:00P |
| | | | | W14 | 4:55P | ***TO ALEUTIAN CHAIN TRIP*** | | | | | |
| | | | | M19 | 10:30P | | | T20 | 12:30P | T20 | 2:00P |
| F23 | 6:30A | F23 | 9:30P | S24 | 12:45P | S24 | 3:45P | SU25 | 3:30P | SU25 | 4:55A |
| | | | | SU25 | 10:30P | | | Ar. M26 | 8:00A | | |
| | | | | M26 | 10:30P | | | T27 | 12:30P | T27 | 2:00P |
| F30 | 6:30A | F30 | 9:30P | S31 | 12:45P | S31 | 3:45P | SU1 | 3:30P | SU1 | 4:55A |

## *M/V Tustumena*

### AUGUST EASTBOUND

| Leave SELDOVIA | Leave HOMER | PORT LIONS | Arrive KODIAK | Leave SEWARD | Arrive VALDEZ |
|---|---|---|---|---|---|
| SU1 6:00A | SU1 9:30A | | SU1 7:00P | | |
| | M2 9:30A | | M2 7:00P | | |
| T3 4:00P | T3 7:55P | W4 6:30A | Lv. W4 4:00P | TH5 9:45A | TH5 11:00P |
| SU8 6:00A | SU8 9:30A | | SU8 7:00P | | |
| | M9 9:30A | | M9 7:00P | | |
| T10 4:00P | T10 11:30P | | W11 9:00A | | |
| ***FROM ALEUTIAN CHAIN TRIP*** | | | M16 8:15P | | |
| T17 4:00P | T17 7:55P | W18 6:30A | Lv. W18 4:00P | TH19 9:45A | TH19 11:00P |
| SU22 6:00A | SU22 9:30A | | SU22 7:00P | | |
| | M23 9:30A | | M23 7:00P | | |
| T24 4:00P | T24 7:55P | W25 6:30A | Lv. W25 4:00P | TH26 9:45A | TH26 11:00P |
| SU29 6:00A | SU29 9:30A | | SU29 7:00P | | |
| | M30 9:30A | | M30 7:00P | | |

### AUGUST WESTBOUND

| Leave VALDEZ | Leave SEWARD | Leave KODIAK | PORT LIONS | Leave HOMER | Arrive SELDOVIA |
|---|---|---|---|---|---|
| | | SU1 10:30P | | Ar. M2 8:00A | |
| | | M2 10:30P | | T3 12:30P | T3 2:00P |
| F6 6:30A | F6 9:30P | S7 12:45P | S7 3:45P | SU8 3:30A | SU8 4:55A |
| | | SU8 10:30P | | Ar. M9 8:00A | |
| | | M9 10:30P | | T10 12:30P | T10 2:00P |
| | | W11 4:55P | ***TO ALEUTIAN CHAIN TRIP*** | | |
| | | M16 10:30P | | T17 12:30P | T17 2:00P |
| F20 6:30A | F20 9:30P | S21 12:45P | S21 3:45P | SU22 3:30A | SU22 4:55A |
| | | SU22 10:30P | | Ar. M23 8:00A | |
| | | M23 10:30P | | T24 12:30P | T24 2:00P |
| F27 6:30A | F27 9:30P | S28 12:45P | S28 3:45P | SU29 3:30A | SU29 4:55A |
| | | SU29 10:30P | | Ar. M30 8:00A | |
| | | M30 10:30P | | T31 12:30P | T31 2:00P |

# M/V TUSTUMENA ALEUTIAN CHAIN TRIPS

| | | | | | | |
|---|---|---|---|---|---|
| LV KODIAK | WED | 4:55PM | LV UNALASKA | SAT | 11:45AM |
| LV CHIGNIK | THU | 1:00PM | LV AKUTAN | SAT | 4:00PM |
| LV SAND POINT | FRI | 12:30AM | LV COLD BAY | SUN | 4:45AM |
| LV KING COVE | FRI | 9:00AM | LV KING COVE | SUN | 7:15AM |
| LV COLD BAY | FRI | 11:55AM | LV SAND POINT | SUN | 3:00PM |
| LV FALSE PASS | FRI | 5:30PM | LV CHIGNIK | MON | 1:45AM |
| AR UNALASKA | SAT | 6:30AM | AR KODIAK | MON | 8:15PM |

Southwestern Ferries

# Southwestern & South Central Fares

# M/V TUSTUMENA CABIN TARIFFS

## FOUR BERTH CABIN — OUTSIDE/COMPLETE FACILITIES — ITEM 4BF

| BETWEEN AND | UNALASKA | AKUTAN | FALSE PASS | COLD BAY | KING COVE | SAND POINT | CHIGNIK | KODIAK | PORT LIONS | SELDOVIA | HOMER | SEWARD |
|---|---|---|---|---|---|---|---|---|---|---|---|---|
| AKUTAN | 23 | | | | | | | | | | | |
| FALSE PASS | 80 | 57 | | | | | | | | | | |
| COLD BAY | 109 | 86 | 29 | | | | | | | | | |
| KING COVE | 122 | 129 | 72 | 43 | | | | | | | | |
| SAND POINT | 152 | 165 | 108 | 79 | 68 | | | | | | | |
| CHIGNIK | 194 | 210 | 153 | 124 | 113 | 80 | | | | | | |
| KODIAK | 282 | 295 | 238 | 209 | 194 | 166 | 124 | | | | | |
| PORT LIONS | 282 | 295 | 238 | 209 | 194 | 166 | 124 | 43 | | | | |
| SELDOVIA | 337 | 350 | 293 | 264 | 250 | 216 | 182 | 96 | 96 | | | |
| HOMER | 328 | 342 | 285 | 256 | 242 | 209 | 175 | 88 | 88 | 43 | | |
| SEWARD | 349 | 362 | 305 | 276 | 262 | 228 | 194 | 98 | 98 | 163 | 155 | |
| VALDEZ | (NO DIRECT SAILINGS) | | | | | | | 164 | 164 | 216 | 209 | 91 |

## FOUR BERTH CABIN — INSIDE/NO FACILITIES — ITEM 4NO

| BETWEEN AND | UNALASKA | AKUTAN | FALSE PASS | COLD BAY | KING COVE | SAND POINT | CHIGNIK | KODIAK | PORT LIONS | SELDOVIA | HOMER | SEWARD |
|---|---|---|---|---|---|---|---|---|---|---|---|---|
| AKUTAN | 19 | | | | | | | | | | | |
| FALSE PASS | 66 | 47 | | | | | | | | | | |
| COLD BAY | 91 | 72 | 25 | | | | | | | | | |
| KING COVE | 102 | 108 | 61 | 36 | | | | | | | | |
| SAND POINT | 127 | 138 | 91 | 66 | 57 | | | | | | | |
| CHIGNIK | 162 | 175 | 128 | 103 | 94 | 67 | | | | | | |
| KODIAK | 235 | 246 | 199 | 174 | 162 | 138 | 103 | | | | | |
| PORT LIONS | 235 | 246 | 199 | 174 | 162 | 138 | 103 | 36 | | | | |
| SELDOVIA | 281 | 292 | 245 | 220 | 208 | 180 | 152 | 80 | 80 | | | |
| HOMER | 274 | 285 | 238 | 213 | 202 | 174 | 146 | 73 | 73 | 36 | | |
| SEWARD | 291 | 302 | 255 | 230 | 218 | 190 | 162 | 82 | 82 | 136 | 129 | |
| VALDEZ | (NO DIRECT SAILINGS) | | | | | | | 137 | 137 | 180 | 174 | 76 |

## TWO BERTH CABIN — OUTSIDE/NO FACILITIES — ITEM 2NO

| BETWEEN AND | UNALASKA | AKUTAN | FALSE PASS | COLD BAY | KING COVE | SAND POINT | CHIGNIK | KODIAK | PORT LIONS | SELDOVIA | HOMER | SEWARD |
|---|---|---|---|---|---|---|---|---|---|---|---|---|
| AKUTAN | 13 | | | | | | | | | | | |
| FALSE PASS | 47 | 33 | | | | | | | | | | |
| COLD BAY | 64 | 51 | 17 | | | | | | | | | |
| KING COVE | 75 | 79 | 45 | 28 | | | | | | | | |
| SAND POINT | 100 | 97 | 63 | 46 | 40 | | | | | | | |
| CHIGNIK | 129 | 129 | 95 | 78 | 68 | 43 | | | | | | |
| KODIAK | 179 | 192 | 158 | 141 | 130 | 110 | 76 | | | | | |
| PORT LIONS | 179 | 192 | 158 | 141 | 130 | 110 | 76 | 28 | | | | |
| SELDOVIA | 213 | 226 | 192 | 175 | 164 | 140 | 115 | 56 | 56 | | | |
| HOMER | 208 | 221 | 187 | 170 | 159 | 136 | 111 | 52 | 52 | 28 | | |
| SEWARD | 218 | 230 | 196 | 179 | 168 | 144 | 119 | 60 | 60 | 101 | 96 | |
| VALDEZ | (NO DIRECT SAILINGS) | | | | | | | 103 | 103 | 144 | 140 | 54 |

# Southwestern & South Central Fares

## PASSENGER 12 YEARS & OVER (Meals and Berths NOT included) — ITEM ADT

| BETWEEN AND | UNALASKA | AKUTAN | FALSE PASS | COLD BAY | KING COVE | SAND POINT | CHIGNIK | KODIAK | PORT LIONS | SELDOVIA | HOMER | SEWARD | WHITTIER | VALDEZ | TATITLEK |
|---|---|---|---|---|---|---|---|---|---|---|---|---|---|---|---|
| AKUTAN | 16 | | | | | | | | | | | | | | |
| FALSE PASS | 46 | 34 | | | | | | | | | | | | | |
| COLD BAY | 62 | 50 | 18 | | | | | | | | | | | | |
| KING COVE | 74 | 66 | 34 | 18 | | | | | | | | | | | |
| SAND POINT | 98 | 90 | 58 | 42 | 32 | | | | | | | | | | |
| CHIGNIK | 132 | 124 | 92 | 76 | 66 | 42 | | | | | | | | | |
| KODIAK | 202 | 194 | 162 | 146 | 136 | 112 | 76 | | | | | | | | |
| PORT LIONS | 202 | 194 | 162 | 146 | 136 | 112 | 76 | 20 | | | | | | | |
| SELDOVIA | 246 | 240 | 208 | 192 | 180 | 156 | 122 | 52 | 52 | | | | | | |
| HOMER | 242 | 236 | 204 | 188 | 176 | 152 | 118 | 48 | 48 | 18 | | | | | |
| SEWARD | 250 | 242 | 210 | 194 | 184 | 160 | 124 | 54 | 54 | 100 | 96 | | | | |
| WHITTIER | 316 | 308 | 276 | 260 | 250 | 226 | 190 | 120 | 120 | 166 | 162 | | | | |
| VALDEZ | 292 | 286 | 254 | 238 | 226 | 202 | 168 | 98 | 98 | 142 | 138 | 58 | 58 | | |
| TATITLEK | 292 | 286 | 254 | 238 | 226 | 202 | 168 | 98 | 98 | 142 | 138 | 58 | 58 | 30 | |
| CORDOVA | 292 | 286 | 254 | 238 | 226 | 202 | 168 | 98 | 98 | 142 | 138 | 58 | 58 | 30 | 30 |

## ALTERNATE MEANS OF CONVEYANCE (Bicycles—Kayaks—Inflatables) — ITEM AMC

| BETWEEN AND | UNALASKA | AKUTAN | FALSE PASS | COLD BAY | KING COVE | SAND POINT | CHIGNIK | KODIAK | PORT LIONS | SELDOVIA | HOMER | SEWARD | WHITTIER | VALDEZ | TATITLEK |
|---|---|---|---|---|---|---|---|---|---|---|---|---|---|---|---|
| AKUTAN | 6 | | | | | | | | | | | | | | |
| FALSE PASS | 10 | 8 | | | | | | | | | | | | | |
| COLD BAY | 12 | 10 | 8 | | | | | | | | | | | | |
| KING COVE | 14 | 12 | 10 | 6 | | | | | | | | | | | |
| SAND POINT | 18 | 16 | 12 | 9 | 8 | | | | | | | | | | |
| CHIGNIK | 23 | 18 | 14 | 15 | 13 | 9 | | | | | | | | | |
| KODIAK | 33 | 23 | 18 | 25 | 23 | 20 | 15 | | | | | | | | |
| PORT LIONS | 33 | 23 | 23 | 25 | 23 | 20 | 15 | 6 | | | | | | | |
| SELDOVIA | 40 | 33 | 23 | 32 | 30 | 26 | 21 | 11 | 11 | | | | | | |
| HOMER | 39 | 40 | 33 | 31 | 29 | 26 | 21 | 10 | 10 | 5 | | | | | |
| SEWARD | 40 | 39 | 40 | 32 | 30 | 27 | 22 | 11 | 11 | 18 | 17 | | | | |
| WHITTIER | 50 | 44 | 42 | 42 | 40 | 37 | 31 | 21 | 21 | 28 | 27 | | | | |
| VALDEZ | 47 | 54 | 52 | 38 | 37 | 33 | 28 | 18 | 18 | 24 | 24 | 10 | 8 | | |
| TATITLEK | 47 | 54 | 52 | 38 | 37 | 33 | 28 | 18 | 18 | 24 | 24 | 10 | 8 | 8 | |
| CORDOVA | 47 | 54 | 52 | 38 | 37 | 33 | 28 | 18 | 18 | 24 | 24 | 10 | 8 | 8 | 8 |

## VEHICLES UP TO 19 FEET (Driver NOT included) — ITEM 719

| BETWEEN AND | UNALASKA | AKUTAN | FALSE PASS | COLD BAY | KING COVE | SAND POINT | CHIGNIK | KODIAK | PORT LIONS | SELDOVIA | HOMER | SEWARD | WHITTIER | VALDEZ | TATITLEK |
|---|---|---|---|---|---|---|---|---|---|---|---|---|---|---|---|
| FALSE PASS | 123 | N | | | | | | | | | | | | | |
| COLD BAY | 169 | O | 46 | | | | | | | | | | | | |
| KING COVE | 200 | | 87 | 41 | | | | | | | | | | | |
| SAND POINT | 269 | Y | 156 | 110 | 80 | | | | | | | | | | |
| CHIGNIK | 370 | E | 257 | 211 | 180 | 110 | | | | | | | | | |
| KODIAK | 571 | H | 458 | 412 | 381 | 312 | 211 | | | | | | | | |
| PORT LIONS | 571 | I | 458 | 412 | 381 | 312 | 211 | 46 | | | | | | | |
| SELDOVIA | 699 | C | 586 | 540 | 509 | 439 | 339 | 138 | 138 | | | | | | |
| HOMER | 687 | L | 574 | 528 | 497 | 428 | 327 | 126 | 126 | 35 | | | | | |
| SEWARD | 706 | E | 594 | 548 | 517 | 447 | 347 | 145 | 145 | 277 | 265 | | | | |
| WHITTIER | 896 | S | 783 | 737 | 706 | 637 | 536 | 335 | 335 | 467 | 455 | | | | |
| VALDEZ | 830 | | 718 | 672 | 641 | 571 | 470 | 269 | 269 | 401 | 389 | 134 | 85 | | |
| TATITLEK | 830 | | 718 | 672 | 641 | 571 | 470 | 269 | 269 | 401 | 389 | 134 | 85 | 76 | |
| CORDOVA | 830 | | 718 | 672 | 641 | 571 | 470 | 269 | 269 | 401 | 389 | 134 | 85 | 76 | 76 |

# INDEX

The author in a blueberry patch in Juneau

## THE AUTHOR

ELLEN SEARBY worked on the Alaska ferries as a shipboard natural-ist for the U.S. Forest Service during the summers of 1975-77. From 1978 to 1990 she worked as part of the ferry crew. Answering questions for thousands of passengers, she learned what the Inside Passage traveler wanted and needed to know—and wrote it in this book, annually revised.

She worked several winters as a research analyst in Alaska's coastal management office. With a B.A. in biology and an M.A. in geography from Stanford, a long-time interest in mountaineering ("I climbed with a lot of good people on their days off.") and a commercial pilot's license (she flies a 1948 Luscombe), she finds the Inside Passage a challenging place to be. In her spare time she started SEADOGS, the Southeast Alaska search and avalanche dog team.

She did the research, wrote, and published *The Costa Rica Traveler* (new 4th edition, 1999) and the Vancouver *Island Traveler*. She is editing and publishing *The Panama Traveler* by David Dudenhoefer. She is married to Henry Jori, a retired forestry pilot. In 1990 she retired to full-time travel writing and publishing, and now lives on the family farm among the California redwoods.

## *Windham Bay Press*

Guidebooks for independent travelers who want to **See More and Spend Less!** Great photos! Clear maps. Fun to read! Easy to use! Perfect gifts.

### The Costa Rica Traveler, Getting Around in Costa Rica (4th ed.) by Ellen Searby.

Tells all you need to know to explore a warm and friendly spot in the Central American sun—how to get there, what to bring, how to explore on your own, when to go with a naturalist guide so you'll see more. Lists nature lodges plus 300 hotels personally inspected, with their prices and facilities (even whether the desk staff speaks English)!

**The Costa Rica Traveler** tells where you'll find wildlife and where to go for the particular birds, monkeys, or sea turtles you want to see. A calendar shows fishing seasons, turtle and bird nestings, Costa Rican holidays, and other special activities you may want to plan for.

If you're thinking of retiring in Costa Rica, investing or volunteering there, **The Costa Rica Traveler** has tips, addresses, and phone numbers *you need.*

**Publishers Weekly Travel Bestseller** for warm destinations 4 years!

Readers and reviewers say: "I've been going to Costa Rica for 18 years, but your book is the best!"

"**The Costa Rica Traveler**, by Ellen Searby, veteran travel writer with a demanding eye for value, who frequently updates her excellent guide, which carefully rates hotels and takes you off the beaten track." *The Tico Times.* "For the armchair traveler, this book is a great read. For the Costa Rica bound—it's a must!" *Marlin Magazine*

### Tropical Beaches And So Much More!

ISBN 0-942297-10-5. 400 pages, maps, over 100 photos. US$ 17.95

## Costa Rica Road Map

**Most complete map of Costa Rica** we have seen, published in Canada, text in English. • 8 miles to the inch. • Shows all beaches, mountains, parks, and biological reserves. • Shows all roads where you can drive even a 4-wheel drive, and all towns big and tiny—even which towns have service stations! • Colors and type show mountain ranges and an incredible amount of information clearly. • Map is about 30 x 30 inches, easy to handle in car or bus. •**Essential for planning your trip and for exploring Costa Rica by car or bus.** Fine for slide and VCR shows when you return. $7.95.

## A Guide To The Birds of Costa Rica, By Stiles and Skutch

•The *only* complete bird guide to Costa Rica—includes 52 color pages.
•Makes bird identification easy—most of the time!

•Highly readable, durable for years of field use, paperback.

•Essential for any birder in Costa Rica. Published by Cornell University Press. US $34.95. Plus shipping charges listed on order blank.

## Special Costa Rica Set—everything the birder needs but his binoculars!
•The Costa Rica Traveler, 4th edition
•Costa Rica Road Map
•A Guide to Birds of Costa Rica
One copy of each of the above sent together to same address. US $60. Very special shipping rate for the set—save $4 to $8.

## The Panama Traveler, From Rainforest Adventures to Canal Cruises, by David Dudenhoefer. New title fall 1999! Your complete guide to fun and adventure in Panama. •Rainforests with more bird species than in all North America. • Indigenous tribes, ancient cultures and arts. •Fishing, diving and snorkeling among tropical fish in warm water. •Hiking in mountains or on secluded islands. •Boat tours around islands, up jungle rivers, and through the Canal. •Hotels, cabins, lodges, restaurants described. •What to bring and how to prepare for your choice of trip.

### All this and the Panama Canal!
Author Dudenhoefer lives in Costa Rica and has traveled in Panama for years. He's your guide to fun and safety in this exciting country. 224 pages, maps, photos, index. ISBN 0-942297-09-1. US$13.95

**Panama Map**, 1:800,000, complete map of the entire country with enlarged section showing the Canal. Historical and cultural notes include information on native tribes. This map amazes Panamanian guides we've given it to! $7.95.

**Panama Canal Map**, pictorial map of the Canal with its history. Photos, drawings, and diagrams show clearly how the locks work to raise and lower your ship. Cruise Map Publishing Co. $7.95.

**Central America Map**, 1:1,800,000. Are you driving through Central America or visiting more than one country on your trip? You *need* this map! From Yucatan through Panama, with enlarged map of the Panama Canal, published by International Travel Maps, Canada. •About 26 miles per inch. •Shows all major and secondary roads. •Complete map of the Interamerican highway. •Sightseeing attractions, archeological sites. Historical notes, geographical information. •Mountains and lowlands, offshore reefs, and islands clearly shown. US $7.95.

**More Maps!** Published by International Travel Maps, in all cases the most detailed ever done of these areas, the maps you *need* before, during, and after your trip!

| | Scale | Price |
|---|---|---|
| **Alaska** | 1:2,500,000 | $6.95 |
| **Vancouver Island** | 1:400,000 | 4.95 |
| **Gulf Islands** (British Columbia) | 1:50,000 | 4.95 |
| **San Juan Islands** (U.S.) | 1:70,000 | 4.95 |
| **West Coast Trail** | 1:100,000 | 4.95 |

(the only map of Canada's famous wilderness Lifesaving Trail.

*Note*: we add maps to this list as useful ones are published, so it's worth writing for our latest list. For example, we expect to add an Inside Passage map soon.

## Alaska's Inside Passage Traveler, See More, Spend Less, 19th ed., by Ellen Searby

**Alaska's Inside Passage Traveler** is the authority for using one of the world's last great travel bargains, the Alaska ferry fleet. Ferries go through "narrows" close to both shores where you can see wildlife on the beach and eagles in their nests. Ferries stop at all the ports, rather than selected ones. Best of all, you can get off at any port, stay as long as you wish, and catch another ship.

You can bring your car or RV, a bicycle, or a kayak. You can reserve a stateroom, or sleep inexpensively on the solarium deck or in reclining chair lounges.

**Alaska's Inside Passage Traveler** tells all you need to know to make the most of the ferries to see the Inside Passage and its towns. Hotels, hostels and campgrounds are listed with their rates. Searby gives suggestions for traveling with children or pets, driving an RV in Southeast Alaska and on the ferry, senior rates, and enjoying the northern wilderness safely.

Author Ellen Searby worked 15 years on the ferries, first as a U.S. Forest Service naturalist and then as a member of the crew.

Readers and reviewers say "This is the insider's guide to the Inside Passage. If Searby doesn't know it, no one does."

"A must for Alaska travelers." "These books are absolutely the most informative and worthwhile." "The book is just what we were hoping for." ISBN 0-942297-13-X  240 pages, maps, photos, index. US$14.95

**The Vancouver Island Traveler**, Guide to the Freshest, Friendliest Place on Earth, by Ellen Searby. All New 2nd Edition!

Cool and forested from nature, but warm and friendly due to its welcoming people, Vancouver Island offers you sightseeing and shopping in Victoria, world class fishing, golfing beside the shore, sea kayaking, beach and mountain hiking, caving, diving, bicycling, camping beside lakes and ocean, and simply relaxing!

Canada's Vancouver Island is just a short ferry or plane ride from Seattle or Vancouver. The perfect place to travel with children, it's clean and has lots for them to do. Distances are short so you don't have to keep them for long in car or RV.

**The Vancouver Island Traveler** gives you all the information you need to plan an exciting or relaxing getaway trip doing what you like best. Hotels, hostels, campgrounds and restaurants are listed, with recommendations, even suggestions for tea shops in Victoria!

"Finally a detailed guide book for the island." *The Province*, Vancouver.

**Safe, Friendly, Nearby!**

ISBN 0-942297-05-9. 224 pages, maps, over 90 great photos, US$13.95. Coming in 1999.

## Zip Close Bubble Bags

**Save your gear in rainforest or desert!** Keep your cameras, lenses, and binoculars clean and dry in the field. Pad such fragile and valuable items from each other in your day pack while you hike, kayak, cycle, or even ride a trotting horse.

**No More Rattles in Your Pack!**

Author Ellen Searby brings her cameras home in good shape from months of field use, keeping each in a separate bag in her pack. "It's great to be able to reach in and grab one for a quick shot of a monkey, leaving the others in their bags. I give the bags to my naturalist friends, too."

Heavy duty inner and outer layers of plastic with a layer of airtight bubbles between. Washable, reusable many trips. Roomy 12" x 12" holds camera or binoculars. #G-1, $2.50 each.

All the books listed here are available in bookstores, especially those emphasizing travel, where you are most likely to find the maps. Stores can order them for you or you can order from Windham Bay Press, Box 1198, Occidental, CA 95465 U.S.A. Phone (707) 823-7150. E-mail for trip comments or to request catalog (I'm very sorry I don't have time to reply and still get field research and books done), ellnsearby@aol.com.

You are welcome to send for our latest catalog. We hope you have a wonderful trip and look forward to your next one.

Order Form (all prices in US $ )

**Windham Bay Press**, Box 1198, Occidental, CA 95465 U.S.A.
Phone (707) 823-7150, Pacific Time.

| Qty. | Item | Price | Amount |
|------|------|-------|--------|
| _____ | Costa Rica Traveler, 4th ed. | 17.95 | _____ |
| _____ | Costa Rica  Road  Map | 7.95 | _____ |
| _____ | Guide to the Birds of Costa Rica | 34.95 | _____ |
| _____ | Special Costa Rica Set (all of above) | 60.00 | _____ |
| _____ | Panama Traveler, 1st  ed. | 13.95 | _____ |
| _____ | Panama Map | 7.95 | _____ |
| _____ | Panama Canal Map | 7.95 | _____ |
| _____ | Central America Map | 7.95 | _____ |
| _____ | Alaska Map | 6.95 | _____ |
| _____ | Vancouver Island Map | 4.95 | _____ |
| _____ | Gulf Islands (British Columbia) Map | 4.95 | _____ |
| _____ | San Juan Islands (U.S.) Map | 4.95 | _____ |
| _____ | West Coast Trail (Vancouver Island) Map | 4.95 | _____ |
| _____ | Alaska's Inside Passage Traveler | 14.95 | _____ |
| _____ | Vancouver Island Traveler | 13.95 | _____ |
| _____ | Zip Close Bubble Bag | 2.50 | _____ |

**Subtotal** $ _____

Sales tax 7 1/2% on orders for CA addresses                $ _____

**Shipping,** see schedule below:                $ _____

(**Books**—Travel guides: U.S. Surface $2 Air $3.50. Air to Canada $5, Latin America $6, Europe $10. Asia/Africa $12. Pacific Rim $13. **Birds of Costa Rica**—US Air $3. Air to Canada $7, Latin America $10, Europe $17, Asia/Africa $22, Pacific Rim $24. **Maps &  Bags**—U.S., $1 ea. Canada $1.50 ea., All other countries $3 ea. **Costa Rica Set** —U.S. Surface FREE, Air $4. Canada Air $5.)

**Total** $ _____

(Please enclose check payable through  a U.S. bank or U.S.  or Canadian postal money order in US $.)

Ordered by

Address


Mail to  (if different address)


Prices and postage rates good through December 31, 1999. After that date, please request new catalog.

## *Travelers, See More, Spend Less!*

Windham Bay Press guidebooks are available
in bookstores, especially those emphasizing travel.
Your store can order our books from us or
our distributors. We will send a list
of distributors to any store or library.
Write us to request our catalog.

We hope you have a wonderful trip
wherever your travels take you!

Windham Bay Press

Box 1198

Occidental, CA 95465 U. S. A.